D0218512

Getting the Most Out of College

SECOND EDITION

Arthur W. Chickering

New England Resource Center for Higher Education,
University of Massachusetts, Boston

Nancy K. Schlossberg

Professor Emeritus, University of Maryland
President, TransitionWorks

Prentice
Hall

Upper Saddle River, New Jersey
Columbus, Ohio

Library of Congress Cataloging-in-Publication Data

Chickering, Arthur W.
    Getting the most out of college / Arthur W. Chickering, Nancy K. Schlossberg.
      p. cm.
    Rev. ed. of: how to get the most out of college. c1995.
    Includes bibliographical references and index.
    ISBN 0-13-060713-4
    1. College student orientation—United States.   2. College students—United States—Life
skills guides.   I. Schlossberg, Nancy K.   II. Chickering, Arthur W.   How to get the most
out of college.   III. Title.

LB2343.32 .C44 2002
378.1'98—dc21   2001021254

Vice President and Publisher: Jeffery W. Johnston
Acquisitions Editor: Sande Johnson
Assistant Editor: Cecilia Johnson
Production Editor: Holcomb Hathaway
Design Coordinator: Diane C. Lorenzo
Cover Designer: Jeff Vanik
Cover Photo: The Stock Market
Production Manager: Pamela D. Bennett
Director of Marketing: Kevin Flanagan
Marketing Manager: Christina Quadhamer
Marketing Assistant: Barbara Koontz

This book was set in Janson Text by Aerocraft Charter Art Service. It was printed and bound by R. R.
Donnelley & Sons Company. The cover was printed by The Lehigh Press, Inc.

Prentice-Hall International (UK) Limited, *London*
Prentice-Hall of Australia Pty. Limited, *Sydney*
Prentice-Hall Canada Inc., *Toronto*
Prentice-Hall Hispanoamericana, S.A., *Mexico*
Prentice-Hall of India Private Limited, *New Delhi*
Prentice-Hall of Japan, Inc., *Tokyo*
Pearson Education Singapore Pte. Ltd.
Editora Prentice-Hall do Brasil, Ltda., *Rio de Janeiro*

Copyright © 2002, 1995 by Pearson Education, Inc., Upper Saddle River, New Jersey 07458. All rights reserved.
Printed in the United States of America. This publication is protected by Copyright and permission should be obtained
from the publisher prior to any prohibited reproduction, storage in a retrieval system, or transmission in any form or by
any means, electronic, mechanical, photocopying, recording, or likewise. For information regarding permission(s), write
to: Rights and Permissions Department.

10 9 8 7 6 5 4 3 2 1
ISBN 0-13-060713-4

Contents

CHAPTER 10

Taking Control and Keeping It   187

CHAPTER 11

Seven Principles for Doing Your Best   207

PART III Moving On   225

Preface

This Second Edition of *Getting the Most Out of College* provides a comprehensive, hands-on guide to the total college experience. It goes beyond study skills, test taking, and time management to help students (1) manage the transition into college, assess their strengths and weaknesses, get a larger perspective on what they can learn, and clarify their purposes; (2) move through college by understanding what we know about learning, maximizing learning from courses and out-of-class experiences, managing personal relationships, and using good study skills; and (3) plan their transition to life after college, reviewing what they are taking with them and anticipating various life challenges.

The new edition features an abundance of illustrative cases and innovative self-diagnostic exercises and planning activities—giving students powerful tools to maximize their learning and personal development by applying basic concepts and strategies to their own condition, situations, and behavior. Throughout the book, basic concepts are presented in straightforward language and illustrated with quotations and examples from contemporary undergraduates.

New materials in this edition cover: (1) "mental models," the ways prior attitudes, values, assumptions, and misinformation interfere with new learning; (2) how the brain functions; (3) multiple intelligences; (4) kinds and levels of learning; and (5) the differences between surface learning and deep learning. The book includes recent work concerning emotional intelligence and self-diagnostic exercises so students can assess strengths and weaknesses in these areas.

Whether you are young or old, first-time student or returning, contemplating college or already enrolled, this book will help you maximize your learning and personal development. You will need to draw on your education time and again throughout your life, and you may make recurrent investments in postsecondary education.

Our aim is to help you meet those needs and profit from those investments. We do so by sharing concepts, exercises, and illustrative quotes from students. Many of our graduate and undergraduate students have told us how much they wish they had known about some of these things much earlier.

Most people who seriously pursue education after high school go to a nearby community college, a four-year college, or a university. More prospective college students than ever before choose their college because it has low tuition or offers financial aid, or it's near home. For many practical reasons, working adults have a limited choice of institutions. Therefore, the critical issue is not choosing the right college, but getting the most out of the available institution.

Although we oriented this book toward the college experience, its content is applicable to many different learning contexts: to graduate and undergraduate education; to getting the most out of corporate education and training; and to independent, self-designed learning projects. Anytime you move through a significant educational endeavor, this book can help you make the transition into new environments, new experiences, new activities. It helps you maximize learning that lasts. It helps you move on with your life in ways that build on your knowledge, competence, and personal growth. This is not a book to read now and then put on the shelf. It is a lifelong resource for planning and action.

One of our problems in writing this book is that there is such diversity in college students. They range in age from 18 to 80, and they vary widely in ethnicity, national origin, and socioeconomic status. We are convinced that the ideas and accompanying exercises can be helpful to all students. However, it is difficult to find quotations and examples that speak to all of you, regardless of your individual backgrounds. So you may run into persons and passages that don't seem quite right for you. When that happens, just skip to the substantive content and exercises, or try to adapt the examples to your own situation.

On the average, people in the United States change *careers*, not just jobs, five times during their lives. The "one life, one job" career pattern of earlier days has passed. It used to be that you went to school, then to college, got a job, got married in your early 20s, bought a house, raised a family, and retired at 65. Now, people create different combinations. Many delay or interrupt their postsecondary education until they are clearer about occupational orientations and lifestyle interests. They put off marriage and child rearing until their mid- or late 30s. Women frequently integrate marriage and child rearing with substantial career responsibilities. Men actively contribute to homemaking and child rearing, albeit less often than women, and they too combine these responsibilities with job choice and work patterns. Important career changes occur when people are in their 40s and 50s. Many persons continue full- or part-time employment and seek further education when they're well into their 70s.

We are living in an information age and a knowledge-driven society. Men and women move in and out of postsecondary education to acquire additional knowledge or competence, to keep current in professional specialties, or to become certified for new work. In the United States more money is spent on corporate education than on college and university education. Successful corporations are "learning organizations." On the average, adults spend about 180 hours per year in formal and nonformal learning projects. For satisfying work and a good life, today and during the twenty-first century, you need to be a lifelong learner.

If you are a high school student contemplating college, this book can help you understand how to get started. It clarifies the range of purposes you can pursue; teaches you how to successfully tackle courses, classes, and other opportunities for learning; demonstrates the time, energy, and emotion required; and suggests the initiatives you can take.

If you are an adult, working, either single or married with a family, and have community responsibilities, this book helps you think more deeply about the trade-offs you face in investing in your own learning and development. It provides a basis for discussions with others about the conditions you will require and the help you will need to get the most from your experiences.

If you are a student already enrolled in a college or university, the concepts, exercises, and student comments can help you make better use of the resources available and get more out of the experiences and activities you undertake. If you are close to completing your college career, you can review how you functioned and think about how you can learn better in the future. You can clarify what you want to do next, and you can identify the knowledge, competence, and personal strengths you take with you as you move on.

If you are a parent, close friend, or spouse or partner of a current student, this book gives you a realistic sense of what good learning requires. You can better understand the support and understanding you need to provide.

As a lifelong student, you will want to keep this book handy, not only as you go through college, but also as you pursue further education. During college you may want to refer to it each semester to review your achievements and make your plans. This review will maximize your learning and personal development as you experience the different stages of your college career. Given your particular purposes, talents, resources, and energy, you will get the most you can out of college.

This book can be useful for a variety of colleges and university administrators, faculty members, and student affairs professionals. Administrators or faculty members designing and carrying out semester- or year-long programs for new or transfer students can use the full text as a basis for helping persons think deeply, and carry out self-analyses, to clarify how they can best profit from the institution's varied resources. Persons responsible for "Senior Year" programs can use Part III as a way to help students seriously explore various transition issues. Individual faculty members can use Chapters 4, 6, 9, and 11—*What You Need to Know About Learning; Maximizing Learning from Courses and Classes; Time Management, Learning, and Test Taking; Seven Principles for Doing Your Best*—to communicate high expectations to students and to provide concrete suggestions for how they can function best to achieve desired outcomes. Advisors can use Chapters 1, 2, 3, 5, and 10—*College Changes Your Life; Your Purposes: You Can Learn More than You Think; Taking Stock; Deciding on a Major; Taking Control and Keeping It*—to help advisees think more clearly about what they want to learn and how that learning relates to larger goals and purposes. Varied Student Affairs professionals can use Chapters 7 and 8—*Maximizing Learning Beyond Courses and Classes; Developing Mature Relationships*—to help students more purposefully connect with a broad range of co-curricular activities and residence hall programs to enrich their academic studies and pursue other levels of learning. Administrators responsible for varied professional development activities can use it as a resource to help faculty members and student affairs professionals achieve a comprehensive overview of what maximizing a college education includes.

Acknowledgments

We are indebted to many who helped make this book a reality. We as authors coordinated writing and sharing drafts long distance, and we required expert assistance from Betty Bowers, Nancy's secretary, and Pat O'Connell, Art's secretary. Betty shifted between the Macintosh and the IBM, and helped in numerous ways. Pat transcribed segments of recorded interviews and early chapter drafts, and critiqued the full manuscript.

We based the book on conceptual frameworks developed in our previous work on transitions, and our observations of the impacts of college on younger students and adult learners. Much of that work, of course, stands on the shoulders of other researchers, many of whom are close and valued colleagues. The interviews with students as they were moving in, moving through, and moving on give the book a vitality and freshness that enlivens our professional prose. We thank all the students who shared so candidly their observations about college experiences. Susan Bourne's interviewing skill and remarkable ability to establish instant rapport with diverse students elicited the rich and spontaneous comments that supplied many meaningful vignettes.

A number of colleagues reviewed the manuscript and gave us very helpful substantive and editorial reactions: Marcia Fallon, advisor to first generation college students at the University of Maryland; David Potter, Dean of Arts and Sciences at George Mason University; and Linda Reisser, Dean of Student Services at Rockland Community College.

Nancy discussed the book with her two children, Karen and Mark, who had recently graduated from Hood College and George Washington University, respectively. Art got helpful reactions from his daughter Susan, an experienced high school guidance counselor. Steve Schlossberg was, as always, 100 percent supportive, grocery shopping and cooking so that Nancy could be at the computer. Art's long-standing collaboration with Jo is well known. She carefully reviewed the full manuscript and supplied multitudinous substantive and editorial suggestions. Her gourmet meals laced with new French sauces and fine wines set the stage for hours of thoughtful exchange.

We also want to acknowledge each other. This has been a true collaboration. We have learned together. We have shared clear, and at times hard-hitting, reactions. We have come out of this joint effort closer friends and stronger colleagues.

Arthur W. Chickering
New England Resource Center for Higher Education,
University of Massachusetts, Boston

Nancy K. Schlossberg
Professor Emeritus, University of Maryland
President, TransitionWorks

How to Use This Book

This is not a typical book. You don't just read it or study it, and then put it on the shelf or pass it on. It's like learning in college. You have to work actively with it. Throughout the book, numerous exercises help you think about yourself, your future plans, and what you want to get out of college, how you learn best, and what you can do to improve your learning. These exercises both illustrate the major concepts and help you apply them to your own particular situation as you move into and through your college career, and as you move on from college. Thus, you will continually go back and forth between reading and then responding to questions based on the best thinking you can muster at the time.

The best way to use this book is to read it straight through first, without doing the exercises. This reading will show you our general orientation, the content we cover, and our basic recommendations. You'll get the flavor of our ideas, exercises, and student comments. Then go back to the particular chapters or sections most appropriate for you at this time. Reread what the students have to say, and digest the conceptual material. Take the time to do each exercise as thoroughly as you can.

The exercises help you clarify your thoughts, make intentional decisions about areas for further development, and undertake activities to achieve your purposes more effectively. The items in the exercises provide concrete illustrations of the basic ideas. You may find it helpful to discuss the exercises with others. It's hard to know ourselves well; we all develop a capacity for self-deception and self-protection. But remember, these exercises aren't going to be graded. You don't have to share them with anyone else if you don't want to. They will serve you well only if your responses are as candid as possible. Think carefully about the implications of the concepts and exercises for your own behavior.

Some of the exercises you will answer right in the book. But many exercises will call for narrative responses that require space and paper beyond that provided in the book itself. If you use this book well, you may also want to come back to several exercises more than once as you pursue college or further education.

Some of the exercises suggest you compare later responses with earlier ones. For these reasons, it would be most helpful if you use a looseleaf notebook in which you can insert the exercises you complete, and then add more copies as you come back to them in the future. Creating this kind of workbook to go along with the published volume will significantly improve the value of the book and the pay-offs from the time and energy you invest.

Part I, *Moving In*, helps you make the transition into the learning situation. All transitions involve learning new roles, new routines, and new relationships. They involve new assumptions about yourself and your future. Moving into college is no different.

Chapter 1, *College Changes Your Life*, shares these ideas and helps you handle that transition.

Chapter 2, *Your Purposes: You Can Learn More than You Think*, helps clarify what you want to get out of college. You don't need to be crystal clear about a particular occupational orientation or educational interest. College is the best place to explore your interests, test future possibilities, pursue many different purposes. Often these turn out to be mutually reinforcing rather than mutually exclusive. You can go after specialized knowledge and skills for a particular job or volunteer activity. You can strengthen more general capacities such as your critical-thinking and conceptualizing abilities, skills in oral and written communication, and interpersonal competence. You can clarify your own motivation and values for your future life and work. You can become more self-confident. General capacities like these are critical for career success.

You can also pursue the dimensions of personal development important for a good life: emotional intelligence, moving through autonomy to achieve sound interdependence, and developing integrity. Becoming clearer about what you want to get out of college helps you plan, and invest time and energy more systematically, to achieve those ends.

The last chapter in Part I, *Taking Stock*, helps you assess your situation, your supports, and your "self," and to take stock of the knowledge and competence you already have. You analyze your situation, your supports, your real self, and your strategies for coping with various challenges or problems as you meet them. You learn about assessing the knowledge and competence you already have from prior work and life experiences.

Part II, *Moving Through*, shares key concepts and orientations for achieving learning that lasts.

It begins with perhaps the most important chapter of the book, *What You Need to Know About Learning*. This chapter summarizes what brain research and the cognitive sciences tell us about how we learn. It describes "multiple intelligences" as well as different levels and types of learning. Self-analytic exercises help you identify your own intelligences and clarify how you can best pursue learning in ways that fit your particular style and background.

Chapter 5, *Deciding On a Major*, provides perspectives to help you decide where to put your primary emphasis. Building on what you've learned in

Chapters 2 and 3, you examine career and lifestyle priorities in relation to the purposes you identified. Chapter 5 helps you consider how to relate a "liberal education" in the arts, humanities, or social and natural sciences to more specific professional preparation.

Chapters 6 and 7, *Maximizing Learning from Courses and Classes* and *Maximizing Learning beyond Courses and Classes*, use David Kolb's experiential learning theory. This conceptual framework shows you how to take charge of your own learning in ways that increase the working knowledge and competence available to you in the future. These chapters help you integrate academic studies with other responsibilities and activities on campus, at home, at work, and in the community, and link academic theories with real-life experiences for more substantial learning.

Chapter 8, *Developing Mature Relationships*, helps you handle close friendships and intimate relations. It also helps you connect with, and learn from, students and others whose backgrounds differ from your own.

Chapter 9, *Time Management, Learning, and Test Taking*, offers nuts-and-bolts advice about how to balance all your various opportunities for learning. It helps you achieve learning that endures, and teaches you how to succeed on tests.

Chapter 10, *Taking Control and Keeping It*, tells you how to profit from challenges by increasing your options and taking control. It helps you appraise challenges and increase your coping strategies.

The last chapter in Part II, *Seven Principles for Doing Your Best*, helps you put it all together. It shares seven basic ways to function that apply across the full range of your college experience: (a) building relationships with faculty; (b) working collaboratively with other students; (c) learning actively; (d) getting prompt feedback; (e) emphasizing time on task; (f) setting high expectations; and (g) respecting diverse talents and ways of learning. Brief inventories for each of these principles help you identify specific ways to get the most from all the varied opportunities and resources available to you.

Part III, *Moving On*, helps you make a smooth, solid transition to the next part of your life. You will be creating your own special mix of work, friends, and relationships; avocational and recreational interests; contributions to your community; and further learning.

Chapter 12, *Where Are You Going from Here?*, helps you clarify your life, career, social, and educational plans and aspirations. It discusses gender differences in integrating career, marriage, and family responsibilities.

Chapter 13, *Taking It with You*, suggests the challenges and tasks that lie ahead. You identify where you are in a "life span" perspective, and the "developmental tasks" you have already achieved, those that are underway, and those that you will likely face in the near future. An exercise called "Personal and Professional Development in a Life Span Perspective" helps you define the kinds of learning and personal development you want to undertake in light of the knowledge, competence, and personal characteristics you have developed through your college experiences.

A Living Example

This book is based on more than 50 years of research on conditions that influence student learning in college. We also wanted first-hand insights and experiences from current students. Therefore, we interviewed 60 freshmen, juniors, and seniors different in age, ethnicity, and national origin. These students shared the rich experiences and thoughtful reactions that we use throughout the book. They often make important points more clearly and effectively than we can. Their comments reveal the real-life complexities behind our abstractions. All agreed to let us quote them directly. We use their exact words, but we substitute fictitious names to protect their privacy. Often their language is eloquent and to the point. Sometimes it's ungrammatical and rambling. But we think you will learn from those interviews just as much as from our professional observations.

Among all the students we interviewed, one stands out. She is an excellent example of how to get the most out of college. She acts in ways highly consistent with the seven principles we discuss in Chapter 11. She was unusually thoughtful and energetic in deciding on her major. She focuses on learning, not just on getting good grades. She regularly pursues learning beyond her courses and classes.

We share some of her comments with you. This is not to say, "Go and do likewise," but to give a flesh-and-blood example as you begin this book. We'll call her Victoria.

"Victoria, if you looked at last week or the week before can you give me a picture of your typical schedule?"

"The way my schedule works out I take two classes each day. Mondays I have Physical Chem and Calculus. Then Tuesdays is Organic Chemistry and English. I do a lot of outside activities, extracurricular activities, like Chemistry Club and the Tutoring Center. I also teach aerobics and ballet. So I'm kind of busy. But generally I go to class and I usually eat after that. Then I begin to study and read ahead. Usually I'm about two or three chapters ahead of the class."

"Is that something you've always done?"

"No. It's something I had to learn to do. I think one reason I get good grades on my quizzes and tests is that I'm ahead of the class. After studying, I relax for a while, then work on the Chemistry Club or socialize. Then maybe I'll go back at night and read a little bit and end my day with some studying."

"That's on Monday?"

"Monday I have about three hours I spend on teaching. So I also reserve time in case I need to go to the tutor or to the teacher to ask questions. I find my planner very helpful. That is what I call my life because it has all the hours for each day. I block out all my times and say, 'Here's when I have this tutor and here's when I can study.' I've gotten a feel for how long it takes me to read something and how long it takes me to understand something."

"Did you use the planner in your freshman and sophomore years?"

"No, I didn't know how to use it then. I was always organized. I would always write down goals and stuff I wanted to do. But I wouldn't have blocked out times in the day. I would lose track of time because I didn't do that. It would just slip away. It's like, 'Oh. Where did all my time for studying go?' When you block it out you can see, 'Here's five hours I can study.'"

"When did it click in for you?"

"Last year. It was definitely last year 'cause I started taping class sessions. I was working full-time, going to school, and doing other things. I was taking hard classes. I really had no other choice but to manage my time. If I didn't, I would've probably failed at everything I was doing."

"How many credit hours did you carry last year?"

"Twelve. Then I dropped down to 11."

"You were saying that Mondays through Fridays are basically the same. How would you rate your percentages between study time and social time?"

"I give myself about two days, 48 hours a week, just to do nothing, be social, get away from school. Percentage-wise—I figured this out—I spend probably 80 percent of my time school-oriented or for things I have to do. But that includes Chemistry Club, my teaching, and all that kind of fun stuff."

"How about Saturdays and Sundays?"

"Generally speaking, Friday night I play around. I take a jazz class on Saturday morning for fun. Then I try and study, but usually I'll end up playing that day too. On Sunday I tutor four people in my Chemistry class for three or four hours. I tell them everything I know and it helps them. I don't charge them. Basically I don't need to do anything more in terms of studying, because if you can explain something to somebody you understand it. I organized a Chemistry Tutoring Center in Organics."

Notice how Victoria balances class time and studying with work responsibilities and " . . . 48 hours a week just to do nothing" and be social. She builds in activities that help her learn and have fun at the same time, like the Saturday jazz class and the Chemistry Club. She does volunteer tutoring to help classmates and to learn better herself. She uses a daily planner to keep herself organized according to her priorities.

Here's how she approaches studying:

"Is the type of studying you're doing different from before, now that you're a junior?"

"Over the years my studying has changed. I used to rely mainly on getting all my information in class. In high school you could do that. In your beginning courses in college, if the teacher really explains things and you take good notes, you can do well. But I've found as I've gone into upper-level classes that I've had to read the book and go for extra help sometimes. I go ask the teacher to explain some things because the lectures are abstract and not real detailed. They expect you to already know the information. So sometimes you have to get a tutor or somebody to help you out."

"How would you describe the standards you set for yourself, and how do you achieve them?"

"I have very high standards. I don't feel good when I slack off or I'm not responsible. I think that's something you learn in college too, responsibility. I tend to take a lot on my plate at one time. It's hard 'cause I want to do so much. I go about achieving them by prioritizing, which I learn to do more and more. It's a trick to do that, because sometimes you really want to go out to dinner instead of studying. But at this stage in the game, school comes first. That comes over all my other activities, including my job. That's how I achieve what I want to achieve."

"Is it easier to prioritize this year than last?"

"Well, last year was the first year I ever worked and went to school. Before that it was always just school. I never had to accept responsibility for anything. My parents were supporting me. I really learned to prioritize when I took control of my own life; when I had to take responsibility, when the creditors would get after me if I didn't pay my car insurance or something. I learned that school's important, but I also learned to set up time so that I can make money to live off."

"Tell me about yourself and other students in relation to your academic work."

"Last year it really started in Calculus. It was great because we would study together. We would do our homework independently and then meet and discuss it. Then we'd come out after the tests and compare."

"How about joint projects and collaborative learning?"

"Yeah. I learned how important it is to work in groups. It's great because everybody gets to understand what's going on."

"When you use a study group, it's in courses you need help to manage more than the easier ones?"

"I use them when the teacher doesn't tell me everything I need to know. Sure, you can work for a grade, but the idea is to really learn something. When my fiancé went to college he was a psychology major. He worked full-time. His grades weren't wonderful. He got Cs and Ds. People kept telling him he wouldn't amount to anything. But when he came out of college he had really learned something. He's very successful now. He makes a really good living and he's very happy in what he does. So I think, although grades are important, the most important thing is to learn. You have to understand that you're here to learn."

"What advice would you give other students about getting the most out of their academic program?"

"I would say don't do a program for anybody but yourself. If you have ownership of your program, you work harder for it and you don't mind doing things. I love learning and I love going to school. I think I get upset or I lose that when somebody demands that I do it for them. So do it for yourself and not for anybody else. Have an idea where you are going with your classes. Don't just take classes 'cause you feel like taking them. Take them with some sort of purpose.

"I'd also say, 'Learn by your mistakes.' I make them all the time. But I think admitting them and learning from them is the best thing you can do. I don't think any leader or person who has succeeded has not made a mistake. I learned that when I cover them up, I'm only hurting myself. When I don't cover them up it makes me a better person."

Victoria brings the same sense of self-direction and assertiveness to extracurricular activities as she does to her academic studies. There's lots of energy and enthusiasm. She's adventurous and open to new experiences, eager to get involved and learn from them. She goes off campus for some of her most important experiences.

Consider how she approaches extracurricular activities:

"What advice would you offer to help other students get the most out of extracurricular activities?"

"I could write a book. I've gotten involved a lot with school and outside things. You can't let life be all school. You need to keep a foot in regular life. I was very active in student government. I did some internships with senators and stuff in Washington and learned a lot of exciting things. It's good to do extracurricular things in school because it makes you feel school spirit and school loyalty. But I also think it's healthy to do things out of school—a job, volunteer work, dance class, or whatever—because it really provides a good balance."

"You seem energized by all your activities."

"Yeah. It started in my sophomore year. I get really excited about something when I engineer it. I like to create things. I started a club called 'The Political Learners Council' and that gave me a boost."

"Do you remember when the light bulb went on? What brought the change?"

"I don't know. A lot of things. Freshman year I just was there, trying to fit in, trying not to mess up anything, worried about school. I had good grades my freshman year. But sophomore year I just kinda took the attitude, 'I don't want to just fit in.' That was what changed. It wasn't right for me just to fit in. It was right for me to do things how I wanted to do them. And I wasn't hurting anybody. So that's why I did all I did."

With all her energy, curiosity, and self-determination, it took Victoria a while to decide on a major. Her initial choice was wiped out for reasons beyond her control. But she did not let that setback deter her from exploring other options and maintaining momentum toward a meaningful choice.

Here's how she decided on her major:

"Anything else about managing your program?"

"Sometimes you have to do, like, spring cleaning. You rearrange your goals and see what you want. I changed my major three times. So I had to do a little cleaning and see what it is I wanted to do."

"You changed your major three times?"

"Do you want the whole story? It's pretty interesting. I came in as a dance major. I always wanted to be a dancer. It was ironic, because I hurt myself and I could no longer keep up with the dance classes. I had to not dance for about two years. So it was choose another major or quit college.

"My freshman year, I was taking biology and a senior course called physiology of exercise. I was interested in that and really studied. It was, like, 'WOW! I have a brain, too!' I didn't realize I had a brain until I started taking these classes. So I declared myself a physical education, physiology of exercise, major. I was planning to go into physical therapy or something of that nature. Then during the summer I thought about it. I thought about biology and I thought about English and I thought about dance, and all these different majors.

"My mom's a nurse and I decided I wanted to be a doctor. But I always had this fear of chemistry. So I said, 'Okay, if I can just get through chemistry I know I can get into med school.' I took chemistry and had this wonderful teacher who just completely opened up my eyes and made me excited. I really started to enjoy chemistry. I was like, 'Hmmm, this seems like a good major.' So it clicked for me.

"I don't want to work in chemistry. I don't love it that much. But it seemed like the best way to work toward med school. And if I don't get into med school when I graduate, I'll probably get into a Masters program in chemistry, which I've left open as an option."

"Tell me a bit about the process of deciding on a major."

"Well, you see, dance was fun and exciting for me and I loved it. I got into college, quite frankly, on a dance scholarship. But when I started tapping into my intellect it was like a completely new thing for me. When I started taking classes and realizing I could learn and that I had intelligence, I really started to get excited about education."

"What type of information did you seek when deciding on med school?"

"I contacted some med schools. I identified their requirements. I talked with a lot of people. I talked with professionals and with my parents. I would say that if you want to go into a particular field you need to find out what the field is about. So I talked to people in the field."

"You just called individual people?"

"I just cold-canvassed. Just called med schools and said, 'Do you have an advisor I can talk to?'"

"And are people really open to that?"

"Oh yeah. I had one person say, 'Why are you calling now?' but it was like, hey, I don't care, I'm making a decision here."

"What advice would you give a student on deciding on a major?"

"The best advice I could give is not to be pushed into something for the wrong reasons. I'm kind of guilty of this 'cause I have a little sister and I tend to push her toward college. I want her to get an education, but if she doesn't she has to do what's right for her. I guess if I were to talk to her I would say, 'Do what interests you. If you don't know what major you want, try everything.'"

"Take a variety of courses the first year?"

"Take everything that may even remotely interest you. Especially take courses that you think are gonna be difficult or gonna be a challenge, something that didn't come easy in high school. Because you learn. The main thing is to do it for yourself, 'cause you can ensure success if you do it for yourself."

Consistent with her advice to do it for yourself and not for somebody else, Victoria invested lots of time and energy exploring alternatives, getting information, testing possibilities and her own ability, in deciding on a major. All that work paid off, so she clearly owns her priorities. She is energized and motivated. There are many things she wants to learn. She is using resources and opportunities for learning in ways that provide lots of enjoyment and satisfaction as well as solid learning and personal growth.

There is more to our interview with Victoria, but this gives you a sense of how she tackled college. She took charge and exercised initiative. Learning that lasts was more important to her than just getting good grades. She reached out for new experiences, and she was open to what she could learn from them. She set high standards for herself. She developed the ability to set priorities and manage her time accordingly. She balanced academic work with other activities that were fun and contributed to her learning. By collaborating with other students as well as offering tutoring, she strengthened her own learning. She coped with the injury that knocked her out of her main interest and initial major by actively exploring other alternatives. To confirm her interest, she found out what she needed to work toward medical school. She learned that she had a good mind, and she enjoyed using it. She learned that she didn't have to "just fit in." Most important, she learned that owning her program, and organizing her time, energy, and enthusiasm for her agenda and not someone else's, was the key to her success.

You certainly are not Victoria. Your background, purposes, priorities, interests, future plans, and aspirations are different, but if you can develop ownership and enthusiasm for your program and invest the same energy as Victoria did, you too will achieve significant learning and personal development.

This book cannot define a program for you. It cannot supply the priorities and energy you will need to pursue it successfully. It *can* help you think all those things through. It *can* help you make an effective transition into college, clarifying your purposes and your strengths and weaknesses. It *can* help you make sound decisions concerning your major, and maximize your learning from courses and other activities. It *can* help you develop more mature relationships and move on to your postcollege career knowing how to continue lifelong learning and further personal development. So use it actively and keep it handy.

moving in

College Changes Your Life

Going to college changes your life. Some students can live at home, others travel hundreds of miles to attend college. Some already know people, others go solo. Some students' concerns center on the dilemmas of college life, others stem from leaving home. Some are first-generation college students; others come from college families. Some are working adults with family responsibilities, and are involved in diverse community activities. Still others have their own special individual, cultural, and family circumstances.

Whether you are moving into college from high school, returning after a few years, or starting for the first time as an adult learner, your daily routines, relationships, and responsibilities will change. You will assume some new roles, engage in a variety of new activities, meet a complex set of new challenges. The changes may feel most dramatic if you are leaving home to be a full-time student living in a college dorm. If you are a young person commuting from home and maintaining contacts with some of your high school friends, the transition may seem less sharp. If you are an adult who enrolls for only one or two courses while continuing your responsibilities to a job and family, it may not seem like much of a "transition" at all. Most of your life may continue pretty much as it has in the past, although meeting course requirements will create substantial added demands. Whatever your status, younger or older, commuter or resident, full-time or part-time, moving into college will have a substantial impact.

In time, your college experiences and activities will change you as well as your life. They will increase your knowledge and competence, and influence your attitudes and values. They will add conspicuously to your career opportunities and modify your avocational interests. Your plans for the future will change. The experiences you encounter, the diverse persons you meet, all will have an impact on the kinds of friends and types of relationships you enjoy. Your cultural and political sensitivities and sophistication will expand, your ability to contribute to your community and to work on other societal issues will grow.

How well you make the transition, how well you manage moving in, will make a big difference to what you get out of college. For some persons, moving in is a major challenge. For others it is less so. Your situation, purposes, and relationship to your college are unique. But you, like everyone else, will experience some changes as you take this step. The students quoted below reflect some typical reactions to this transition:

Mariella reported, "In the car coming to college I was scared. I was scared out of my mind. I knew who my roommate was. We talked a couple of times, but I didn't know what she was like. I didn't know what to expect. I thought the seniors were going to be mean to us. I was scared to see my mom drive away. I was really on my own now. I was scared I wasn't going to be able to make friends. I didn't think I was going to fit in."

Mel saw it differently. The summer passed quickly and suddenly " . . . it's time to go to school. You're a little nervous inside about what it's going to be like, but mostly excited. Actually, it won't be too different because I'll be living at home."

And Tawanda sighed: "I was looking forward to being on my own, having no one there to yell at me, to get away from my parents. Now that I'm here I miss my mom's always making sure I was on top of things. Now I have to do that for myself."

But all students are not just out of high school. As Pat told us, "I was cheated as a young person and unable to go to college right after high school. I was raised by my mother, a single parent who thought I should become a nurse. After most of my children were grown, I decided to return to school and get the degree I never had. You ask how I felt. Excited. Not scared, just concerned about getting into the groove of serious reading. I am enrolling half-time. My kids are all in school and my husband has agreed to help with the shopping and cleaning. I know I will have less time with the family, but in the long run our life will be better. I will be able to contribute more and enrich life for all of us."

A letter from Kay, a high school graduate, suggests some of the issues she is facing making the transition:

Dear Mom,

First of all, I really miss you. It's so scary to be away at college now. I hate that I'm having to grow up and learn to 'be responsible.' I am not sure I can ever get used to dorm living after the comforts of home. It's noisy. My roommate wants to have her boyfriend stay over and that makes me feel really uncomfortable. Oh Mom— what should I do? But, I can't go running home to you anymore. You're ready to get on with your life now that I'm gone. So I feel I have no one to turn to when I feel overwhelmed by all this newness and strangeness. Does everybody go through this? Maybe it's especially hard for me because we were so close. But then again, and here's the part that's the hardest to say, we had stopped being that close any-way—you had your new boyfriend, and your own job pressures. I feel like I went from being 'first' to being 'third.' Now I'm afraid that with me here I won't be any-thing to you at all, and the bonds connecting us will snap completely. Then what? I don't feel that I know enough to hold my own with all these new people, these huge classrooms, and the workload. Do you think I can handle it? I don't want you to worry about me. I'll feel guilty if I let you down. At the same time, I do want you to worry about me. I want somebody to worry about me.

Well, I guess that's enough. Is it okay with you if I come home next weekend?

Love, *Kay*

Kay's letter shows the ambivalence that often accompanies a change. Kay is afraid of the challenge, of losing her mother's attention, of growing up, yet there she is in college. She wants to be there; yet she wants to be home.

Although each person we interviewed had a unique story, all of them, com-muters or residents, young or old, coming from high school or work, recognized that college was a new experience. The process of making the transition, although anticipated by most, was an unknown. Entering a new environment, taking on new responsibilities, running into new experiences—even when you desire and look forward to all those things—require changes in your routines of when to get up, how you spend your time, where you go, how you relate to others. It triggers new roles, new relationships, and new assumptions about yourself. All these changes require major adjustments.[1]

The Transition Process

Moving into college, adding college to an already full and busy life, calls for "transitions." Transitions vary in how they affect each person.

Most of us like to begin at the beginning, focusing on the new job, the new relationship, the new dream, the new college. But every beginning, every transi-tion, begins with an ending. So it is with you. Your transition really begins with ending high school, ending full- or part-time work, ending being a full-time par-ent. William Bridges, in his book *Transitions*, writes " . . . endings are the first phase of transition." The second phase is " . . . a time of lostness and emptiness before 'life' resumes an intelligible pattern and direction, while the third phase is that of beginning anew." [2]

Entering college involves letting go of the way you were and creating a new identity. If you are coming directly from high school you may feel as if you are in limbo—no longer a high school student, but not fully a college student; no longer a child, but not yet an adult; no longer dependent on parents, but clearly not inde-pendent of them. As Myra said, "I'm still in between. I'm a college student, on my own outside the class, but inside the class I still feel like a high school student. I still feel like I don't understand what's going on somehow." If you are starting college after working full-time, there can be a big discrepancy between being identified as a wage earner and responsible adult, and being treated as a student with a lot to learn. This in-between time can last from a semester to a year.

Some persons delay the transition until they feel more ready. Many high school graduates wait a year or two until they become clearer about whether to go to college and what they want to accomplish. Others enter and then step out for a while. The percentage of students who enter college right after high school and finish in four consecutive years is steadily dropping, because more students are taking time off to figure out why they are going to college, and to clarify their purposes.

Delays or interruptions can be very helpful. You can take the time to become clearer about your purposes, to become more ready for the change. You can create a breathing space between your old life and the new one ahead, and give yourself a chance to reflect on this transition.

Whether you move right into college or delay it somewhat, when you let go of high school, or change the balance between work, parenting, and other activities, the change will stimulate many feelings.

Many mourn or grieve for what is lost. Some incoming students we interviewed did just that. They were confused about feeling sad when they were supposed to be so excited. It is helpful to remember that grief often occurs when leaving one setting for another, or trading off one set of activities and responsibilities for others, even when these changes are desired and voluntary. First-year college students often grieve for the past. At the same time, they are excited about the future. Or they can be scared of the future, but excited about leaving the past. Adults miss colleagues at work, or time with the children when they come home from school. Whatever it is for you, there are going to be conflicting and competing emotions.

Mariella, who felt scared to see her mom drive away, reported a few minutes later how much she was looking forward to college. She said, "All I wanted to do is get away from home. My sister and I fought every single day. My mom would get mad and I was always the one getting into trouble. I was so happy I was getting away from home, and getting away from my parents, and having personal freedom finally."

When asked what he might say to peers, Joe said, "You're going to feel like you're lost for a couple of days. But that's okay, it's a normal feeling. You're going to think it's a lot of work. The big classes are going to feel awkward."

Another student, Tyrone, says, "College is the biggest change I have ever had. Even though I still live at home, still see my high school friends, it is a completely different cultural environment."

THE IMPACT OF CHANGES ON YOUR LIFE

Think of the many changes in your life. Some were bigger than others. Some affected every aspect of your life, others required only a change of routines. The more change, the more coping is required. Transitions change lives in different ways. To evaluate the impact of a particular transition, you can examine the degree to which it changes:

- your roles as student, family member, friend, child, parent, worker
- your daily routines of studying, playing, and working
- your relationships with friends, teachers, parents, spouses
- your assumptions and the ways you think about yourself

Here are some examples of how these changes affect college students.

New Roles

Let's start with those leaving high school:

You are forced to disengage from a role that was central to your identity—being a high school student. You begin to establish an identity in a new role that builds on the old one. You need to let go of old expectations and dreams if you are going to adopt new roles and expectations.

When Gemeil went to college, he left high school as a football hero, the quarterback of his high school team. It was hard for him to be identified as a student rather than someone identified with sports. Gemeil was a first-year student trying to find a substitute for the football, macho identity. In contrast, his roommate was a first-year student with the behaviors and assumptions of a "grind." They both had to establish new roles and new identities. The process was somewhat different for each because their past identities were so different. Football is clearly not everyone's identity; it could be the theater, music, science experiments, cars, basketball. It could be your family and children, church work, volunteering in a hospital. In short, your focus shifts in new settings. Establishing a new identity will be unique for you and for each other person who takes college seriously.

Kay had a different concern as she thought about her changed role. She was afraid that her relationship with her mother was going to remove her from being her mother's number one concern. In fact, she thought she had moved into third place. Her role as close daughter, she felt, would change now that she had left home. Her mother would become closer to her boyfriend. On the other hand, look at the cases where parents are afraid their sons and daughters will separate. They want the children to grow up, but they have trouble letting them do just that.

One father told us that he hated being at home this summer. His daughter was about to go off to college. The mother and daughter were having terrible fights. He said, "My wife can't give up control and my daughter wants to start having more say about her life. My daughter keeps screaming that in one month she will be on her own and cannot wait." This student couldn't wait for the role change with mother. Neither could her father!

Many students live at home. Seung Woo expressed concern that her roles would not change. She felt that her family would expect her to be the same daughter meeting the same expectations. They had not been to college. They would want her to do the same jobs she had done before, and might not understand the time she needed for study or for just being with other students. She wanted some changes.

Or you may be a returning adult like Pat. You'll take on the role of student; your roles as parent and spouse will change. You may give up a role as coworker. You may back off teaching Sunday school or drop out of your weekly bridge game or tennis dates.

Your experience may not mirror any of the examples listed. But everyone can look at a new transition—in this case, starting college—and see that roles have changed.

New Routines

All our students reported changes in their daily routines. These changes were very unsettling, whether they involved late-night studying after dinner and the dishes were done, skipping favorite TV shows, getting used to sleeping in the college dorm without their dog beside them, class schedules very different from those in high school, the time they woke up and went to sleep, fitting in grocery shopping, car pooling, and classes.

Like Seung Woo, commuter students complain that their routines at home stay the same while their routines at school are changing. Dormitory students report that they no longer have a parent or sibling to get them up if the alarm clock fails. No school official calls home to report that you missed a class. You no longer need to explain or get permission from parents to socialize all night. You do not have to sneak a member of the opposite sex to your room. In short, each day and night are more in your control. Commuter students try to figure out how to have their parents loosen up and not expect them to do the same reporting they had to do as high school students. Single parents try to figure out day-care arrangements and how to get kids to and from school.

A returning student with children at home reported great difficulty getting a schedule together that attended to both her family needs and her own needs. Another student said, "In high school I was up and ready by 7:30. Here I sleep later and have more time to study because my classes are spread out. In high school my days were filled with classes, then sports, and by the time I ate dinner it was 9:00 P.M." Another student reported: "It can be distracting to see 100 people around you in class. They come in late and the teacher doesn't say anything and they can leave class when they want. Before, the teacher would probably send you to the principal. Now it's coming and going, eating, and doing whatever, whenever you want."

New Relationships

Going to college involves new relationships—meeting new friends, teachers, advisors. It also means letting go of some previous relationships, and changing others. For some students, meeting new friends and developing meaningful relationships is not easy; for others, redefining old relationships is difficult. But friends are central figures in the continuing drama of becoming and staying an adult. Whether we are young or old, friends provide a framework against which we measure and judge ourselves. New friends help us when we are separating from old relationships and activities, and they support us as we adapt to new roles.

Going to college requires separating from parents and friends who define you a certain way, from siblings who may have categorized you as the shy one, the loner, or the joker. It means changing relationships with partners or spouses who have expectations about you as a wife, mother, and homemaker available to nurture all, or as a husband, father, and provider, available for family outings after work.

Remember Kay's letter? She worried about her changing relationship with her mother. She was afraid of separating, yet acknowledged that it was inevitable. Eventually, she will rework that relationship from being a dependent child to becoming a young adult in a mature, interdependent relationship.

On the other hand, Carlos, a first-generation college student, reports problems changing his relationships with his family. His family is very close. Even now, he visits them once a week and calls them every other day. Carlos reports that they are constantly "nagging" him for not calling more. They cannot understand why he can't come home more often. "They keep saying, 'Why don't you come? What's wrong?' It's hard for them to understand what it's like to be a college student. Maybe I should have gone further away. Being so close makes it less understandable to them."

The way relationships change or stay the same varies with the individual. Martin still feels connected to his high school friends. They get together regularly. However, his high school friends are not a studying group. He feels pressure to party with them. "Some of the fellows at college suggested I stay and go out with them. I'm torn. [I want] to be with my old friends or start really making new friends." Competing demands and conflicting loyalties are often part of transitions.

New settings like college provide opportunities to meet people whose life styles and backgrounds are entirely different from yours. Diversity can be challenging and exciting, but also threatening. If you are a minority member in your new setting, you might feel particularly marginal, not part of the new community. This marginal status can be a difficult challenge, but over time it can, and usually does, change. This book describes many ways students become involved and central. But transitions take time. If you are among the majority on campus, you need to figure out how to relate to others who differ from you in skin color, religious values, sexual orientation, or national origin. Learning to honor and embrace diversity is part of your college transition. As one of our interviewees said, "Before, I stayed in my little square. Here, the guys are terrific. They are the friends I will have for the rest of my life. I do not call my high school friends. Here I talk to everyone. I am meeting guys from all over. There's one from Mexico, a guy from Russia, someone from New Jersey."

New Assumptions

Transitions not only change roles, relationships, and routines, they can change the way you see yourself and the world. You go from the status of high school senior to starting over; from being a manager at work to an apprentice student. This status change can influence how you see yourself.

Some students who were well known in high school find that coming to campus can make them feel anonymous. Kay was confused and suffered from a lack of self-confidence because she now saw herself as someone who "can't handle it," whereas in the safe comfort of her home she never experienced herself this way.

Mariella put it this way: "It was really hard for me to accept that I had graduated. I still thought of myself as a high school senior. It was all a big shock. But when I finally got here, I realized that I'm in college now and it's so totally different. It was hard for me to break away from the high school senior to the college freshman. I thought it was all a dream and I'd wake one day and be in high school."

Evaluating the Impact of College

Calvin moved into the dormitory right after high school. His roles remained the same as friend, brother, child, student, athlete, but his role as best friend changed. He was pulling away from his high school best friend and moving closer to new friends in the dorm.

His routines changed considerably. He was no longer in class from 8 to 3. His schedule varied. He had much more time to use as he wanted. His evening schedule also changed. Now he could go out drinking beer at night with some of his new friends. Before, he had to be home unless he was at a school function.

His relationships were definitely changing. He didn't see his parents or siblings often. He was making new friends and relating to dorm counselors, faculty, and student development professionals. In Calvin's case, his assumptions about himself were shakier than before. In high school, he felt okay about himself. Now he was afraid, wondering if he could make it. He wished that someone had explained the changed routines before he was thrown into what appeared to be "free" hours during the day.

The following exercise, "The Initial Impact of College on Your Life," will help you do just that. By filling out the form you can visualize how college has changed your roles, routines, relationships, and assumptions. Shauntee, for example, added the *role* of student to her existing roles as mother of twins, spouse, child of aging parents, best friend, and coworker. Before returning to school, her *routines* included working, car pooling, cooking, getting the kids to bed, and watching television with her husband in the evenings. Now, she works less, is not car pooling, and in the evenings is doing her homework. Her *relationships* with her husband, children, mother, and coworkers get less time and energy. Her husband, initially supportive of her return to school, has become increasingly irritated that they spend less time together and that he has more responsibility with the children. Despite the tensions at home, her *assumptions* about herself changed from feeling like she was treading water to experiencing a surge of confidence and pride that she can handle the course assignments well and is going to get a college degree. Here's how Shauntee evaluated the impact of college on her roles, routines, relationships, and assumptions about herself.

EXERCISE 1.1   *Shauntee*

THE IMPACT OF COLLEGE ON YOUR LIFE   name

1. Your Role Checklist

    a. Please check the roles that were most important before you entered college.

    ☑ a friend   ☐ a grandchild   ☐ an athlete
    ☑ a best friend   ✗ ☐ a student   ☑ a coworker
    ☐ a sibling   ☑ a parent   ☐ other
    ☑ a child   ☑ a spouse

    b. Now put an X by those that have changed.

    c. Indicate how they have changed.

    I added a new role.

2. Your Changed Routines

    a. Please describe the routines of a typical day in your past life as a high school senior, as a working adult, as a homemaker.

	IN PAST LIFE	IN COLLEGE
9:00 A.M. to noon	*Work*	*Work*
NOON TO 4:00 P.M.	*Work*	*School*
4:00 P.M. to 8:00 P.M.	*Carpool, cook*	*Library, cook*
8:00 P.M. on	*Help with homework, children to bed, TV*	*Homework, children to bed, my homework, TV?*

    b. What are the major differences?

    I watch no TV, spend less time with children, less time at work, lots of time in class, in the library and studying.

3. Your Changing Relationships

    a. In two or three sentences describe how your relationships have changed with:

    ■ Your parents

    I see them less.

    ■ Your siblings

    I hardly see them.

- Your family—children, partner, spouse

  I do less for them.

  _____

- Your boss

  No real change here.

- Your best friend from high school, work, or community

  We talk on the phone but rarely have lunch together. Get together for dinner occasionally.

- Your other long-term friends from high school, work, or community

  They are mostly "on hold." Have an evening together once in awhile.

- Your high school teachers and advisors

  Not relevant.

- Others in your home community

  On hold.

b. Describe relationships that are new this year.

   I've made two new friends at college. I'm part of a study group before class. I'm getting to know my advisor.

4. Your Assumptions

   a. Describe the way you saw yourself last year.

      I was a frazzled worker and parent.

   b. Point out any changes this year.

      Now I'm even more frazzled but I feel I am making something of myself.

   c. Describe how you think others saw you last year.

      As a competent worker and caring parent.

d. Describe how they see you now.

Often unavailable. Giving more time to myself. Maybe less caring.

5. As you look at the changes in your life, rate them on a 5-point scale with 5 being a big change and 1 being no change. For those you rated 3, 4, or 5, describe how they have changed.

   a. Change in roles   ① ② ③ ● ⑤
   How have they changed?
   I have cut back on some and added a new one as a student.

   b. Change in relationships   ① ② ③ ● ⑤
   How have they changed?
   I feel less available and am not as good a spouse.

   c. Change in routines   ① ② ③ ● ⑤
   How have they changed?
   In lots of ways to make time for school. Time with the children and helping with their homework has dropped. Less time to do house work. Miss my nightly TV programs.

   d. Change in assumptions   ① ② ③ ④ ●
   How have they changed?
   I feel great about myself and the possibilities for the future, for both me and the family.

NOTE: The more these have changed, the bigger your transition.

6. As you think about your changes in roles, relationships, routines, and assumptions, what advice would you have liked from counselors, faculty and administrators, partner or spouse, or family to help you make this transition?

I wish my family understood better what I am going through and how demanding it is. I wish someone at the college had met with me and my family to discuss the changes that would be necessary for all of us.

By filling out the form, Shauntee has pinpointed the changes in her life. She wishes that someone had told her to better prepare her children and spouse for the changes in store for all of them. She also wishes she had better skills in negotiating so that her husband would be a more complete support. But . . . she is proud of herself, and that can go a long way to counterbalance the stress of studying and the irritations at home.

As you can see, for some the transition affects every aspect of life; for others, the changes have less impact. We don't want you to do anything about these changes. We just want you to realize that every transition will affect your roles, routines, relationships, and assumptions. This very fact explains why change requires coping—even when it is desired, expected, and positive. Now complete Exercise 1.1 to pinpoint how going to college changes your life.

EXERCISE 1.1

THE IMPACT OF COLLEGE ON YOUR LIFE   name

If you wish, use a separate piece of paper for the narrative responses called for by items 1c, 2, 3, 4, 5, and 6.

1. Your Role Checklist

   a. Please check the roles that were most important before you entered college.

❏ a friend	❏ a grandchild	❏ an athlete
❏ a best friend	❏ a student	❏ a coworker
❏ a sibling	❏ a parent	❏ other
❏ a child	❏ a spouse	

   b. Now put an X by those that have changed.

   c. Indicate how they have changed.

   _____

   _____

2. Your Changed Routines

   a. Please describe the routines of a typical day in your past life as a high school senior, as a working adult, as a homemaker.

THE DAY	IN PAST LIFE	IN COLLEGE
9:00 A.M. to noon		
NOON TO 4:00 P.M.		
4:00 P.M. to 8:00 P.M.		
8:00 P.M. on		

3. Your Changing Relationships

    a. In two or three sentences describe how your relationships have changed with:

       ■ Your parents

       ■ Your siblings

       ■ Your family—children, partner, spouse

       ■ Your boss

       ■ Your best friend from high school, work, or community

       ■ Your other long-term friends from high school, work, or community

       ■ Your high school teachers and advisors

       ■ Others in your home community

    b. Describe relationships that are new this year.

4. Your Assumptions

    a. Describe the way you saw yourself last year.

    _____

    _____

    b. Point out any changes this year.

    _____

    _____

    c. Describe how you think others saw you last year.

    _____

    _____

    d. Describe how they see you now.

    _____

    _____

5. As you look at the changes in your life, rate them on a 5-point scale with 5 being a big change and 1 being no change. For those you rated 3, 4, or 5, describe how they have changed.

    a. Change in roles   ① ② ③ ④ ⑤
        How have they changed?

    _____

    _____

    b. Change in relationships   ① ② ③ ④ ⑤
        How have they changed?

    _____

    _____

    c. Change in routines   ① ② ③ ④ ⑤
        How have they changed?

    _____

    _____

    d. Change in assumptions   ① ② ③ ④ ⑤
        How have they changed?

    _____

    _____

NOTE: The more these have changed, the bigger your transition.

6. As you think about your changes in roles, relationships, routines, and assumptions, what advice would you have liked from counselors, faculty and administrators, partner or spouse, or family, to help you make this transition?

_____

_____

_____

_____

_____

The Bottom Line—Learning the Ropes

You've moved from an environment where you knew what was expected of you to one with changed expectations. You've begun to let go of high school or work, or you're adding college to an already full life as a parent and wage earner. Now you're making the transition to new—or modified—roles, relationships, routines, and assumptions. Identifying the degree of these changes indicates how big this transition is for you.

Mariella has had to adjust to a big school after being in a small school. She has had to adjust to communal living, and that has been hard for her: "I'm not used to having a roommate. I'm not used to having to be quiet while I'm getting ready to go out. I have to go to the bathroom if I want to blow-dry my hair and [my roommate's] still sleeping. It's hard to adjust to being away from home and from the family security. It's been real hard to adjust to so many people here because I graduated from a class of 47 with a student body of 200. Here there are 20,000 people."

In between the old you and the new you, the old school and the new school, you may feel tentative, even unsure. You may think everyone but you is making new friends and having a wonderful time. However, people's outsides and insides sometimes differ. You may find that the person you thought was really confident is just as unsure as you.

Adjusting to a new setting takes time. Changes in roles, relationships, routines, and assumptions don't happen overnight. Eventually, you'll incorporate your new identity and "learn the ropes." By next year, you'll be a college veteran rather than a "new student." You'll be a person who can balance work, family, and school rather than someone overwhelmed by multiple roles.

Learning to manage this transition will provide a base for you as you negotiate any new situation. This book will take you through:

- Understanding the impact of change on your life

- Taking stock of your resources for coping with change
- Taking charge of your life

Wrap-Up

We are *not* saying that the transition into college will be easy or hard. We *are* saying:

- You are not alone
- It is normal to have lots of conflicting feelings during a period of change
- Today is not forever; how you feel today is not how you will feel next year, or the year after
- Be kind to yourself for change is not always easy

REFERENCES

1. Schlossberg, N. K. (1998). *Overwhelmed: Coping with Life's Ups and Downs.* New York: Lexington Books.
2. Bridges, W. (1980). *Transitions.* New York: Addison-Wesley, p. 17.

Your Purposes:
You Can Learn More
Than You Think

Here's what Bill says about why he is going to college:

"I wanted to go to college to get a good job in the future. Both my parents graduated from college and encouraged me to go. All through my senior year I was taking the SATs and we'd send the scores to different colleges."

"Did you have any idea what you wanted to do at that time?"

"Yes. I had an interest in environmental sciences, possibly working with a wildlife conservation society or something."

"Look at your purposes for coming to college. You mentioned environmental science. Name your three main goals and list them in order of importance."

"The first one would be the job. You want to do something you like and get paid well for it. Next would be the people, the relationships. Possibly meeting a girl, because I guess it would be kind of hard meeting a girl in the workplace. Then just taking advantage of the things a college has, like getting more out of it."

"How is college going to help you achieve these goals?"

"With the services and resources, like computer knowledge. The college supplies them. It's your duty to go out and get it."

Bill is like many entering college students. He is in college because his parents encouraged him to go. He has a general interest in environmental science, wildlife conservation, and social issues. He wants to meet other people and find a girlfriend. But he is not very clear about how college can help him, how to translate these general purposes into concrete plans and action.

Juan starts quite differently:

"I wanted to go to college because I'd be the first one in my family. It makes me feel good and proud. My parents love it. They're so happy I am here to take advantage of the opportunity. So that's what I'm trying to do."

"As you worked toward your decision to go to college, did you have a major in mind?"

"No. I still don't. It bothers me, but I don't have one yet. I applied here because it's close to home. I knew the campus so I just said, 'I'm going here.' I live real close, but I still wanted to live on campus. It's been in my head since the eighth grade. You just want to be here bad. Because it helps you. My goal is to finish in four years."

"How can college help?"

"I'm not really sure."

Juan has no clear—or even vague—purposes for his education. The main thing is that he is the first one in his family to go to college. He doesn't have much sense of how college can help him on his way, beyond having accepted him.

But there are others more like Mary.

"I remember when I was a sophomore or junior in high school. I was like—I'm not going to college. I am sick of school. But then I started thinking, since I want to be a lawyer, I have to continue. My mom always said—because I wanted to take a year off—'If you take a year off you won't go back.' I thought, 'Yeah, she's probably right.' Both my parents wanted me to go to college so it was like, 'Okay, I'm going to have to go just to get it over with.' It was the beginning of my junior year that I finally decided I was going to go."

"How did you decide on law?"

"I've always loved law. When my parents got divorced I decided I'd like to go into domestic law, because I like handling families and stuff. Higher education is a big must. You used to be able to get a good job with a high school diploma. Now you need a college degree. So that leads to my second reason. To get a good-paying job. The third reason is to experience being away from home."

"Let's take these goals and explain how college will help."

"Basically, I'm going to study a lot harder courses than I had in high school. It's going to give me stuff I didn't know before. I'm going to learn just through the courses in government and politics. I hear with a government and politics degree you can do about anything. I think it will help me get into a good law firm."

"Where did your purposes come from?"

"I think it was a lot of things. It was stuff I hear from people already in college, people that have gone through college. The main thing is how our society is coping with recession and stuff like that. My family always wanted me to go to college, whether it was near home or away. They wanted me to have a better education so I could be better and get a good stable job. I think it's a good time for me to go because I know what I want to do. I just want to get into it and get it over with so I can start my career."

Mary's reason for going to college is clear: she wants to be a lawyer. She went right from high school, even though she was "sick of school," because her mother persuaded her that if she took a year off she wouldn't "go back." She picked a major that keeps open diverse opportunities. She expects to learn a lot from hard courses, but her main orientation is to get in and "get it over with."

Let's hear from one more entering student, Ito.

"When do you first remember deciding you wanted to go to college?"

"I've prepared for it since elementary school."

"So it's something you always wanted to do?"

"Yeah."

"If you were to name three goals for coming to college, what would they be, in order of importance?"

"Number one would be the Japanese program. Number two would be the location. Number three would be the cost. I'm interested in Japanese culture and I want to learn Japanese. The Japanese program here will teach me about these things. And the college is nearby and relatively low cost."

"Where did these goals come from? Were they part of what your family expected, your friends, a combination?"

"The location and cost were because my family is not rich and I don't want them to have to pay a lot for me. The Japanese business program is my own choice because I'm very interested in Japanese."

Ito knew from elementary school on that he wanted to go to college, and that his parents expected him to. Unlike Bill's general interest in the environment, Mary's orientation toward law, and Juan's absence of clear goals, he has a very sharply defined focus, based on his strong interest in Japanese, which links to a career in business.

Bill, Mary, Juan, and Ito are going to college for the same reasons most persons give: because someone assumed they would. Because they have a career goal that requires college. In one case, because it's an opportunity his parents didn't have. But all these students can get much more out of their college experience than they think.

You may be clear about a future career, a special interest, or a major. Or you may not have any clear goals at the outset. Whatever your position, to really experience career success and to be the best you can be, there are significant areas of competence and personal development you can pursue during your college years. This chapter describes those areas of learning. They will serve you well no matter what your future plans for work, marriage, family, or social contribution. They will serve you well whether you are coming to college straight from high school, or as an adult coming to college either for the first time or after some time out. The knowledge, competence, and personal characteristics addressed here will be useful throughout your life. So whatever your age or condition, we urge you to give them serious thought. Our aim is to help you become more purposeful about this learning, for by taking charge of it you can get much more from the time, money, energy, and emotion you invest. We start with larger learning for career success. Then we turn to larger learning for a good life.

Larger Learning for Career Success

No matter what your specific interests and goals, no matter what your major may be, you need to develop three critical areas: cognitive skills, inter-personal competence, and motivation. If Bill, Mary, Juan, and Ito make significant progress in these areas, their chances for outstanding careers will increase dramatically.[1]

COGNITIVE SKILLS

Cognitive skills, the mental processes we develop in acquiring and using knowledge, are the most important factor in career success. One respected researcher studied many occupations: small businesses, counseling, military services, police, sales, civil service, industrial management. His most consistent—and completely unexpected—finding was that the amount of knowledge one had was *not* related to superior or even marginally acceptable performance. Instead, cognitive skills were the most significant factor in occupational success.

What are these skills?

Written and Oral Communication

Writing and speaking are at the top of the list. These skills are critical in most complex work settings. Without good communication skills, it's hard to work productively with others. You can't think clearly unless you can express ideas, feelings, and personal reactions in rich, complex ways.

Communication skills are a stumbling block for many students. It's hard to admit you don't write or speak clearly and forcefully. Try to overcome any embar-rassment you may have. Practice presentations and ask others for critical reactions. Read your papers aloud to a friend or classmate. You'll be surprised how often you hear awkward expressions or recognize things that are unclear or poorly stated. Ask teachers and fellow students to critique your writing. Revise and tighten. Then revise again. Edit as though every word is your enemy.

As authors, we each have 30 years of writing practice. Even so, we revised each chapter four or more times before sending it to the editor. Every chapter will be revised again before it goes for final publication. Then we will get further sug-gestions from a copyeditor. We are still learning.

Critical Thinking and Conceptualizing Skills

We are constantly flooded with information from television, newspapers, maga-zines, books, friends, and relatives. Conceptualizing skills help us make sense of this chaos. They involve skills such as:

- determining the factual accuracy of a statement
- distinguishing between verifiable facts, value claims, and reasoned opinions
- distinguishing relevant from irrelevant information, claims, or reasons

- determining the credibility of a source
- identifying ambiguous claims or arguments
- identifying unstated assumptions
- detecting bias
- identifying logical fallacies
- recognizing logical inconsistencies in a line of reasoning
- determining the strength of an argument or claim
- identifying problems and defining them in clear workable terms
- inventing answers rather than simply searching for them
- understanding many sides of a controversial issue
- learning from experience (translating observations from varied experiences into general propositions that can guide future action)

Mary's success as a lawyer will depend heavily on top-notch critical thinking and conceptualizing skills. Bill won't be successful in environmental sciences if he can't identify unstated assumptions, detect biases and logical fallacies, and understand many sides of complex issues. Remember the range of information and issues Victoria thought through when deciding on her major. Mary, Bill, Juan, and Ito will make sound decisions about their majors and college programs only if these skills are well developed.

Use the following "Inventory" to assess your "good thinking." You already have some of these "good thinking behaviors" well established, but there may be others that aren't typical of you. Check your responses and select the most important things to work on. Then identify courses, classes, extracurricular activities, or other opportunities where you can strengthen these behaviors. If you don't have a sense of appropriate opportunities, talk with other students or ask faculty members or student personnel services professionals for their suggestions.

Exercise 2.1 is the first of a number of reflective exercises you are asked to complete as you work your way through this chapter. Try to give each one adequate time and thought. Discuss them with other students, or with friends, faculty members, your advisor, or student personnel professionals. They can help you get a better perspective and see other angles. At the end of the chapter you are asked to review them and set priorities among the areas you identify for further work.

EXERCISE 2.1

GOOD THINKING BEHAVIORS INVENTORY   name

Check the appropriate column for each item.

	VERY OFTEN	OFTEN	SOMETIMES	RARELY	NEVER
1. I define goals or problems clearly.	❏	❏	❏	❏	❏
2. I make clear plans for doing a task.	❏	❏	❏	❏	❏
3. I persist in thinking things through.	❏	❏	❏	❏	❏

	VERY OFTEN	OFTEN	SOMETIMES	RARELY	NEVER
4. I am flexible in the ways I think through a problem or task.	❏	❏	❏	❏	❏
5. I seek out supporting information or reasoning.	❏	❏	❏	❏	❏
6. I continuously check the accuracy of my information.	❏	❏	❏	❏	❏
7. I spot and correct errors or mistakes.	❏	❏	❏	❏	❏
8. I use precise language.	❏	❏	❏	❏	❏
9. I draw on my past knowledge and experience.	❏	❏	❏	❏	❏
10. I apply my existing skills appropriately to new situations.	❏	❏	❏	❏	❏
11. I examine data, situations, and problems from a variety of viewpoints.	❏	❏	❏	❏	❏
12. I seek alternatives beyond the first "best" answer.	❏	❏	❏	❏	❏
13. I raise questions when causal relationships don't seem legitimate.	❏	❏	❏	❏	❏
14. I try to identify my own biases and faulty logic.	❏	❏	❏	❏	❏

The most important items for me to work on are:

_____

_____

_____

_____

Some of the most useful courses, classes, extracurricular activities, or other opportunities to strengthen these behaviors are:

_____

_____

_____

_____

_____

_____

_____

INTERPERSONAL COMPETENCE

Interpersonal competence is the ability to work cooperatively with others, to seek and offer help, to influence others, to perform well in various situations and relationships. It is the second most important factor in successful careers and a satisfying life. What does this kind of competence include?

Nonverbal Communication

About 80 percent of communication is *nonverbal*. It is the feelings behind the words, the signals sent by gestures, posture, dress, personal mannerisms. It is the messages sent by material possessions, how they are organized, how they are displayed. Writing and speaking well are important, but usually the nonverbal communication has greater impact, whether we are sending or receiving. If we are in doubt, if the verbal communication is ambiguous, we usually trust the nonverbal communication.

You hear pots and dishes banging in the kitchen and your spouse says, "How about a little help with the dishes!" Your father says, "Will you turn that stereo down or shall I turn it down for you!" You know you aren't being asked simple questions. You see two people talking, heads close together, or walking hand in hand. You recognize the intimacy. You have to get past a secretary and through a closed door to see a school principal or a faculty member. You understand that person is important or busy, or wants to appear that way. And when you find that person leaning back behind a big desk, looking at you silently without offering you a seat, you know you'd better state your business and be quick about it. You know you are not likely to get a full hearing, that you are not meeting a warm, friendly person who is apt to be sympathetic. Thus, skill in "reading" nonverbal communications can be very important.

More important, perhaps, is awareness and control of your own nonverbal signals. We send many mixed signals because our verbal and nonverbal messages don't match. If, when face-to-face, someone says, "It's been great talking with you. I'd really like to get together again," but never returns your calls or gets in touch, it can be confusing. But it's not surprising if we soon put more stock in the lack of follow-through than in the nice words.

Accurate Empathy

Accurate empathy is the ability to sensitively diagnose what people are experiencing or where they are coming from, based on what they say or do. It includes the ability to respond to people in ways that let them know you understand. This skill is obviously important in any service or helping occupation like sales, teaching, counseling, law, medicine, and such. But it also is central to working with others in any job, volunteer activity, church, or community group. Accurate empathy is critical for developing and sustaining long-term relationships, for being an effective parent, for coping with family problems.

In college you need to develop mature, supportive relationships with other students. You will meet many people whose backgrounds, beliefs, and behaviors differ from your own. You may live closely with roommates or housemates off campus. You will be in study groups, both giving and receiving help. You will participate in diverse extracurricular activities, internships, and other learning opportunities outside of courses and classes. In all these varied contexts, accurate empathy will be key to effective collaboration and contribution.

Strengthening Others

Strengthening others, helping them feel and be more effective, is another key part of interpersonal competence. You are able to strengthen others through accurate empathy. In fact, one reason accurate empathy is so important is that it helps others know you have understood them, that you have tried to respond appropriately.

There are three ingredients here, the most important of which is respect and positive regard no matter how much a person differs from you. It rests on the belief that, with help and encouragement, people can do good things and be effective. We know, for example, that having positive and high expectations of students in schools and classrooms leads to better performance.

The second ingredient is the ability to give help, whether it is asked for or not, in ways that help another person not just solve a problem or do a task, but become more confident and effective. Finally, and most difficult for some of us, is the ability to manage our frustration and anger so we don't vent it inappropriately.

MOTIVATION

In addition to cognitive skills and interpersonal competence, appropriate motivation is critical for career success.

"Motivation" refers to whatever seems to lead you to do what you do, think what you think. Some motives are rooted in basic impulses and needs for things like food, security, sex, and love and respect from others. Other motives are based on interests, aspirations for the future, talents, or personal characteristics we want to express. People who succeed in meeting their needs and achieving their goals share several characteristics. They are clear about what's driving them, what they want to do, where they want to go. They have clear purposes. They set high standards for themselves, work hard, and take risks. They have self-confidence.

Clear Purposes

"When the going gets tough, the tough get going." But you don't do that without *clear purposes*. Clear purposes that can help drive your college education include (a) vocational plans and aspirations; (b) personal interests; and (c) issues concerning values, lifestyle, and family. Being clear about these areas releases energy and excitement about academic studies, extracurricular activities, friends, and working relationships that help you make progress.

We use the term "vocational plans" in the broad sense of a "calling." There is a huge difference between a "vocation" and a "job." You can think of your career as a succession of jobs, or you can think of various jobs as all contributing to some larger work or contribution. How you think makes all the difference. The key problem is finding a meaningful vocation within the job structure of our society. Alienation from work typically occurs because we can't find that calling within the jobs available. Work that is a vocation is the way many of us add meaning to our lives. It's the way we redeem our lives from futility, boredom, and aimlessness.

Bill's career in environmental sciences or wildlife conservation can add much meaning to his life. Mary's career as a lawyer can give significance and purpose to her existence. Ito's business career, making use of his Japanese studies, can provide a framework for ongoing identification with his own cultural heritage.

Interests in sports, the arts, theater, literature, social problems, games, travel, and foreign countries can give you a lot of satisfaction and stimulation. They enrich your life, provide opportunities to share experiences with others, make you a more interesting and enjoyable friend and partner. A good life results when you cultivate and balance these interests with your vocation. Using college to develop personal interests as well as your vocational plans requires setting clear priorities that recognize both.

Issues concerning lifestyle and family also come up. Do you want to make a lot of money, have a fancy house on a spacious lot, two cars in the driveway? Or will a modest income without lots of expensive things be okay? Do you want to get married and have a family? How important to your life are frequent contacts with close friends? What trade-offs will you make to maintain an important relationship? Your goals need to recognize these diverse, and often conflicting, alternatives.

Between one- and two-thirds of all students (depending on the college) change career plans and aspirations during college. That's good. It often means they have become clearer about themselves and what is important, about their own strengths and weaknesses. It means they are having experiences that raise useful questions, that they are open to those experiences and trying to profit from them.

Balancing vocational plans and aspirations with personal interests, and at the same time taking account of lifestyle and family issues, is a complex task. It never gets settled once and for all. The trick is to be clear enough about your purposes so they give meaning and coherence to your existence; so your motives provide good drive for your time, energy, and emotion. It's also important not to be so inflexible that you resist changing those purposes when you feel it is appropriate.

Thinking about what you enjoy doing and what you are like is a good way to get purposes in perspective. Exercise 2.2, the "Who Am I—Who Do I Want To Be?" worksheet, helps you identify some of the activities you've enjoyed in the past, the skills those activities called for, and the personality characteristics associated with them. It also helps you think about what kinds of activities you want to enjoy in the future, together with the skills and personal characteristics you will need to pursue them. You can reexamine and rethink your responses when you find yourself becoming less motivated, less clear, more confused about why you are in college and what you want to get out of it. Sharing your responses with a friend or two, getting their reactions, will be helpful as well.

Here's what some of Bill's responses to this exercise might be:

One of his most enjoyable activities during early childhood was going hiking and camping in the mountains with his parents. Some of the skills called for were learning how to use an ax and hatchet, how to build cookfires and keep them going, how to organize a knapsack so it is comfortable to carry, how to set up and take down the tent. One of the personality characteristics he developed was stoicism, the ability to suffer discomfort—from blisters, mosquito bites, and sleeping on hard ground—without complaining. He also developed the ability to keep going even when he was tired, sore, hungry, or thirsty; to carry an appropriate share of the weight; and to work with others setting up camp and doing other chores.

This activity continued into adolescence, when he became old enough to go off on expeditions with friends and trek off the beaten paths through high country. In addition to strengthening the skills and characteristics developed in childhood, he learned how to read a compass and a topographical map, how to anticipate changing weather conditions, how to make collaborative decisions, and how to follow through under difficult circumstances. During adolescence he also enjoyed fixing up the cars and off-road vehicles that he used to get himself and friends out into the wilderness. He became a skillful auto mechanic, able to drive through various types of terrain, and knowledgeable about getting out of mud holes and snow drifts. He became resourceful, able to keep calm in emergencies and to be creative about dealing with difficult conditions.

Now, as a young adult, he is into rock climbing. He has learned how to use mechanical aids and developed technical skills to handle difficult pitches. His arms and fingers have developed strength. He can keep cool and function smoothly when exposed to sheer drops.

While he's been in the mountains he's seen the effects of wasteful forest management, run across piles of litter by an isolated lake, and found himself surrounded by people when he sought solitude. His interest in cars and off-road vehicles has dropped away as he has observed some of the damage caused by unrestrained use. He thinks a career in environmental sciences might give him a chance to continue his enjoyment of the outdoors while he helps preserve those opportunities for others in the future. He recognizes he will need to learn a great deal about the complex interactions among people, wildlife, land use, and business interests. He will need to become politically skillful, develop a long-range perspective, and sustain effort in the face of compromise and failure. In later adulthood he hopes to explore the Andes and apply his knowledge and competence to global environmental issues.

That limited hypothetical response for Bill is clearly very different from the responses that Juan, Ito, or Mary might give. Your responses will have their own unique character. If you try to set down some of your key areas of enjoyment, skills, and personality characteristics and describe their future shape, you may find trajectories similar to Bill's that will enrich your purposes for college.

EXERCISE 2.2

Complete the worksheet for "Who Am I" up until your current age. Switch to "Who Do I Want to Be" at the appropriate interval. Use a separate piece of paper to write out your responses for each period.

	MOST ENJOYABLE ACTIVITIES	SKILLS CALLED FOR (musical, creative, good with people, mechanical ability, etc.)	PERSONALITY CHARACTERISTICS (sense of humor, cooperative, dependable, leadership, risk taking, serious, independent)
Early Childhood			
Adolescence			
Young Adulthood			
Middle Adulthood			
Later Adulthood			

Having purposes consistent with your *values* helps orient your life toward things you feel are worthwhile and desirable. The values that underlie Bill's choice of wildlife conservation will differ in important ways from those underlying Mary's decision to be a lawyer. They both will differ from the values associated with Ito's orientation toward Japanese studies and business.

In large measure, your values are what make you unique. You are not born with them. They are shaped as you grow up with your particular parents, in your particular community and culture. Some people, for example, place a strong value on material possessions, a fine house, a new car every two or three years, the latest appliances, and so forth. Others value freedom, flexibility, and pursuing personal interests more than money or possessions. Some people place a high value on friendships or on spiritual well-being and give these priority when they invest their time and energy. To make life, career, and educational decisions that lead you in satisfying directions, you need to be clear about which values are most important for you. Without that clarity, or if your decisions are based on what someone else thinks is worthwhile or desirable, you usually end up bored or frustrated.

Again, we can use Bill as a hypothetical example. The value he listed first was being out in nature. It originated early, in sharing the frequent hiking and camping trips with his parents and their joy in those times together. This value is important to him because it provides a chance to get away from pressures of school, to test himself under challenging conditions, to experience the beauty of the peaks and valleys, woods and streams. He reflects this value in his life by spending a major portion of his limited funds on quality equipment, and by allocating many weekends and vacations to hiking and camping activities. This value was one of the primary factors in his choice of a major and future career orientation.

The value he listed second was making a substantial income. His parents were well-off, with a nice suburban home, a van for their camping trips, and ample time and money for those excursions. They felt comfortable underwriting his hiking and camping because it was a healthy outlet that stopped him from smoking and kept him in good physical shape. The high school friends he went hiking and camping with were similarly affluent and didn't have to worry about pinching pennies when they went on their trips together.

He reflects this value in the way he spends his money and by his part-time employment at a sporting goods store where he can get his equipment at discounted prices. It influences his career and educational planning because he assumes he will go directly to work after graduation for a government agency or conservation organization.

He listed his third value as open, clear, honest communication. He developed this value during the wilderness excursions with his friends, and in rock climbing. He learned that you can't pull together under difficult circumstances unless everyone can be clear about what they think and how they feel. Grudging agreement, passive resistance, and ignoring fear, frustration, or anger, all can break up the group, kill a trip, or result in serious difficulties. Open, clear, honest communication is important to him because he's uncomfortable if he doesn't know where he stands with friends or authorities, and he doesn't feel very skillful in reading between the lines. His directness and occasional emotional confrontations with friends and acquaintances reflect this. He looks forward to a career where he can use solid research and hard facts to confront people and practices destructive to nature.

You can probably suggest some alternatives for Bill's fourth and fifth values, where they came from, how they might be reflected in his life, and the potential influences on his future.

Use the "Value Analysis" worksheet to clarify your five most important values. When you have done this, look at them in relation to your responses for the "Who Am I—Who Do I Want To Be?" worksheet. These two exercises can provide a solid basis for thinking about courses you want to take. They can help you set priorities among varied extracurricular activities and learning opportunities beyond courses and classes. When it comes time to decide on a major, you will want to review and update them. If you take them seriously you will be in a much better position to act on Victoria's advice, and "do it for yourself." You

EXERCISE 2.3

VALUE ANALYSIS   name

On separate sheets of paper, answer the following questions about each of your five most important values.

First value:

What is this value?

Where did it come from (parent, peer, culture, yourself, other)?

Why is it important to you?

How is it reflected in your life? If it is not reflected, explain why.

In what ways will this value influence your life, career, and educational planning?

Now do the same for your second, third, fourth, and fifth values.

can manage your college career in ways that strengthen your ability to pursue both work and a lifestyle that you most enjoy and that reflects your most important values.

Self-Confidence

Self-confidence plays a vital part in whatever you do. We've all seen people choke under pressure. A champion tennis player double-faults at a critical point, or goes from "being in the zone" to hitting everything out or into the net. An expert golfer shanks a crucial drive into the rough. A person asked a difficult question stumbles and rambles, looking down or away. Our minds go blank and we blow an easy exam question.

Strong motivation depends on your sense that you can do what you set out to do, influence others, have an impact on events. It rests on past successes and on learning from failures. Cognitive skills and interpersonal competence are important to a successful career. But they won't add up to much without self-confidence, without a strong sense of your own competence. Persons who can take action to solve problems and cope with difficulties have successful careers and satisfying lives. Persons who experience the world as a series of insurmountable obstacles do not.

Use the "Self-Confidence Inventory" to see whether there are things you would like to work on during college. Here again, you may be very confident about some of these activities and less so about others. The college environment is full of challenges where you can test yourself and practice. Intentionally taking on some of the challenges to broaden and strengthen your self-confidence can have lasting payoffs.

EXERCISE 2.4

SELF-CONFIDENCE INVENTORY name

	VERY OFTEN	OFTEN	SOMETIMES	RARELY	NEVER
1. It's hard to ask my teachers for help.	❑	❑	❑	❑	❑
2. I talk easily with people in high positions.	❑	❑	❑	❑	❑
3. I try to avoid oral presentations.	❑	❑	❑	❑	❑
4. I contribute to class discussions.	❑	❑	❑	❑	❑
5. I confront persons in authority when I think I'm right.	❑	❑	❑	❑	❑
6. I don't let important officials intimidate me.	❑	❑	❑	❑	❑
7. I take on difficult problems.	❑	❑	❑	❑	❑
8. I seek leadership positions.	❑	❑	❑	❑	❑
9. When I disagree with teachers I say so.	❑	❑	❑	❑	❑
10. I "block" on exam questions.	❑	❑	❑	❑	❑
11. I seek out new experiences.	❑	❑	❑	❑	❑
12. I seek out new relationships.	❑	❑	❑	❑	❑

Some of the things I would like to work on are:

_____

_____

_____

_____

Some of the most useful courses, classes, extracurricular activities, or other opportunities for me to develop interpersonal competence are:

_____

_____

_____

_____

_____

_____

_____

Larger Learning For a Good Life

The larger learnings we discussed previously are necessary for career success and for a good life. But they're not enough. High-level critical thinking skills, interpersonal competence, and strong motivation anchored in clear purposes and values, all supported by self-confidence, are excellent cornerstones. But you need other building blocks for a solid foundation. You need to amplify emotional intelligence, move through autonomy toward interdependence, and develop integrity. College experiences can contribute as powerfully to these kinds of larger learnings as to those required for career success.

EMOTIONAL INTELLIGENCE

Daniel Goleman, psychologist and former reporter for *The New York Times*, asks why some people with high IQ flounder and those with modest IQ do surprisingly well?" Goleman argues that the difference can be found in what he labels "emotional intelligence." Amplifying emotional intelligence is a challenge for all of us throughout life. It is an especially critical task for adolescents and young adults.[2]

Emotional intelligence includes three major elements:

1. Self-awareness. Recognizing your feelings as they happen and being able to monitor them from moment to moment is the cornerstone.

2. Managing emotions. After self-awareness comes the ability to handle or express feelings in ways appropriate to the situation, or to pursue activities that help burn off, soothe, or temper the feelings. Emotional self control— curbing impulses, delaying gratification, restraining anger, expressing respect and appreciation—are critical ingredients for any complex relationship or achievement.

3. Self-motivation. Harnessing powerful feelings in the service of larger goals powers creativity, mastery, or significant achievement. Being "in the zone," "in the flow," characterizes peak performance in most domains. Persisting in the face of frustrations, delays, and complications is part of most complex tasks.

Anxiety, anger, depression, lust, and shame can derail any of us. You can't learn when grabbed by powerful emotions like these. Becoming more sensitive to your feelings, more aware of how they are influencing your behavior, is the starting point.

Anger and fear trigger primitive reactions. Adrenal glands go to work. The heart rate accelerates. Muscles tense. Blood sugar flows into muscles. Digestion slows down. Pupils dilate. We sweat to cool off the heat generated by the impending struggle with the exam or the rival team.

Delicious food makes us salivate. Impending intimacy makes our hearts race. These innate reactions from the autonomic nervous system were once biologically relevant. Now, too often they are over-reactions that can build up powerful pressures if they are not recognized and dealt with. They cause tension, resentment, and suffering. We need to learn how to release these feelings before they explode.

There are other kinds of emotions like love, rapture, sympathy, longing, grief, wonder, awe. Sometimes laughter or tears are the only signs. Some cultures and some families see these as signs of weakness or vulnerability. They don't express such feelings easily, and so you may not be able to identify them easily. These emotions are not related to the survival of the fittest, but they provide the basic substance for a rich and satisfying life.

Many of us are not fully aware of our sexual or aggressive impulses. When they aren't explicitly recognized and expressed, they come out in other ways. We overeat or diet, sleep a lot or lie awake, drown ourselves in work or escape to the TV, deaden ourselves or get high with drugs or alcohol. So our first task is to become more aware of these impulses. Then we can try to find more productive ways to handle them.

We all need to learn to cope with fear and frustration. All students face these emotions. A little can help you get "psyched up" for a test or a game. Too much can freeze you, or provoke the "fight or flight" reaction. Unreasoning parents, arbitrary authorities, impersonal institutions, and inflexible rules can frustrate strong needs. We have to work or study with people who have backgrounds, tastes, habits, and values different from ours. Most of these forces don't give in easily. Temper tantrums and sulking don't help, and often make things worse. There are no guidebooks for handling infatuation, seduction, disdain, or rejection. Whether we are powerfully attracted or repelled, we need to develop more appropriate responses than those brought with us from childhood.

Use the "Emotional Intelligence Inventory" to see if there are characteristics in this area you would like to work on. You may not be accustomed to thinking about your emotions in these ways. You may not feel comfortable considering some of these responses. Often, however, those feelings of discomfort are clear signals of something worth further exploration. So try to be open with yourself to identify areas worth pursuing.

For example, you might want to work on the combination of numbers 3 (When I'm sad I try different ways to get beyond it) and 8 (If I get depressed I explore the reasons with others). To address these you might want to ask a faculty member or advisor about some helpful readings, or set up an independent study for a more detailed examination of depression, its causes, symptoms, and useful responses to it. There may be an appropriate support group among the activities at the university. Or you might want to talk with one or two friends about being sounding boards for each other when you're feeling down. Perhaps you want to work on blowing off steam in ways that don't hurt you or others. You might want to get more involved in a contact sport, or maybe develop a schedule to jog or work out at the fitness center.

EXERCISE 2.5

EMOTIONAL INTELLIGENCE INVENTORY   name

Check the appropriate column for each item.

	VERY OFTEN	OFTEN	SOMETIMES	RARELY	NEVER
1. When I'm frustrated I try to be clear about what caused it.	❏	❏	❏	❏	❏
2. When I'm strongly attracted to someone I try to understand why.	❏	❏	❏	❏	❏
3. When I'm sad I try different ways to get beyond it.	❏	❏	❏	❏	❏
4. When I get angry I understand why.	❏	❏	❏	❏	❏
5. I can tell the difference between wanting a sexual relationship and really caring for someone.	❏	❏	❏	❏	❏
6. When I feel frustrated I find a solution and go on to something else.	❏	❏	❏	❏	❏
7. I understand what makes me happy.	❏	❏	❏	❏	❏
8. If I get depressed I explore the reasons with others.	❏	❏	❏	❏	❏
9. When I'm feeling hurt by another person I examine why that should be.	❏	❏	❏	❏	❏
10. I blow off steam in ways that don't hurt me or others.	❏	❏	❏	❏	❏
11. I express love and affection in ways appropriate for the relationship.	❏	❏	❏	❏	❏
12. I can let people know I'm angry with them without hurting them.	❏	❏	❏	❏	❏

Some of the most important items for me to work on are:

_____

_____

_____

_____

_____

Some of the most useful courses, classes, extracurricular activities, or other opportunities for me to work on managing emotions are:

_____

_____

_____

_____

_____

_____

_____

_____

THROUGH AUTONOMY TOWARD INTERDEPENDENCE

"Autonomy" means to be self-governing, self-determining, independent. "Dependent" means relying on others for support. "Interdependence" occurs when there is mutual support, when others rely on us as we rely on them. Becoming an adult means moving beyond individual independence to relationships of mutual respect and support. Most young persons entering college feel a new sense of freedom and independence. Too often it's the independence of a hog on ice. You're on new and slippery territory. There can be some clumsy thrashing around or awkward immobility. You're free from familiar restraints and outside pressures. You can stay up all night and sleep all day. Go to class or not. Study hard or goof off. Often an outside observer's dominant impression is instability.

The independence of maturity is different. You are secure and stable. You coordinate actions to serve immediate and longer-range purposes. This kind of maturity requires both emotional independence and instrumental independence, and then recognition and acceptance of interdependence.

Emotional independence means you don't have pressing needs for reassurance, affection, and approval. You begin by disengaging from your parents. Perhaps for the first time you begin to see parents for what they are, middle-aged persons, neither all-knowing nor all-powerful. Your childhood faith in these strong and reliable guides confronts evidence of weakness and fallibility. Doubt, disillusion, anxiety, and anger may set in. Peers become more reliable sources of support and counsel. Other adults who don't seem to share your parents' limitations often play key roles. With time, you don't need these supports so much. You can risk losing friends, suffer disapproval, or lose status to pursue a strong interest or stand by what you believe.

Instrumental independence has two elements: the ability to carry on activities and to solve problems your own way, and the ability to be mobile to satisfy your own needs and desires. It means the ability to think for yourself and translate your ideas into action. It means taking off for a weekend, week, summer, semester, or longer to travel, get a job, pursue a relationship, or do some important volunteer work.

Maturity in this area comes when you recognize that you can't operate in a vacuum, that your life is inevitably connected to others and to society. You realize you depend on those relationships and societal supports. Connections with parents get reexamined. You realize they can't be dispensed with, except at the price of continuing pain for all. You recognize that you can't be supported indefinitely without working for it, that the benefits of a social structure require contributing to it. Caring and being cared for, loving and being loved, must go hand in hand.

As this change occurs, your relationships become more equal and reciprocal. You can better balance your needs to be distinctive and to be part of a larger whole. You respect the autonomy of others while finding ways for give-and-take with an expanding circle of friends. You become clearer about how much giving and receiving you can handle. But because conditions and relationships change, autonomy and interdependence are never settled once and for all. You must continually re-create your own mix.

Use the "Achieving Interdependence Inventory" to see if there are things in this area you want to work on. Perhaps, for example, you might want to work on items 6 (I have friends who depend on me), 7 (My friends and I have different opinions), and 9 (My friendships include giving and taking, caring and being cared for). You might set up something like Victoria's tutoring group, or create a study group with persons from diverse backgrounds where you explore alternative points of view as you examine key concepts or experiences. You might want to get involved in ride-sharing or exchanging child care. Like Bill, you might want to join outdoor activities or other clubs that involve team work in challenging situations.

EXERCISE 2.6

ACHIEVING INTERDEPENDENCE INVENTORY   name

Check the appropriate column for each item.

	VERY OFTEN	OFTEN	SOMETIMES	RARELY	NEVER
1. I feel comfortable going to a party alone.	❏	❏	❏	❏	❏
2. I express opinions different from those of my parents.	❏	❏	❏	❏	❏
3. I do things contrary to my parents' wishes.	❏	❏	❏	❏	❏
4. I think seriously about advice I receive from my parents.	❏	❏	❏	❏	❏

	VERY OFTEN	OFTEN	SOMETIMES	RARELY	NEVER
5. My parents and I agree to disagree about some attitudes and values.	❏	❏	❏	❏	❏
6. I have friends who depend on me.	❏	❏	❏	❏	❏
7. My friends and I have different opinions.	❏	❏	❏	❏	❏
8. It is okay when some people don't like me.	❏	❏	❏	❏	❏
9. My friendships include giving and taking, caring and being cared for.	❏	❏	❏	❏	❏
10. I contribute to college or community organizations.	❏	❏	❏	❏	❏
11. I seek opportunities to volunteer my time and services.	❏	❏	❏	❏	❏
12. I take trips alone.	❏	❏	❏	❏	❏
13. I seek opportunities to experience new places.	❏	❏	❏	❏	❏
14. I seek employment to help support myself.	❏	❏	❏	❏	❏

The most important items for me to work on are:

_____

_____

_____

_____

_____

Some of the most useful courses, classes, extracurricular activities, or other opportunities for me to move through autonomy toward interdependence are:

_____

_____

_____

_____

_____

_____

_____

_____

DEVELOPING INTEGRITY

The dictionary defines "integrity" as "the quality or condition of being whole or undivided; completeness." When you have integrity, what you say or do in one situation is consistent with what you say or do in another. The beliefs you express to one person or in a particular context are consistent with the beliefs you express to another person elsewhere. Most importantly, the words you say, the beliefs you describe, the values you assert, are consistent with your actions. You "walk your talk." You have integrity when word and word, word and deed, deed and deed, all hang together. They ring true like a well-made bell.

Like the expectations and behaviors in relationships with others that get built into us while we're growing up, we also acquire attitudes, values, and beliefs from our parents and culture. Most of these are implicit and unconscious. They are hard to identify. As we grow up, our lives extend beyond our family and community into different worlds and relationships. We run into information about other cultures and ways of living. These confrontations often challenge our own unquestioned assumptions. They suggest beliefs and behaviors that may seem more appropriate for your generation, more suitable for the times and places in which you find yourself. Developing integrity means examining the attitudes, values, beliefs, and behaviors you have unconsciously acquired. It means discarding some, modifying others, adopting new ones, so that finally you have something that fits you well.

It's like taking your high school clothes to college. You see lots of different styles and outfits. Some are appealing, some turn you off. Most people spend a lot of time and energy trying out different combinations, creating mixes of the old wardrobe with new items. You check out how this fits and feels, how others react, what seems to work when and where. Gradually you sort out what you want to keep and what you want to throw away. Often it's hard to part with old favorites, those well-worn jeans or shirts that have shaped themselves to your special contours. Sometimes you take them out again to see how they feel, how well they seem to represent you. Eventually you develop your own style and build a new wardrobe that is truly yours. You have invested in it. You know it will last awhile. Of course, as time passes and circumstances change, there is perpetual renewal and replacement. It's never settled forever.

That's what developing integrity is like when it comes to your beliefs, your values, and your actions. The arts, humanities, and sciences are filled with works and issues that raise questions of value and meaning. A study group where participants share their own points of view and examine their own backgrounds in relation to them provides useful insights on many of these items. You can design term papers and class projects that address the moral and ethical position taken by different characters, or which are embodied in various professional decisions. Writing and thinking about such issues, discussing them with classmates and friends, will also increase understanding and retention of the ideas themselves. You can ask a spouse, child, or friend to point out your inconsistencies. You can get involved with social action groups or volunteer activities that put your action behind your beliefs. Use the "Integrity Inventory" to check out where you seem to be in this area. Then identify what you want to work on and how you might proceed.

EXERCISE 2.7

Check the appropriate column for each item.

	VERY OFTEN	OFTEN	SOMETIMES	RARELY	NEVER
1. Morally right action varies with the context or situation.	❏	❏	❏	❏	❏
2. When experts differ it helps me clarify my own thinking.	❏	❏	❏	❏	❏
3. I examine several sides of an issue before making a decision.	❏	❏	❏	❏	❏
4. Unjust laws should be disobeyed.	❏	❏	❏	❏	❏
5. I question the values and beliefs I grew up with.	❏	❏	❏	❏	❏
6. Hearing the experience of others has changed my beliefs.	❏	❏	❏	❏	❏
7. I discuss my most important attitudes and values.	❏	❏	❏	❏	❏
8. My internal standards guide my actions more than others' judgments.	❏	❏	❏	❏	❏
9. I make my daily life consistent with my most important beliefs.	❏	❏	❏	❏	❏
10. People know where I stand on most issues.	❏	❏	❏	❏	❏
11. Key beliefs and values give meaning to my life.	❏	❏	❏	❏	❏
12. It's hard to know the right thing to do.	❏	❏	❏	❏	❏

Some of the most important items for me to work on are:

_____

_____

_____

Some courses, classes, extracurricular activities, or other opportunities for me to work on so I can increase my integrity are:

_____

_____

_____

_____

_____

Wrap-Up

You've covered a lot of territory and looked at ways to think about larger learnings for a career and a good life. As you have seen by now, there are many college experiences, resources, and opportunities that can work on some of these. But it's hard to tackle them all at once. It's better to focus on some of the most important learnings for awhile and then to turn to others. Ideally, you will achieve balanced learning and personal development across all these areas as you move through college, and you will continue to grow and learn when you go on to the next part of your life. Exercise 2.8, "Priorities for Career Success and a Good Life," can help you get started on some of the key areas you want to pursue. Here is an example to give you a sense of how to proceed.

EXERCISE 2.8   *Greer*

PRIORITIES FOR CAREER SUCCESS AND A GOOD LIFE   name

Directions: Take time to look over your responses to the exercises you have completed for this chapter. For each exercise you identified one or more areas to work on. Pick your top priorities from each one and list them under the headings below. Then decide which ones you want to work on now and some ways you might do so.

Because you may want to continue addressing some of these areas for personal development, conclude the exercise by identifying a time when it would be good for you to complete it again, identifying other priorities and ways to work on them.

Good Thinking Behaviors Inventory

   Examine data, situations, problems from a variety of points of view.

   Try to identify my own biases and faulty logic.

Self-Confidence Inventory

   Talk easily with people in high positions.

   Seek leadership positions.

Emotional Intelligence Inventory

   Blow off steam in ways that don't hurt me and others.

   Express love and affection in ways appropriate for the relationship.

Achieving Interdependence Inventory

Contribute to college or community organizations.

Seek opportunities to volunteer my time and services.

Seek opportunities to experience new places.

Integrity Inventory

Discuss my most important attitudes and values.

Make my daily life more consistent with my most important beliefs.

My top priorities for now are:

Try to identify my own biases and faulty logic.

Talk easily with people in high positions.

Contribute to college or community organizations.

Discuss my most important attitudes and values.

Make my daily life more consistent with my most important beliefs.

Some ways I can pursue these are:

Organize study groups with persons in my courses whose
backgrounds are different from mine.

Participate in student government and work toward a leadership role.

Volunteer to help at the Senior Citizens' Center.

I think a good time for me to redefine these priorities would be:

Next spring, when I am thinking about my summer activities and how
I want to organize my time for the next academic year.

Now complete the exercise yourself. Your priorities for your own develop-ment, for the larger purposes you want to pursue, and the ways you think you can pursue them, will obviously be different from our example. If you take this exer-cise seriously and follow through with the activities you identify, then these larger purposes for career success and a good life will not simply be academic abstrac-tions. They will take on real meaning as part of your college experience.

If you have trouble identifying activities or approaches you might take to work on your priority areas, consult your advisor, a faculty member, or a student services professional. They can supply some good ideas.

EXERCISE 2.8

PRIORITIES FOR CAREER SUCCESS AND A GOOD LIFE   name

Directions: Take time to look over your responses to the exercises you have completed for this chapter. For each exercise you identified one or more areas to work on. Pick your top priorities from each one and list them under the headings below. Then decide which ones you want to work on now and some ways you might do so.

Because you may want to continue addressing some of these areas for personal develop-ment, conclude the exercise by identifying a time when it would be good for you to complete it again, identifying other priorities and ways to work on them.

Good Thinking Behaviors Inventory

Self-Confidence Inventory

Emotional Intelligence Inventory

Achieving Interdependence Inventory

Integrity Inventory

My top priorities for now are:

Some ways I can pursue these are:

I think a good time for me to redefine these priorities would be:

The next chapter, *Taking Stock*, helps you become clearer about where you stand as you address these purposes.

REFERENCES

1. The concepts and language in this chapter borrow heavily from Chickering, A. W., and Reisser, Linda, *Education and Identity.* Copyright © 1993. San Francisco: Jossey-Bass.

2. Goleman, D. (1995). *Emotional Intelligence.* New York: Bantam Books.

Taking Stock

Think back on the transitions in your life. Some you probably handled well, others less smoothly. You may find it puzzling that you pulled through one change like a trooper only to flounder in the face of another. People react differently to different transitions because of their unique strengths and resources. Each of the students we interviewed approached college with different resources.

We have developed a "4 S System" as a guide for taking stock of your resources. Your potential resources include:

- Your Situation—your situation at the time of the transition
- Your Supports—those people and assets that bolster you
- Your Self—who you are, your optimism and ability to deal with ambiguity
- Your Strategies—what you do to cope

Often, people complain about not understanding how they are handling change. The 4 S System is designed to take the mystery out of change. Understanding the system will not necessarily make the change more enjoyable or less miserable, but by taking stock of your resources—your Situation, Supports, Self, and Strategies—you get a picture of your strengths and deficits as you negotiate the college transition. By looking at them together, you can see which are your strengths and which resources need strengthening.

One person might have lots of Support from home and school; another might have little Support but lots of coping Strategies. Another might see the Situation and Supports as very low, but knows that he has the inner resources, the Self, to make it work.

You can see how the system works by contrasting the different resources Kathleen and Josh brought with them to college. Josh's Situation when he entered college was positive. He came from a family where college was the norm. College came at a good time in both his and his family's lives. He had no real stress, other than the usual pains of growing up and separating. His Supports in college were low. He knew no one and felt out of it. He wondered how he would become part of a crowd. When looking at his Self, he knew he was an optimist and saw the glass as half-full. Because of that, he felt that his Supports would increase if he just gave them time. He felt he was a good coper. His high school counselor had commented on his ability to get along with anybody. In summary, his Situation, Self, and Strategies were strong resources as he entered college. His low resource was Supports but he felt he could and would be able to change that.

Kathleen's family had moved from Ireland to Virginia three years before she entered college. She was the first person in her family to even consider college, let alone apply. Her high school counselor identified her as a student with great potential. The counselor took special interest in Kathleen, helped her complete the applications, and convinced her parents that college would be valuable. Kathleen felt her Situation was problematic. Although everyone finally agreed she should go to college, there was underlying resistance. She felt her family needed her to stay home, to work, to contribute financially. She was frightened that college would be too much for her. Although Kathleen's Supports were weak at home, they were very strong at college. The high school counselor had contacted the admissions director and set up a special mentor for her. Her mentor found two other students, also the first in their family to attend college. Kathleen felt well supported by the mentor and the students. She was pessimistic, afraid of the big change in her life. She also did not know which Strategies to use. The ones she used at home did not seem appropriate in this new setting. Kathleen's strength was her Supports at college. She needed to work on her home Situation, her Self, and her Strategies.

Examining your Situation, your Self, your Supports, and your Strategies helps you see if the balance of resources at a particular time will make the change possible and positive. You can use this process all through college—in fact, all through life. In Chapter 10, "Taking Control and Keeping It," we discuss how to increase your coping strategies, and how to turn the S's that are not your strengths into resources that work for you. But for now, just enjoy your strengths and understand that your 4 S's can change, do change, and will work for you. By taking stock of your mix of resources, you can assess how well equipped you are to deal with any transition—in this case, the college transition.

The 4 S System

The 4 S System rests on several assumptions:

- No one factor is necessary for coping with change; rather, many factors play a role: your Situation, Supports, Self, and Strategies.

- Everyone has a balance of resources and deficits for facing transitions.
- These potential resources and deficits are not permanent but change over time.
- There are things you can do to turn the deficits into resources.

TAKING STOCK OF YOUR SITUATION

Students' situations, when they come to college, vary greatly. For some, it is a good time to come to college, for others it poses enormous problems because of family pressures and difficulties. Whenever you make a transition, you must look at the total Situation. Are you going to college at a good time in your life, or are there too many other problems? Is attending college your choice, or do you feel pushed by peers, family, employer, or other external circumstances? Do you assess your college Situation as positive, negative, or in-between? Do you assess the rest of your life as positive, negative, or in-between? Are there other pressures in your life or is this a calm period?

How you assess your transition can make a tremendous difference in how you cope. Your Situation is not static; it is constantly changing. This means that you need to reassess your Situation with each change, deciding whether or not it is a resource or deficit. A few examples of different Situations illustrate the importance of taking account of this particular S.

Vincent: "This is both a good and bad time for me to come to college. This is a good time because if I sat out a year, I might have not wanted to go. But it is really a bad time because my parents had to buy two cars and we were up against it financially. But my father said, 'We can handle it; so go ahead.'"

Betsy: "Thank heavens I got into college. I needed to get away from my family. My parents fight all the time and I feel caught. Being at college is great. It is a relief."

Aurelia: "I really wish I had control over my life. I would have liked to take a year off and not come right to college."

Carlos: "College is what I always wanted, but I feel very torn. My mother is dying of cancer, my father is falling apart. I go home every weekend and feel as if I am not doing anything right."

Vincent, Betsy, Aurelia, and Carlos all have different Situations that will influence how they handle college. It is possible that Carlos's Situation of family illness might interfere with his initial success. If it does, that does not mean he is not college material or that he will not be a great success when his Situation has calmed down. Someone else might have financial problems, another might have everything in place.

We'll fill in the "Situation Review" for Kathleen so you can see how it works.

EXERCISE 3.1   *Kathleen*
                                                         name

YOUR SITUATION REVIEW

1. Give examples of ways you evaluate this transition of coming to college as:

   ❏ positive   ❏ negative   ☑ mixed

   It is mixed because my family needs me at home. I am new to this country.
   Even though my high school counselor thinks I can manage I am not sure I
   can handle all the reading and writing.

2. In what ways is this a good or a bad time in your life to come to college?

   It's as good a time as any for me I guess. But it would be a better time
   for my family if we were more established and my father had a
   better job.

3. What do you control in this transition?

   I can work hard at my studies and try to make friends.

4. What seems out of your control?

   My parents feelings and limited money. All the long homework assignments
   they give me.

5. Was coming to college your choice? If yes, what was your thinking? If no, whose choice was it?

   It was my high school counselor's idea. I went along when he talked
   my parents into it.

6. In what ways were you strongly influenced by someone else? Some external circumstances?

   I did pretty well in high school and my counselor helped a lot.

7. In what ways do you feel hopeful or pessimistic about your chances of handling this transition positively?

   Sometimes I feel hopeful. Then when my work piles up and I don't do well
   on tests I feel pessimistic.

8. What areas of your life are:
   very stressful?

   The courses and heavy homework assignments. My parents' feelings.

moderately stressful?

least stressful?

My mentor and student friends. Life in the dorm.

9. Taking everything into account, do you feel your situation is:
   - ❏ a high resource?   ❏ a low resource?
   - ☑ a mixed bag?   ❏ okay?

   Please explain.

   It's a mixed bag.

10. As you make this assessment, can you identify what you base it on?

    Just my feelings and my experiences so far.

11. What are the implications of your responses?

    It would probably be a good idea to discuss it more with my mentor.
    Probably I should go to the study skills center.

As you can see, Kathleen's Situation is mixed. It has both positives and negatives. If she can arrange a meeting between her mentor, herself, and her parents, perhaps she can begin to take control of her Situation and make it less of a mixed bag.

By answering the following questions you can clarify whether your Situation is working for or against you *at this time*. We emphasize *at this time* because Situations change. For this exercise, and for Exercises 3.2, 3.3, 3.4, and 3.5, you will need to use separate sheets of paper.

EXERCISE 3.1

YOUR SITUATION REVIEW   name

Use a separate sheet of paper to complete this exercise.

1. Give examples of ways you evaluate this transition of coming to college as:
   - ❏ positive   ❏ negative   ❏ mixed

2. In what ways is this a good or a bad time in your life to come to college?

3. What do you control in this transition?

4. What seems out of your control?

5. Was coming to college your choice? If yes, what was your thinking? If no, whose choice was it?

6. In what ways were you strongly influenced by someone else? Some external circumstances?

7. In what ways do you feel hopeful or pessimistic about your chances of handling this transition positively?

8. What areas of your life are:
   very stressful?
   moderately stressful?
   least stressful?

9. Taking everything into account, do you feel your situation is:
   ❏ a high resource?   ❏ a low resource?
   ❏ a mixed bag?   ❏ okay?
   Please explain.

10. As you make this assessment, can you identify what you base it on?

11. What are the implications of your responses?

TAKING STOCK OF YOUR SUPPORTS

Most people need Support from others to help negotiate a transition. In fact, for many, social Support is the key to handling stress. People receive Support from their intimate relationships, their family units, their larger network of friends, and their institutions through faculty, student personnel services professionals, peers, or administrators.

Support can include any of the following:

1. Affection—respect, love, caring, understanding
2. Affirmation—agreement that what you have done is appropriate or understandable
3. Assistance or aid—tangible help like tutoring, editing, study groups, party mixers for finding dates
4. Feedback—responses that reinterpret situations, provide a different perspective, challenge or reaffirm your interpretation

Those we interviewed illustrated a variety of Supports:

■ "My Supports are my mom, my dad, my pastor, my boyfriend, and my boyfriend's mom—so you see, I have lots of Support. Even more than in high school because my dad has gotten more involved. My mother listens for any slight change in my voice and is always asking, 'Are you okay?' My dad is totally supportive because he has taken sociology, psychology, and biology, and he's there. My boyfriend is in his second year of college in another state, but he understands what I am going through and he helps keep me focused."

- "My mom calls and tries to give me Support. She keeps telling me that I'm going to make it through. That helps me give myself Support. Also I get lots of Support from my grandmother. I feel I need more faculty Support to help me adapt to college."

- "I have a confusing Support system. My parents are divorced. My mother and stepfather Support me financially. My dad is just there for moral Support. But I get more emotional Support now than in high school because I'm going to be the first one in the family to go to college. I am a male Hispanic and this is a big deal in our family."

- "When you ask what Supports I need, I need a computer. I talked to my dad and maybe he will get me one for Christmas."

- "I owe credit to my high school counselor for writing such wonderful letters of recommendation. I am getting little Support from my parents. I am doing it on my own. I have gotten a loan. If I had a problem, I would not go to my parents, I would go to a friend. My father doesn't ask me how I am doing, and my mother always asks. She worries too much."

- "My Support comes from church. I go home every other week and go to church with my folks."

- "The university has been very supportive. They go out of their way to help us, especially new students. They create extra programs to make students more aware of the different groups here. I am Asian American, meeting all kinds of different people. Also, they have many programs, like special tutoring. I do not plan on using any of these extra services but it makes me feel more secure knowing that they're there."

- "I got Support from the Black Student Alliance. This gave me a group with whom to identify. I was scared that I would be the only African American, but I soon saw that I was not alone. There is a counselor in the Minority Student Services who is like my mentor. She is always there for me at any time. She is my main Support."

On the other hand, some students felt they were not getting the Support they needed:

- "I feel I need more faculty Support to help me adapt to college. I wish there was someone who could check on you at times to make sure everything is going okay, and if not, then give you advice on different services the campus offers."

Support from family, friends, school officials, employers, and others are critical for college students. The same student might experience both Support and sabotage. For example, Marie, a returning student, felt she got great Support from her husband, children, and parents when she decided to return to school. At first, she was delighted and felt fortunate. After six months of writing papers on weekends and evenings, she began getting negative comments from her husband like, "I see the dishes are not even washed," and from her children, "You're no fun anymore." Marie was terribly upset by these comments, felt guilty, and was about to withdraw from school. Her faculty advisor gave her so much encouragement—her grades were all A's—that she decided to stick with it.

We all need Support, but there are times when we get it from one person and not from another. As we have also seen, there are times when those giving us Support take it away. Support is not one-dimensional; it comes from many sources, in many ways. To one person, getting a computer would be the needed Support; to another, talking to Mom; to another, a husband and children who will help with the shopping, cooking, and cleaning. What we strive for is to have our overall Support be more positive than negative.

Let's see how Kathleen's Supports are working for her.

EXERCISE 3.2   *Kathleen*

YOUR SUPPORT REVIEW   name

1. Describe the kind of support you are receiving.
   Affection I am getting includes

   My high school counselor, my college mentor, my two friends, and
   my roommate.

   Affirmation I am getting includes

   My mentor and roommate think I am doing OK in my studies,
   even though sometimes I only get C's on my tests.

   Aid I am getting includes

   My two friends help me meet other people. My mentor sometimes
   helps me with my studies.

2. In any of the areas listed above, do you feel you need more support?

   I wish I had more affirmation from home. I need more help
   with getting my homework done and managing my time.

3. Describe the friends you talk to. What about?

   I talk a lot with my two friends who are also the first to go to
   college. We talk about different ways to get homework done,
   about what kinds of extracurricular activities to do, and about
   boys we like. We also talk about our problems with our parents.

4. Describe the family members you talk to. What about?

   So far I only really talk with my mentor. She has encouraged me to ask my teachers questions when I don't understand and I have done that with one teacher twice after class. We also talk about my parents and what I might do for a major.

5. Describe the faculty members or other college personnel you talk to. What about?

   I don't talk with any other faculty members. My advisor seems very busy so I use my mentor for choosing my courses.

6. Do you sometimes feel that the people in your world are undercutting you? Please explain.

   My parents do really undercut me. I always have the feeling they would rather I was home.

7. Do you feel you are able to initiate support by telling others what you need? Please explain.

   It is hard for me to ask for help. I am used to being pretty much on my own and managing for myself. In Ireland we lived in a small town and everybody knew everybody else and helped out without you asking for it. Here we live in a suburb and nobody knows anyone else or helps them.

8. Do you feel your support system is
   - ❏ a high resource?
   - ☑ a mixed bag?
   - ❏ a low resource?
   - ❏ okay?

   Please explain.

   It's a mixed bag because of my parents' attitudes and limited money.

9. What are the strongest parts of your support system?

   My mentor and my student friends.

10. What are the weakest?

    My family and my teachers.

11. Are there ways you can strengthen your support system?

    I don't have any good ideas about how to do this right now.

As you can see, her main problem was guilt about not helping out at home. She doesn't have ideas about how to strengthen her Support system. She would find suggestions in Chapter 10, "Taking Control and Keeping It," about how to strengthen her Supports. Complete your own "Support Review." Go to Chapter 10 if Supports seem to be a low resource or mixed bag.

EXERCISE 3.2

YOUR SUPPORT REVIEW   name

Use a separate sheet of paper to complete this exercise.

1. Describe the kind of support you are receiving:
   Affection I am getting includes
   Affirmation I am getting includes
   Aid I am getting includes

2. In any of the areas listed above, do you feel you need more support?

3. Describe the friends you talk to. What about?

4. Describe the family members you talk to. What about?

5. Describe the faculty members or other college personnel you talk to. What about?

6. Do you sometimes feel that the people in your world are undercutting you? Please explain.

7. Do you feel you are able to initiate support by telling others what you need? Please explain.

8. Do you feel your support system is
   ❏ a high resource?   ❏ a low resource?
   ❏ a mixed bag?   ❏ okay?
   Please explain.

9. What are the strongest parts of your support system?

10. What are the weakest?

11. Are there ways you can strengthen your support system?

TAKING STOCK OF YOUR SELF

What personal characteristics do you bring to the college transition? When you try to answer that question, you get into the challenging task of defining who you are. Psychologist Martin Seligman asserts that whether you are an optimist or a pessimist is central to how you handle life. As Seligman writes, "The defining characteristic of pessimists is that they tend to believe bad events will last a long time, will undermine everything they do, and are their own fault. The optimists, who are confronted with the same hard knocks of this world, think about misfortune in the opposite way.

They tend to believe defeat is just a temporary setback, that its causes are confined to this one case. Optimists believe defeat is not their fault."[1]

Those who feel they have control over their lives, who are optimistic about their power to control at least some portions of their lives, tend to experience less depression and achieve more at school or work. They are even in better health. Seligman suggests that the individual's "explanatory style"—the way a person thinks about the event or transition—can explain how some people weather transitions without becoming depressed or giving up. Since many transitions are neither bad nor good, but a mixture of both, a person's explanatory style becomes the critical key to coping. A person with a positive explanatory style is an optimist, while one with a negative style is basically a pessimist. The good news is that pessimists can learn the skills of optimism and improve their lives.

Another way to assess your Self is to identify times when you are challenged and when you are overwhelmed by change. For example, if your grades placed you on probation, would you assume that they will never get better, that you are a failure, that maybe you are not college material? Would you feel overwhelmed and defeated, or challenged and determined to do better?

It is interesting to see how our interviewees saw themselves:

- "I define the transition of coming to college as challenging rather than overwhelming. I feel confident that I will make a 3.0."
- "I wish I were more of a resource for myself, but I'm rather shy. I don't speak up a lot. I need help in this area."
- "Although I feel in control of the decision to come to college, I still think I need to become more independent. My way of dealing with stress is very unorthodox, because I only study right before the test and I don't worry about it until then. The only thing I worry about is my car breaking down. I approach most transitions with underconfidence. I set very high standards and am afraid I will not meet them."
- "I have the confidence I can do it, but then I still feel a little fear. I am trying to do it on my own, without help. I wish I just had a little more confidence."

Exercise 3.3, "Your Self Review," helps you reflect on how you respond to challenges and how you rate your Self as a resource. Before filling it out let's see how Kathleen sees herself.

EXERCISE 3.3   *Kathleen*
YOUR SELF REVIEW   name

1. In what ways do you feel challenged by the college transition? Please explain.

Learning to do all the course work has been my biggest challenge. At the beginning it was very uncomfortable not knowing anyone except the two students my high school counselor found for me. I wasn't used to all the noise and partying in the dorm.

2. In what ways do you feel overwhelmed by it? Please explain.

   I feel overwhelmed when I can't keep up with my studies and when my parents want me to come home and help out.

3. Do you feel both challenged and overwhelmed? Which is the predominant feeling?

   More overwhelmed I guess, most of the time.

4. Do you generally feel a sense of control or mastery as you face transitions? Give examples.

   In the past I've generally felt pretty much in control. I knew my way around our village and county in Ireland and was a good student. After we got here from Ireland I was able to do my school work and help out at home with odd jobs.

5. Do you usually face life as an optimist rather than a pessimist? Give examples of some things that lead you to feel optimistic or pessimistic.

   Generally, I have been pretty happy-go-lucky. I used to sing a lot. And I felt I did quite well in high school and was popular enough. When I got good grades and was chosen for the glee club that made me fell optimistic. Now, when school work piles up, when I don't get good grades, and when I run out of money I get more pessimistic.

6. Do you define your Self as resilient in the face of change? Give examples.

   Yes. My mother got sick soon after we arrived here, and I was able to take a lot of responsibility for shopping and cooking. I did not have a lot of trouble getting accepted in school and doing the work.

7. Have you uncovered ways to make your prior learning count? If so, what are you doing? Note: To answer this question, please go to Exercise 3.4, "Assessing Your Prior Learning." After you fill that out, you will be able to decide whether to apply for such credit.

   I haven't tried to do this. There might be a possibility because I know Gaelic and have read quite a lot of Irish plays that seem to be part of some of the literature courses.

8. Taking into account all of the above, do you rate your Self as:
   - ☑ a high resource?
   - ☐ a low resource?
   - ☐ a mixed bag?
   - ☐ okay?

Please explain.

I have been able to come through a number of difficult situations and changes so far. I think if I work real hard and am patient with myself and my parents, I will get through college OK.

9. If you do not see your Self as a high resource, do you have any ideas about how to strengthen your Self? How to become more of an optimist?

I think I am OK as an optimist.

Kathleen sees college as overwhelming. But her past experience of coping with the move from Ireland and helping her family makes her feel somewhat optimistic about being able to cope with the various challenges. Now see how your Self review comes out.

EXERCISE 3.3

YOUR SELF REVIEW   name

Use a separate sheet of paper to complete this exercise.

1. In what ways do you feel challenged by the college transition? Please explain.

2. In what ways do you feel overwhelmed by it? Please explain.

3. Do you feel both challenged and overwhelmed? Which is the predominant feeling?

4. Do you generally feel a sense of control or mastery as you face transitions? Give examples.

5. Do you usually face life as an optimist rather than a pessimist? Give examples of some things that lead you to feel optimistic or pessimistic.

6. Do you define your Self as resilient in the face of change? Give examples.

7. Have you uncovered ways to make your prior learning count? If so, what are you doing? Note: To answer this question, please go to Exercise 3.4, "Assessing Your Prior Learning." After you fill that out, you will be able to decide whether to apply for such credit.

8. Taking into account all of the above, do you rate your Self as:
   - ❏ a high resource?   ❏ a low resource?
   - ❏ a mixed bag?   ❏ okay?

   Please explain.

9. If you do not see your Self as a high resource, do you have any ideas about how to strengthen your Self? How to become more of an optimist?

Your resources include the knowledge and competence you already have. This learning comes not only from formal schooling, academic studies, or special courses, but also from prior work and life experiences. Some of our most powerful and useful learning has occurred on a job, through a volunteer activity, pursuing some special interest or hobby, or because of some special circumstances you have faced.

Your particular supply of knowledge and competence provides the building material already available as you construct your college experience. It's like building a house. You already have some cornerstones, perhaps even a solid foundation. You have some scaffolding, perhaps some walls, or a room or two nearly finished. You probably have some finished trim or nicely designed doors or windows. You may have a floor plan or a general design—or perhaps you're still looking for one.

Whatever your condition, it is very helpful, as you are taking stock of your Self, to become clearer about the knowledge and competence you already have. Then you can make better judgments about the additional things you need to know, new abilities you want to acquire, personal qualities you want to strengthen. With this awareness, you can use your time, energy, dollars, and emotions more efficiently. You can capitalize on what the college has to offer, create your own opportunities for special learning, and get much more from your total experience. In many institutions, you can save time and money by getting credit for the college-level learning you already have acquired.

Barry is an adult who decided to assess his prior learning. He wanted to finish his coursework for the Bachelor of Science degree, with a major in "Information Processing Systems" from the night school. As an older student, Barry was eager to complete college as fast as possible. While attending Evening College, he heard about "Life Experience Portfolio Evaluation." After discussing his background with a counselor, he registered for the "Portfolio Development" class. Here he developed skills in analyzing, identifying, articulating, and documenting experiential learning for academic credit. His completed portfolio consisted of a résumé, autobiography, chronology, competency statements, and extensive documentation. Barry, who had been a computer operator and systems software programmer, discovered that his prior learning could be applied to his degree.

Here are some guidelines that will help you decide whether to seek such credit:

1. Credit is not awarded for the experiences you have had, but for the learning that has resulted from those experiences. It is important to keep that distinction in mind as you consider evaluation.

2. The learning should have general applicability outside of the specific situation in which it was acquired. For example, you may have learned the specific procedures for processing personnel applications at one company. If you also learned principles and techniques that would apply at other companies, then this may be a situation where you can receive college credit.

3. The learning should include both theoretical and practical understanding. Even though you may not have applied the knowledge you possess to a prac-

tical situation, you should be aware of how to do something; you should understand why you are able to do what you do. You should not expect to receive college credit for application of a manual skill or a narrowly pre-scribed routine or procedure. Simply being able to manipulate a machine or carry out a practical activity without understanding the concepts, principles, or theoretical underpinnings is not sufficient.

4. It should be possible to evaluate the learning. You should be able to describe precisely what you know and can do, and what appropriate attitudes you have developed as a result of your experiences. You should be able to demonstrate on tests, through actual performances or products, or to an expert in the field, that you currently possess the learning you claim to have.

5. Your knowledge must be current. You should have attained from your expe-riences at least the same degree of knowledge or competence as has been attained by others through their college experiences and activities.

6. What you have learned must be related to courses, disciplines, academic areas, or academic programs offered at your university.

Exercise 3.4, "Your Self Review: Assessing Your Prior Learning," can help you decide whether it is appropriate to seek credit for the knowledge and com-petence you have already achieved from previous work and life experiences. You might want to explore, with an appropriate faculty member, advisor, or student development professional, the alternatives available at your institution.

EXERCISE 3.4

YOUR SELF REVIEW: ASSESSING YOUR PRIOR LEARNING   name

Use a separate sheet of paper to complete this exercise.

1. Do you think you have acquired college-level skills or knowledge?

    For example, you may have run a business, written for a newspaper, worked in a political organization, acted in community theater, traveled and learned a foreign language, read a lot of history or classical literature on your own. If you can document or demonstrate what you have learned from activities and experiences like these, you may receive college credit for your knowledge of accounting practices, your journalism skills, your knowledge and under-standing of local political practices, your acting ability, your language skills and literary understandings, after they have been appropriately evaluated.

2. Can you supply a realistic appraisal of your prior learning that satisfies the following questions?

    a. Does it have general applicability?

    b. Can it be documented, demonstrated, and evaluated?

    c. Does the learning you received relate to specific majors, programs, or courses in the cur-riculum?

    d. Does it include both theoretical and practical understanding?

    e. Is it current?

3. Are you aware of the following ways to assess prior learning for college credit?
   a. College level examination program (CLEP) (yes, no)
   b. Documented competency statement (yes, no)
   c. Portfolio (yes, no)
4. Looking at your prior learning, do you feel that you have some that merits college credit? If yes, consult your advisor or counselor for help in selecting the right approaches for you.

TAKING STOCK OF YOUR STRATEGIES

There are many actions you can take to cope with a Situation that is taxing or challenging.

1. You can change the stressful Situation. For example, you can say to yourself, "I got an F on that paper, but I am going to try to get the instructor to give me a chance to rewrite the paper so I don't have to get the F."
2. You can change the meaning of the stressful Situation. For example, "I got an F on that paper. I am disappointed, but I see it as a warning, and even as an opportunity to get extra help. I would rather have the F my first year when there is time to do something about it."
3. You can relax in the face of stress. For example, "I got an F. I am going to try to improve it, but mostly I am going to try to stay relaxed so I do not freeze and keep getting F's. To stay loose, I might go for a run, work out, go out with a friend, watch TV, meditate."

As you can see, some of these Strategies are problem-focused, designed to alter the situation that causes distress: "I received an F in the course. I am going to try and have that changed." Others are emotion-focused, designed to regulate your feelings: "I can try to deal with my feelings about receiving the F and explain it so that I do not feel diminished."[2]

The good news is that there is a cognitive framework for thinking about coping. The bad news is that there is no magic coping Strategy. The effective coper uses lots of Strategies flexibly, depending on what is going on. For example, if there is hope of getting the F changed, then use one of the problem-focused Strategies. You can drop the class, for example. If, however, there is no hope then try to regulate your emotions.

When we asked students what Strategies they used to cope with the newness of college, they responded in a variety of ways:

- "I live four hours away and can't talk to my folks every day. But I am having to write letters. This, for me, is a new way of relating to my parents."
- "I used to be embarrassed asking questions if I did not understand something in class. Now I am learning to ask instead of sitting around and doing nothing. I used to sit by myself if I was lonely. Now I'm learning to talk to a few people."

- "I write everything I need to do in a weekly planner. Then if someone asks me to go somewhere, I look at my schedule and then give the answer. I am in a special program because my English is not good. I need to develop more Strategies in language and also need help in motivation. My family is motivated for me. I wish I had more motivation. I have some but I need a lot more."

- "I need help in time management. I need to spend less time with my friends. I know it's hard, but it has to be done."

- "I need help with motivating myself to study. I need help not to watch too much TV. I am trying to get in an isolated area so I won't be able to turn the movie on or lay on the bed. I am torn between studying and friends. I want to be with my friends but I know I should study. I need some Strategies for sorting this out."

Kathleen was not unlike some of the students just described. Her "Coping Strategies Review" made it clear she did not have many ideas about what to do.

EXERCISE 3.5   *Kathleen*
YOUR COPING STRATEGIES REVIEW   <small>name</small>

1. Describe Strategies you use to take action, to change the Situation.

   I work hard to try to get on top of it.

2. Describe ways you try to change the meaning of the Situation.

   I have talked with my mentor and my friends about the Situation, and with my parents. That has helped me understand it a bit better, although I still don't really accept it.

3. Describe ways you try to control or regulate your emotional reaction to the Situation.

   I just try to keep busy and not let it get me down.

4. Which Strategies seem to work best for you?

   Working hard and keeping busy.

5. Do you see ways to increase your coping repertoire?

   No, I don't see any right now. Maybe my mentor or friends could help.

6. Taking all of the above into account, do you rate your Strategies as:
   - ❏ a high resource?   ☑ a low resource?
   - ❏ a mixed bag?   ❏ okay?

Please explain.

I guess I would rate them as a low resource, because all I seem to know how to do is keep working away, hoping it will get better.

Filling out the exercise, "Your Coping Strategies Review," will give you an idea about whether or not you use lots of Strategies flexibly. If your responses are similar to Kathleen's, the chapter on "Taking Control and Keeping It," gives you specific information on ways to increase your coping Strategies.

EXERCISE 3.5

YOUR COPING STRATEGIES REVIEW   name

Use a separate sheet of paper to complete this exercise.

1. Describe Strategies you use to take action, to change the Situation.
2. Describe ways you try to change the meaning of the Situation.
3. Describe ways you try to control or regulate your emotional reaction to the Situation.
4. Which Strategies seem to work best for you?
5. Do you see ways to increase your coping repertoire?
6. Taking all of the above into account, do you rate your Strategies as:
   - ❏ a high resource?   ❏ a low resource?
   - ❏ a mixed bag?   ❏ okay?

   Please explain.

Wrap-Up

You face each transition with potential resources: your Situation, Supports, Self, and coping Strategies. These 4 S's are not static. You are likely to pursue significant learning several times during the course of your life. Every time you start a new program, your Situation differs. You might enter college the first time as an unmarried person, dependent on parents, or you might enter as a married person with children. You also bring different Supports each time you pursue serious learning. You may use different Strategies. You probably are the same in terms of Self, but even that changes over time. Very simply, you can break down the components of change in order to evaluate what makes things work for you, what hinders your adaptation. You can discover clues as to what to do next.

The final exercise, "Taking Stock of Your 4 S's—A Summary," helps you visualize each S, marking which ones need strengthening.

Jim had retired from the army. He returned to school to prepare himself for a new career. His Situation was a plus. He had a family, his wife was working, his children on track. This was a good time for him to return. He felt Support from the army in terms of retirement benefits, and from his wife and children. He was optimistic about his ability to handle college. He had been unaware of the possible credits for prior learning and saw that as a plus. But he was concerned about his need to learn more about Strategies. By taking stock of his 4 S's, Jim could focus on what he needed to do.

Unlike Jim, Kathleen's summary of her 4 S's shows she needs help. In Chapter 10, "Taking Control and Keeping It," we'll see what kinds of help she might get.

EXERCISE 3.6	*Kathleen*
TAKING STOCK OF YOUR 4 S's—A SUMMARY	name

To summarize your resources, go back over each S and rate it either as a strength or as a resource needing strengthening.

	A STRENGTH	NEEDS STRENGTHENING
1. Your overall Situation	❏	☑
2. Your overall Supports	❏	☑
3. Your overall Self	☑	❏
4. Your overall Strategies	❏	☑

5. List the S's that you need to strengthen. Keep them in mind as you complete this book.

I need to strengthen my situation with my parents and with improving my school work and studying more effectively. I need to learn more strategies for coping with challenges other than just working, working, working.

Each person has different resources, some of which need strengthening. The summary exercise provides the information you need to highlight where you are and identify which S needs strengthening. Taking stock is the first step to changing.

EXERCISE 3.6

TAKING STOCK OF YOUR 4 S's—A SUMMARY   name

To summarize your resources, go back over each S and rate it either as a strength or as a resource needing strengthening.

	A STRENGTH	NEEDS STRENGTHENING
1. Your overall Situation	❏	❏
2. Your overall Supports	❏	❏
3. Your overall Self	❏	❏
4. Your overall Strategies	❏	❏

5. List the S's that you need to strengthen. Keep them in mind as you complete this book.

_____

_____

_____

_____

REFERENCES

1. Seligman, Martin., E. P. (1991). *Learned Optimism*. New York: Alfred A. Knopf.
2. Lazarus, R. S., and Folkman, S. (1999). *Stress and Emotion: A New Synthesis*. New York: Springer.

II

moving
through

What You Need to Know About Learning

College is about learning. Moving through college depends on it. How you think about learning, and how you act on that understanding, will heavily influence what you get out of college. It will determine how well you achieve your purposes. Your larger learning for career success—cognitive skills, interpersonal competence, motivation—will rest on those decisions. So will your larger learning for a good life—amplifying emotional intelligence, moving through autonomy toward interdependence, developing integrity. The choices you make about how you invest your time, energy, and emotion can be more sound—or less—depending on how well you understand and apply what we know about learning.

Mental Models

"Know thyself." That age-old precept is the cornerstone for effective learning. Socrates said, "An unexamined life is not worth living." Current cognitive psychologists document the powerful ways our prior beliefs, our "mental models," influence how and what we learn. We are all "meaning making" creatures. From our earliest days we are trying to makes sense of our world. The meanings we make—and remake and remake—provide an ongoing, increasingly complex and increasingly solidified, context against which new experiences are interpreted and assimilated.

Most of us assume we respond like a camera and tape recorder. Sights and sounds that hit our eyes and ears get faithfully reproduced in the brain. Not so. Using new technologies, scientists—neurophysiologists, molecular biologists, neuroanatomists, chemists, medical researchers—now can directly observe mental activity. They can record how the brain responds to varied stimuli, how it carries out varied tasks. Certainly there is not yet agreement on a comprehensive theory about how the brain functions. But there are findings that help us know more about learning. One major finding, consistent with a substantial body of psychological research, is that the brain does not simply reproduce external reality. Instead, apparently, about 80 percent of what we perceive and think we have understood is rooted in prior attitudes, information, ideas, emotional reflexes. Only about 20 percent comes from the "external reality."

Learning is a whole-person, whole-brain activity. Intellect and emotion are inseparable. That's why knowing thyself is so important. That's why examining your own prior history, prior knowledge, preconceptions, attitudes and values, and emotional reflexes is critical for significant learning.

Your Brain

Cognitive scientists and brain researchers give us insights about brain functioning and learning. Here are two lists. The first comes from Dee Dickinson, head of Seattle's New Horizons for Learning Project, based on the work of Marian Diamond at the University of California, Berkeley:

- The brain is remarkably plastic across the life span.
- Powerful learning is prompted when all five senses are engaged.
- Adequate time is needed for each phase of information processing (input/assimilation/output).
- Emotional well being is essential to intellectual functioning, indeed to survival.

The second list comes from K–12 research summarized by Geoffrey Caine and his wife Renate:

- Body, mind, and brain exist in dynamic unity.
- Our brain is a social brain.
- The search for meaning is innate.
- The brain establishes meaning through patterning.
- Emotions are crucial to patterning.
- Learning involves conscious and unconscious processes.

- Complex learning is enhanced by challenge, inhibited by threat.
- Every brain is uniquely organized, with resulting differences in talent and preference.

Take special note of the next-to-last item on this list. When we are threatened, emotions take over. We usually revert to more primitive responses. New learning drops away. We choke. Every athlete recognizes this dynamic. It's why serving out a tough tennis match can be so hard. It's why that smooth, relaxed rhythm gets lost when we look down a steep pitch of deep moguls. It's why final exam performance often falls seriously short of what we really know and can do. We need challenges to learn, but not threats.

Your Intelligences

Ted Marchese—a long time friend and colleague, whose brilliant overview *The New Conversations About Learning* supplies much of what we are sharing— gives a nice example, which helps us move such findings closer to how you can manage your own learning.[1]

> Imagine an experiment in which rats are being raised in a series of five boxes. In the first box you have a single rat, raised the usual (sterile) way. In box two, you have a rat raised the same way, except that it is given toys to play with. In box three, same idea, except that the rat's toys are changed every week. Box four, same idea, changed toys, but there are several rats growing up together. In box five, you have several rats, rich toys, but each rat is removed from the cage every day and lovingly stroked for 15 minutes. At the end of a time period, all these rats are given learning tasks to accomplish: pushing levers for food, finding their way through mazes, and so on. The findings, when you look at their respective abilities to learn these tasks, is a learning curve that goes up steadily from the first box to the fifth . . . a 25 percent gain in "rat intelligence" if you will, attributable to differences in upbringing.

Now, you are probably saying, "Yeah, but I'm no rat." True. But it's also true that rats and humans share about 95 percent of their genetic material. The important thing about these findings is not just what they tell us about educationally powerful environments for learning. They also demonstrate the brain's ability to develop new capacities, depending on the environments it encounters, the situations it experiences. These findings demonstrate that "intelligence" is not a given, fixed at birth. Given the right conditions we all can become more complex, fully functioning persons, across the life span. Certainly early experiences, genetic dispositions and capacities are important. Yet, except for cases of extreme deficit or deformity, they do not determine what or how much you can learn.

And of course, one major difference between you and a rat is that you have the capacity to create your own environments for learning, for increasing your own intelligence. You can take action to fashion the combinations of challenges and supports—the rich mix of new toys, companions in learning, and loving strokes—that will maximize the learning, the increased capacities, called for by your purposes. And the good news is that there are several kinds of "intelligence" you can build on and strengthen.

There has been a growing consensus that IQ is not the whole intelligence story. True, it might predict certain language and math skills, but it does not reflect intelligence in living. The links between IQ and other test scores like SAT tell only a partial story—yet that is the part of the story on which admissions directors rely. And more important, many learners evaluate their own intelligence based on such scores.

In other words, colleges and universities tend to think of intelligence as the part of us that enables us to do the academic tasks set forth by the curriculum and the faculty.

Wrong. Intelligence, according to Howard Gardner, Professor of Education at Harvard, is not a one-dimensional factor.[2, 3] His theory of "multiple intelligences," which proposes different kinds of capacity, supports many types of intelligence—each legitimate, each to be honored. The problem is that the educational system focuses on only one or two kinds. But in life you will utilize many different kinds of intelligence.

Gardner, of course, includes verbal and mathematical skills but also includes spatial capacity, kinesthetic, physical fluidity, musical, personal, interpersonal, and intrapersonal. "The operative word in this view of intelligences is *multiple*."

Knowing these different kinds of intelligence might help you understand yourself better. As you read about them, think about which intelligences you use.

1. Linguistic—Capacity to use words, "Word Smart."
2. Logical-Mathematical—Capacity to use numbers, "Number or Logic Smart."
3. Spatial—Ability to perceive the visual-spatial world accurately, "Picture Smart."
4. Bodily-Kinesthetic—Expertise in using one's whole body, "Body Smart."
5. Musical—Ability to appreciate and express in musical forms, "Music Smart."
6. Interpersonal—Sensitivity to others' feelings and moods, "People Smart."
7. Intrapersonal—Self knowledge, "Self Smart."

Thomas Armstrong developed a checklist for assessing the variety of your intelligences.[4] Martina, overwhelmed with the necessity to write papers with proper footnotes, began to feel "stupid." Her profile on the checklist showed that she excelled in interpersonal and intrapersonal intelligences. This was confirmed when she took a temporary job organizing a political campaign. At first she was reluctant to interrupt her studies, but after two weeks of receiving kudos from the officials of the organization, commenting on her "people skills," she said to her advisor, "I am really very smart. It just doesn't show in the conventional way." Her renewed self-confidence enabled her to return to her master's thesis. She realized she would never be an academic scholar but that she was "Self and People Smart."

To develop your own profile complete Exercise 4.1 to assess the kinds of intelligence that currently work for you.

EXERCISE 4.1

ASSESSING YOUR MULTIPLE INTELLIGENCES*   name

Check items that apply.

LINGUISTIC INTELLIGENCE

- ❑ write better than average for age
- ❑ spin tall tales or tells jokes and stories
- ❑ have a good memory for names, places, dates, or trivia
- ❑ enjoy word games
- ❑ spell accurately
- ❑ appreciate nonsense rhymes, puns, tongue twisters, and so on
- ❑ enjoy listening to the spoken word
- ❑ have a good vocabulary for age
- ❑ communicate to others in a highly verbal way

What other linguistic strengths have you?

_____

_____

LOGICAL-MATHEMATICAL INTELLIGENCE

- ❑ ask a lot of questions about how things work
- ❑ compute arithmetic problems in your head quickly
- ❑ enjoy math class
- ❑ find math computer games interesting
- ❑ enjoy playing chess, checkers, or other strategy games
- ❑ enjoy working on logic puzzles or brain teasers
- ❑ enjoy putting things in categories or hierarchies
- ❑ like to experiment in a way that shows higher order cognitive-thinking processes
- ❑ think on a more abstract or conceptual level than peers
- ❑ have a good sense of cause–effect for your age

Other logical-mathematical strengths:

_____

_____

*From *Multiple Intelligences in the Classroom*, by Thomas Armstrong. Alexandria, VA: Association for Supervision and Curriculum Development. Copyright © 2000 ASCD. Reprinted by permission. All rights reserved.

SPATIAL INTELLIGENCE

- ❑ report clear visual images
- ❑ read maps, charts, and diagrams more easily than text
- ❑ daydream more than peers
- ❑ enjoy art activities
- ❑ like to view movies, slides, or other visual presentations
- ❑ get more out of pictures than words while reading
- ❑ doodle

Other spatial strengths:

_____

_____

BODILY-KINESTHETIC INTELLIGENCE

- ❑ excel in one or more sports
- ❑ move, twitch, tap, or fidget
- ❑ mimic other people's gestures or mannerisms
- ❑ love to take things apart and put them back together again
- ❑ enjoy running, jumping, wrestling . . . running to class, jumping over a chair
- ❑ show skill in a craft
- ❑ have a dramatic way of expressing yourself
- ❑ report different physical sensations while thinking or working
- ❑ enjoy working with clay or other tactile experiences

Other bodily-kinesthetic strengths:

_____

_____

MUSICAL INTELLIGENCE

- ❑ notice when music sounds off-key or disturbing in some other way
- ❑ remember melodies of songs
- ❑ have a good singing voice
- ❑ play a musical instrument or sing in a choir or other group
- ❑ have a rhythmic way of speaking or moving
- ❑ unconsciously hum
- ❑ tap rhythmically on the table or desk

❏ are sensitive to environmental noises

❏ respond favorably when a piece of music is played

Other musical strengths:

_____

_____

INTERPERSONAL INTELLIGENCE

❏ enjoy socializing with peers

❏ seem to be a natural leader

❏ give advice to friends who have problems

❏ seem to be street-smart

❏ belong to clubs, committees, or other organizations

❏ enjoy informally teaching

❏ like to play games

❏ have two or more close friends

❏ have a good sense of empathy or concern for others

❏ other seek out your company

Other interpersonal strengths:

_____

_____

INTRAPERSONAL INTELLIGENCE

❏ display a sense of independence or a strong will

❏ have a realistic sense of his strengths and weaknesses

❏ do well when left alone to play or study

❏ march to the beat of a different drummer in your style of living and learning

❏ have an interest or hobby that you don't talk much about

❏ prefer working alone to working with others

❏ accurately express how you are feeling

❏ are able to learn from your failures and successes in life

❏ have high self-esteem

Other intrapersonal strengths:

_____

_____

Nancy recounted her daughter Karen's experience when she was writing her master's thesis on Howard Gardner's work. Since Karen's strong suits are spatial and artistic, Nancy suggested to Karen that she present her master's thesis as an artistic presentation, rather than written in the required academic form. Karen immediately replied: "You must be crazy. They teach Gardner; he is their Guru, but they grade the old-fashioned way." Despite Karen's realistic warning, we are including this section for conscious-raising purposes. Whether or not your professors stick to a monolithic view of intelligence as verbal and mathematical, if you do not fit in that mold do not, we say DO NOT assume that you are not intelligent. Do assume that you have other intelligences, many of which will more directly lead to career and life success.

Now that you have a richer sense of the kinds of intelligence you can bring to bear to accomplish your purposes, you need to determine what kind of learning you want.

KINDS OF LEARNING, LEVELS OF LEARNING

There are different kinds of learning, different levels of learning.

Learning can mean to gain knowledge, comprehension, or mastery through experience or study, or to memorize. It can mean to acquire experience of, or skill in, to be informed of, or to find out.

These definitions don't make distinctions important to you. They do not distinguish between transient or enduring learning, between surface and deep learning, or between learning that is context-specific or broadly applicable. They do not distinguish among types of learning. There can be change in verbal behavior without change in other behaviors, in underlying attitudes or values, in ways of making meaning, ways of knowing, or "orders of consciousness." There can be changes in specific skills without concurrent changes in more broad-based abilities. Pieces of information can be acquired without increasing general understanding.

Distinguishing among levels and types of learning is critical for improving your learning and for evaluating what you have learned. We can think about "levels" in two ways: (a) different levels of competence; and (b) different capacities for learning.

Levels of Competence

Several levels of competence are required for responsible citizenship, career success, a healthy marriage, and effective parenting. A nice fat Bermuda onion gives us a useful metaphor. The layers go from simple to complex. They go from those most susceptible to change and context specific to those that are most generic, nourishing and supporting the outer layers, slow to develop and slow to change. Learning in the outer layers can be dealt with as discrete, separable elements; learning in the core layers is necessarily multivariate and interdependent. Each layer interacts most closely with those adjoining.

Survival or life skills, the outer layer, are learnings that most immediately meet the world. They involve caring for health needs, planning and managing time,

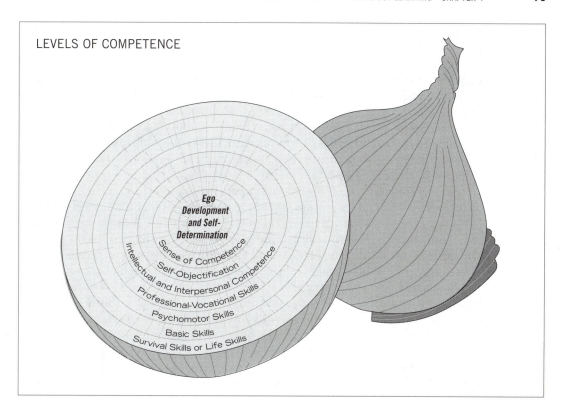

LEVELS OF COMPETENCE

choosing an occupation, finding and keeping jobs, buying and selling, and dealing with welfare, health, employment, government agencies and organizations.

Basic skills—reading, writing, speaking, numeracy—are critical in our knowledge society. Without them survival is possible, but very difficult.

Psychomotor skills may be more important than basic skills in some contexts, but those are becoming rare. For young persons coping with city streets and playgrounds, good coordination, strength, stamina, and fast reactions are probably more important than reading, writing, and arithmetic. Athletic ability and dancing may provide more ready routes to recognition, self-esteem, and status than good control of standard English. On the farm and in the shop, handling tools and machinery precisely and sensitively can sustain employment and income.

Professional-vocational skills depend heavily on adequate basic skills. Most professions and vocations require high-level verbal or quantitative skills to reach positions of significant responsibility.

Intellectual and interpersonal competence are so functionally interdependent that they are properly two parts of a single layer. Professional-vocational success, effective citizenship, healthy marriage and family relationships depend on both.

Intellectual competence is a spacious umbrella. Bloom's taxonomic hierarchy includes knowledge and comprehension, application, analysis, synthesis and evaluation. Others have added problem solving and problem identification.

Interpersonal competence is equally spacious, including such variables as verbal and nonverbal communication skills, diagnosing and responding effectively to another's needs or purposes, positive regard for others, the ability to help others in ways they feel strengthened, and the ability to control impulses and hostile feelings so they are not unleashed to make others feel diminished, powerless, or ineffective.

Self-objectification, self-assessment, and tendency to learn are required if survival skills, basic skills, professional-vocational skills, and intellectual and interpersonal competence are to grow. They all depend on the ability to objectify and describe one's purposes, to assess one's strengths and weaknesses, and to learn in response to these diagnoses.

Sense of competence, self-confidence, provides the foundation for self-objectification, self-assessment, and learning. Some of the major elements are confidence in one's ability to work with others, in one's judgment and decision-making ability; confidence that one can handle unanticipated problems, can find the information one needs, can augment the knowledge, skills, attitudes called for by new situations, can help others release energy to pursue shared goals.

Ego development and self-determination have to do with being purposeful, having a solid sense of one's identity and values, secure in one's ability to manage emotions. This core of the onion is where we make and give meaning to our lives. It is from this core that we take charge of our existence and create our future.

Well, that Bermuda onion is one way to think about levels of competence. Others would cultivate a strain with more or fewer layers, reject some and add others, use a different sequence. The metaphor does not pretend to be exhaustive or definitive.

The critical point is that we have an onion. We have multiple layers that interact. In learning you can start with one layer and go toward others. You can start with a particular professional or vocational skill, and also strengthen the most pertinent psychomotor and basic skills. And you can go toward the core, identifying the most critical types of intellectual and interpersonal competence, the areas for self-objectification and self-assessment, where sense of competence needs strengthening, and the pertinent purposes, values, and identity issues that need to be addressed.

Neither the core nor the skin can survive alone. A flourishing, zesty onion requires soils for growth that nourish and strengthen all the layers.

Capacities for Learning

Kolb's (1984)[5] experiential learning model of personal growth suggests that human development occurs by achieving "higher level integration through dialectical conflicts" generated by increasing perceptual, affective, symbolic, and behavioral complexity. We like to think of these as different dimensions for learning, or as "capacities for learning." Our capacity to learn, to convert life's challenges into broadly applicable learning that lasts, grows as we develop increasing perceptual, affective, symbolic, and behavioral complexity.

Increasing perceptual complexity means that we can see distinctions, recognize subtleties, taste differences, and feel gradations that were formerly not accessible. The differences between a novice and an expert wine taster, or appreciating good music or art rest on recognizing increasingly fine or subtle distinctions in form, taste, texture, and expression.

Increasing affective complexity means recognizing and responding to internal stimuli in less totalistic and more differentiated fashion. A powerful personal attraction may become understood to result from a mix of lust, caring, respect, affection, and longing for a past love. An angry outburst may be seen to contain defensiveness bas:ed on low self-esteem, hostility toward authority carried on from childhood, or a desire to look strong and impress others.

Increasing symbolic complexity occurs when our knowledge base, conceptual sophistication, and cognitive skills help us name the parts of things formerly seen as unitary. When we come to understand interactions underlying apparently simple cause-and-effect relationships, we can give meanings to what we are experiencing as a result of increasing perceptual and affective complexity.

Increasing behavioral complexity occurs when our words and deeds become more finely responsive to the situations we encounter, when they more accurately reflect perceptual, affective, and symbolic complexities that characterize the context that calls for action. Think of the differences on the basketball court between a Michael Jordan and a high school star. Think of two teachers. One commands a wide range of exercises, group processes, print, visual and technological resources, and evaluation strategies, enriched by solid human relations skills. The other commands lecture notes, a text, and midterm and final exams that combine multiple choice and essay questions. There is an enormous difference in the behavioral repertoires available to each. And it is likely that there are large differences also in perceptual, affective, and symbolic complexity with regard to students, learning, and teaching.

These "capacities for learning" apply across all levels of competence. Strengthening these capacities is necessary for many areas of complex learning. To grow a healthy onion means continual growth in these four capabilities. When your learning achieves increasing complexity in all four areas, you greatly strengthen your capacity to learn at whatever layer of the onion you wish to address.

aximizing Your Learning that Lasts

Once you have become clear about the kinds of learning and levels of learning you need pertinent to your larger learning for career success and a satisfying life, the question becomes, "What do I actually do?"

SURFACE LEARNING AND DEEP LEARNING

Perhaps the most important thing to understand is the difference between "surface learning" and "deep learning." Surface learning relies primarily on short-term memorizing. Cramming facts, data, concepts, and information to pass quizzes and exams. You know how to do it. Highlight texts. Make lists. Create outlines. Develop mnemonics. Rehearse, alone or with friends. Ask questions about things you don't understand so you have the right answers. Surface learning does NOT rely on seeking meaning. In contrast to deep learning, it does not ask how the texts, ideas, information, concepts, or data relate to your own thinking, your own attitudes, your own behavior in the world. It does not ask you to reflect on your particular mental models, your own preexisting prejudices. It does not ask how this new learning builds on, connects with, or challenges your prior knowledge and competence. It is that meaning making that is the primary characteristic of deep learning. It asks that you create and re-create your own personal understandings. It asks that you apply new information to varied real life settings and reflect on what those experiences tell you about the validity of the concepts, the limits of their applicability, the shortcomings of your own understandings. It is through recurrent cycles of such behaviors that you generate deep learning that lasts.

Studies in Scotland, Canada, and Australia find that 90 percent of students' study was characterized by surface learning. From what we know about teaching in the United States, that figure is probably not far off for us as well, because most of our teaching only calls for surface learning. It emphasizes covering large amounts of material, rather than examining, applying, and reflecting on a few key concepts. Most course work is required, in the same amount, at the same pace, for all students in a class. So students have little choice and little influence on what they are asked to learn, regardless of their prior knowledge and competence, or the motives that bring them to the course. Quizzes, exams, assigned papers and projects, with "grading on a curve," create competitive, threatening environments. These approaches to teaching, and the surface learning that accompanies them, also generate anxiety, fear of failure, low self-esteem.

In *The Power of Mindful Learning*, Ellen Langer, a Harvard psychologist, recognizes the limited value of rote learning, canned assignments, and hurried coverage.[6] Students get on autopilot. With mindful learning you are open to new information, can construct your own categories, and can recognize and try to reconcile diverse perspectives and points of view. You make choices about how you will pursue your learning, devise your own assignments and challenges, identify your own products and performances, consider how you will evaluate those to ascertain what and how much you have learned.

The second important thing to understand is the importance of practice. The most important kind of knowledge for strong performance is "tacit." Tacit means "expressed or carried on without words or speech," and "implied or indicated but not actually expressed." Tennis players talk about being "in the zone." That's when everything is flowing smoothly, naturally, when you are not talking your way through a serve, backhand, overhead, or volley. Studies comparing newcomers and experienced workers show that newcomers try to solve problems by reasoning from laws or principles, going to the text. Experienced workers draw on stories, on sharing information with others. They reason from causal models but are always pitting those models against their own experiences in practice. Novices are typically trained to produce the "right answers." Experts work from socially constructed, experience-based understandings, appropriate for the specific situations they confront. That kind of tacit knowledge comes from rich experiences in varied situations, and from repeated practice over time.

Wayne Gretsky, the star hockey player said, "A good high school player can take the puck down the ice. A good college player can skate to where the puck is. A good professional player skates to where the puck will be." High performance knowledge is always connected to specific activities, contexts, cultures. Theories and abstractions are helpful conceptual organizers, but effective application depends on tacit knowledge. And that only comes with practice.

Here are some summary principles, in the form of an exercise, that can help you diagnose and strengthen your learning. They are adapted from the Joint Task Force Report from the American Association for Higher Education, the American College Personnel Association, and the National Association of Student Personnel Administrators, *Powerful Partnerships: A Shared Responsibility for Learning.*

EXERCISE 4.2

MAXIMIZING YOUR LEARNING

name

Learning is about *making and maintaining connections:* biologically through neural networks; mentally through concepts, ideas, and values; and experientially through interaction between the mind and the environment, self and other, generality and context, deliberation and action.

	VERY OFTEN	OFTEN	SOMETIMES	RARELY	NEVER
1. I seek out a variety of world views.	❏	❏	❏	❏	❏
2. I try to experience culturally diverse perspectives.	❏	❏	❏	❏	❏
3. I try to create relationships among my different courses and between those courses and experiences in college and out.	❏	❏	❏	❏	❏
4. I try to make connections between what I am learning and my own circumstances and needs.	❏	❏	❏	❏	❏
5. I seek out relationships with persons whose backgrounds differ from my own.	❏	❏	❏	❏	❏

Learning is enhanced when it *takes place* in the context of a *compelling situation* that balances challenge and opportunity, that uses the brain's ability to conceptualize quickly and its capacity for contemplation and reflection upon the experiences.

	VERY OFTEN	OFTEN	SOMETIMES	RARELY	NEVER
1. I deliberately enter new situations I have not experienced before.	❏	❏	❏	❏	❏
2. I take on new tasks that involve things I do not know how to do.	❏	❏	❏	❏	❏
3. When I see problems or conflicts I try to help solve them.	❏	❏	❏	❏	❏

	VERY OFTEN	OFTEN	SOMETIMES	RARELY	NEVER
4. I set high standards for myself in academics and in other aspects of my life.	❏	❏	❏	❏	❏
5. I take responsibility for leadership when I see the need.	❏	❏	❏	❏	❏

Learning is *developmental,* a cumulative process *involving the whole person,* relating past and present, integrating the new with the old.

	VERY OFTEN	OFTEN	SOMETIMES	RARELY	NEVER
1. I try to plan my courses so later ones build on what I've learned before.	❏	❏	❏	❏	❏
2. I keep journals, portfolios, and other devices that help me keep track of what I've learned and how it relates to past learning.	❏	❏	❏	❏	❏
3. I set aside time each day or week to reflect on what I'm learning and on how it relates to past knowledge and experiences.	❏	❏	❏	❏	❏
4. I discuss what I'm learning with classmates, friends, and relatives to see what they think and whether my own thinking makes sense.	❏	❏	❏	❏	❏
5. I create metaphors and analogies that help integrate and give meaning to different things I am learning.	❏	❏	❏	❏	❏

Learning is done by *individuals* who are *tied to others as social beings* in competitive and collaborative relationships, enhancing learning through cooperation and sharing.

	VERY OFTEN	OFTEN	SOMETIMES	RARELY	NEVER
1. I join, or help form, study groups in my courses.	❏	❏	❏	❏	❏
2. I seek out opportunities to tutor or to help informally other students.	❏	❏	❏	❏	❏
3. I try to establish relaxed relationships of mutual respect and shared learning with faculty members.	❏	❏	❏	❏	❏
4. I share my confusion, uncertainty, mistakes, misunderstandings with fellow students, faculty members, or student affairs professionals.	❏	❏	❏	❏	❏
5. I participate in varied clubs, organizations, and student activities pertinent to my interests and purposes.	❏	❏	❏	❏	❏

Learning requires *frequent feedback, practice,* and *opportunities to use* what has been learned.

	VERY OFTEN	OFTEN	SOMETIMES	RARELY	NEVER
1. I ask for feedback from classmates and teachers about the strengths and weaknesses of my work.	❑	❑	❑	❑	❑
2. I reflect on evaluations of my work to understand better what I need to do to improve.	❑	❑	❑	❑	❑
3. I rehearse out loud key facts, concepts, and principles to myself or to others.	❑	❑	❑	❑	❑
4. I use practical problems or real-life situations to apply and practice what I have learned.	❑	❑	❑	❑	❑
5. After a course or unit is over I review it to fix it in my mind for the future.	❑	❑	❑	❑	❑

Learning involves *applying* knowledge and skills *to different contexts* and circumstances.

	VERY OFTEN	OFTEN	SOMETIMES	RARELY	NEVER
1. I list a range of specific examples, stories, and pictures that illustrate and enrich abstract concepts and principles.	❑	❑	❑	❑	❑
2. I take advantage of opportunities for off-campus service learning, internships, volunteer activities, and field research.	❑	❑	❑	❑	❑
3. I participate in on-campus programs and activities that help me develop skills, competence, and perspectives pertinent to my purposes and interests.	❑	❑	❑	❑	❑
4. I enroll in interdisciplinary programs and courses that ask me to apply academic concepts to practical problems or social issues.	❑	❑	❑	❑	❑
5. I ask faculty members to explain relationships among different concepts and principles, and how they apply to specific situations.	❑	❑	❑	❑	❑

Learning involves *monitoring* one's own learning, *understanding* how knowledge is acquired, *developing strategies* for learning consistent with one's capacities and limitations, and *being aware* of one's own ways of knowing.

	VERY OFTEN	OFTEN	SOMETIMES	RARELY	NEVER
1. I think about how I learn particular subjects or skills best.	❏	❏	❏	❏	❏
2. I consider how my own background and prior experiences influence what I am trying to learn.	❏	❏	❏	❏	❏
3. I seek to understand the different ways knowledge is generated in different disciplines and subjects.	❏	❏	❏	❏	❏
4. I evaluate my own work in relation to the teacher's criteria or expectations.	❏	❏	❏	❏	❏
5. I develop my own criteria for evaluating whether I have reached the standards I set for myself.	❏	❏	❏	❏	❏

Wrap-Up

When you can answer Often or Very Often to most of these statements, you will be on your way to maximizing what you get out of college. You will be taking charge of your own learning. You will be achieving the purposes you set for yourself. You will realize the most value you can from the time, energy, and emotion you invest.

Most important, perhaps, you will be doing that even when you encounter poor teaching, or teaching approaches that don't match how you learn best. You will be creating your own educationally powerful environments for learning, even if the particular place you find yourself does not encourage such learning.

REFERENCES

1. Marchese, T. (July 2000) *The New Conversations About Learning*, Presentation at the 2000 American Association for Higher Education Summer Academy, Snowbird, Utah.
2. Gardner, H. (1983). *Frames of Mind: The Theory of Multiple Intelligences.* New York: Basic Books.
3. Gardner, H. (1999). *Intelligence Reframed.* New York: Basic Books.
4. Armstrong, T. (1994). *Multiple Intelligences in the Classroom.* Alexandria, VA: Association for Supervision and Curriculum Development.
5. Kolb, D. A. (1984). *Experiential Learning: Experience as the Source of Learning Development.* Upper Saddle River, NJ: Prentice Hall.
6. Langer, Ellen. (1998). *The Power of Mindful Learning.* Perseus.

Deciding
on a Major

When Ito entered college he was clear about his major. He wanted to learn about Japanese culture and prepare for a business career that related to Japan. He planned to study in Japan as part of his program. Bill was less certain. He thought he might like environmental sciences so he could pursue work in wildlife conservation. Mary aimed to become a lawyer, but was thinking about majoring in government or politics to keep a wide range of future options open. Juan had no major in mind, and felt a bit bothered by that. Victoria changed her major three times before settling on chemistry as a route toward medical school.

When it comes to deciding on a major, college students, whatever their age, vary greatly in how clear they are. Here is what some of the juniors and seniors we interviewed had to say about their choices:

Dorothy said, "I declared my major as a freshman. In my senior year in high school I took Spanish. We were watching movies and reading about the Aztecs in Mexico. They showed us the museums, and the sites and digs the archaeologists went on. It was really fascinating. I thought, 'I would really like to do that.' I didn't realize people could do that for a living. I came up for the summer and talked to a professor about the program."

"You feel firm about that now that you're a junior?"

"I never wanted to change my major. When I came I wanted to be ready to go to Peru right after college and dig or whatever. Now there are other things I'd like to pursue with it. So I could end up doing different things."

"Which roads are you looking at?"

"I'll probably go to graduate school. I want to travel and this is a good field to travel in."

"Have you ever volunteered on a dig or anything?"

"No. I wanted to. I need to do that to get my certificate in archaeology and I plan to do it this summer. But you don't make any money doing it. I have to earn money to go to graduate school."

"You talked to a faculty member to explore it. Are there other people who helped you clarify your major?"

"Not really, just my family. I told them and they were like, 'Oh, that's really neat.'"

"Have you explored where you can go with the major once you get out?"

"Last year I went to the Career Development Center and worked on the computer to get ideas about what I could do, what the requirements are, and what I need to take."

"What advice would you give students about deciding on a major?"

"Decide on something that you're going to have fun with, that you're going to enjoy. I know a lot of people just decide on a major where they're gonna make a lot of money or something. Maybe that might give them a little joy, but I wouldn't want a job that was not exciting and interesting; something I can always explore, find out new information, and not just the same old thing."

So Dorothy, like Ito, brought a clear interest to college. She has learned that there are a range of possibilities and that graduate study will be necessary. Her college experiences have reinforced and clarified her future plans.

Amanda's choice, though built on an early interest, only really emerged during her first two years.

"I will go to graduate school and study physical education with a specialization in physical therapy."

"How did you come to choose physical education and your ultimate goal of physical therapy?"

"The main part was that I was an athlete. In fact, when I was 12 years old, I liked to work with people's bodies. I would put a sling on my sister, or work on my mom or dad. That kind of helped out. But I didn't want to be a physical therapist. It was just something in the medical field; a doctor or something like that. Then as I got older I realized what you had to go through to be a doctor and I changed it. When I was at my other college I was going to be an athletic trainer. Then I got here and changed it to physical therapy."

"How did you go through that process of change?"

"I thought that with physical therapy I could be a trainer or a physical therapist. There is more I can do as a physical therapist than if I was just a trainer."

"More options?"

"Yes."

"How firm do you feel about your decision?"

"I am strong minded on it. I don't think I would change it right now. I think I will enjoy it because I have been working with some physical therapists. I enjoy that."

"How have you been working with them?"

"My mom's best friend works in a nursing home. I go there and help out. She got me more interested. Then during the summer I volunteered at a hospital for kids. That was sad, but fun, too."

"You get reward out of helping others?"

"Yeah I do, and from seeing their progress, from being real weak to getting strong. That's what I like about it."

"When did you decide for sure?"

"Last year, my sophomore year, I really, really decided. Because when you get into the classes and you get more interested in it, it is, like, 'Yeah, this is it.' I was glad. It was like, 'Whew, what a relief.'"

"Whom did you talk with? Who was most helpful?"

"I talked to my mom's best friend. And with my roommate and her father. They live just down the street from my mother. She is more experienced than me."

"Did the people you were working with help you define what you wanted to do?"

"Yeah. The supervisors who made sure we did everything right helped."

"What advice would you offer other students about deciding on a major?"

"I would just tell them to do something that they really like to do. Think about when you were young or something that you now enjoy doing."

"Why is it important that persons enjoy what they do?"

"If you don't, you won't put your all into it. You won't get the best out of it. You won't put forth that effort. You don't want to get up in the morning and feel, 'Oh, I've got to go to work again today.' But if you like it, like, 'Oh yeah, I want to go and help her today,' then you want to get up and do it."

"Anything else?"

"Do something you know you can do. Don't pick something you're not good at. Be realistic. Don't take something you don't have any clue about or that you struggle with."

"And salary?"

"Yeah. You've got to make sure that you get paid. Money is not everything. But these days you've got to have some kind of money unless you have a husband to support you."

So Amanda, like Dorothy, now has a clear target, a specific occupation. She built on an earlier general interest. She talked with her mother, her mother's friend in the occupation she was exploring, and with a "more experienced" roommate. Importantly, she did volunteer work to see what the work was really like and found it satisfying. She feels firmly committed to her decision and is unlikely to be surprised when she reaches her goal. She recognizes the need for income, but, like Dorothy, emphasizes getting into work you enjoy. Like most college students who find that kind of clarity, she heaved a big sigh of relief.

Amos's experience, as with many students, was less tidy, more difficult.

"One of the hardest things through college is picking your major. When I came I always had wanted to go to law school. This university does not have a pre-law program. I was, like, 'Just pick a major,' something that if I don't go to law school I can still use to get a job. I picked public administration but didn't like it. I went to government courses. I did okay but I did not like what I was learning. Then I thought about an English major, but gee, that is not really me. So I went back and looked at my score card. By then I had taken a class in every type of subject. I thought, 'This history looks pretty good and I always had fun in it.' So I said, 'What the heck.' That's how I became a history major. Because I liked it. The only thing is that I am in no way cut out for teaching. I've seen a lot of teachers. You see what it does to them. You know what you have done to teachers, especially when you were a kid. Then you hear about teachers' salaries. I have had this debate with a lot of my friends. High school and middle school teachers are the most underpaid human beings in the world. With the abuse they take and what they have to put up with from kids and parents—and from the administration—they are really underpaid. I think I will not put myself through that. I mean, I won't lie. I am somewhat—I won't say materialistic—but you know, I want the big house, the nice car, the little family. It's the American dream. I want it. I can't get that through teaching."

"So you changed from public administration to history. But you are still interested in law school and not being a teacher. What type of jobs do you think your degree will lead to?"

"I'm a gambler. I know straight out I am gambling. It is one of those things you just have to do. If I get out with a history major, I am holding nothing. I can try to become a teacher or whatever. If I don't get into law school right away I will need to look around and say, 'What can you do with a history major?' Am I going to become a curator at a museum or what? But it's just throwing the dice."

"What advice would you offer students about choosing a major?"

"Do something you like. Don't torture yourself, don't pick a major and see dollar signs. 'I don't like it but it pays well.' Because you won't last. You will say to yourself 'This stinks.' Pick something you want to do. It's hard to learn something when you are not interested. That's why I got out of government. I just lucked out into what I happen to like. Okay. I have always liked history."

Amos picked his major because he found an area he liked learning about. He is still interested in going to law school, but he's willing to "roll the dice" for future jobs with his history major if that doesn't work out. His view is to go for whatever you find most enjoyable and will want to learn about now. Then take the next step as it comes.

Betty is like many students. A junior, she made a decision because the college bureaucracy asked for it. But she is still uncertain. She has other interests that might be better alternatives.

"I might have been influenced by my roommate. She was gung ho and knew exactly what she was doing. She came in here saying, 'I'm going to be a biology major and I'm going to med school.' I came in having no clue, left high school having no clue. I took those little occupational interest tests and they kept saying administrative or some other kind of professional work. But they didn't lead me anywhere. I enjoyed my introductory biology classes so I thought I would continue with that. I kept enjoying it until I hit chemistry and then I hit a rut. But the B.A. in biology only requires two semesters of chemistry. Yet I'm still questioning, do I want to continue with this. If I take the right number of elective classes I can get a certificate in environmental management. So I might do that. I'm not quite sure."

"You've just said you're not quite sure, but it sounds like you have been exploring what you can do with different majors."

"Just a little. I haven't done enough to set my mind at ease saying, 'Okay, this is what I wanna be.' Like the other day, when I got out of my biology exam it was like 'Do I really want to do this?' It could be anything else. Why did I choose biology? So I'm still questioning myself."

"So what are you going to do now?"

"I am going to research and find work. I need to talk to my advisor and find out what I can do with it. Is there any future in it? If not, I hope he will help me orient myself. Environmental issues are going to be there in the future. So it's going to be a future somewhere, somehow."

"What kinds of information have you sought?"

"Honestly? None. I've been to the library once or twice to look up what I could do with environmental biology and I didn't really get very far. I had other things to do. My long-term future isn't as important to me as my immediate future right now."

"Tell me about that."

"I look at each semester. I don't look any further. I have to start looking at the next semester since we have to put in our course requests . . . which actually makes me have to look further into the future because if I don't want to continue with this it's going to mess up my whole schedule."

"What's it feel like?"

"Stressful. It's like I'm making an immediate decision, like, 'Oh God, my future!'"

"What advice would you offer other students?"

"Take it slow. Don't rush into anything. Don't feel you have to declare a major immediately. I jumped into biology and now I wonder. Take as many different classes as possible. Get a feeling for everything. Like, this is my first communications class this semester. I wish I had taken one in my freshman year to get a feeling for it. I enjoy it. Maybe an administrative class or something like that would have been nice. Just get your feet wet the first few years and don't worry about declaring unless you're a diehard and you already know. A lot of people graduate and go into a job where they're not even doing anything they got their degree in because the job market is so tight. But it will definitely help your grades if you are in a major you enjoy so you want to study and want to do it. Actually, lately I've been thinking maybe I'll go into a French major. I was coming from a French class the other day. I sat down and said, 'Yeah, I really enjoy this class.' So who knows!"

"What's it feel like to say, 'Who knows?'"

"It's kind of scary, because you don't know what you're going to be doing or where you're going to end up. But in another way it's exciting because who knows, something different may come along. Everything is still out there. I think that's why I was scared to declare a major, because then I'm stuck. But I could change my major. I can take four more years if I need to and find something I thoroughly enjoy. That's why 'who knows' is both ways. It can be scary, or it can be exciting because you can try something new."

Despite her uncertainty, Betty seems comfortable keeping an open mind about her choice of biology. She recognizes that she has limited information and needs to get more; that she needs advice about possibilities. She admits to a variety of interests and is ready to spend the necessary time to find something she thoroughly enjoys. Institutional timing required her to declare a choice. She conformed to that institutional convention, but she has not let the institutional need close her mind or preclude changing her major.

Your Major and Your Purposes

Defining your major can be one of your most important decisions. It determines many of your course requirements. It also limits the range of other courses you can take if you stay within the number of credits typically required for graduation. So selecting a particular major is not only a decision to study a particular area in more depth, it's also a decision *not* to explore a wide range of other potential interests. Betty, for example, is uncertain about her biology major because she has other interests she would like to explore further. The extensive course requirements of some majors allow very few "electives." Other majors allow more flexibility. If you are choosing among two or more virtually equal alternatives, you might want to choose the one that gives you greatest flexibility and freedom.

There is another important point. We use the word "defining" for a good reason. Most persons assume they can only *select* from among the predefined alternatives. If one of those really fits your interests, fine. But many persons have interests, or occupational orientations, that don't conform to the ways academics "box" knowledge and competence. Many of those boxes don't fit the real world of work and effective living very well. Many of them have become outdated. If you don't find one that fits your particular needs, design your own. Many institutions have processes that allow for "individualized majors." Even those that don't will often respond to your initiative if they see that you really are motivated to pursue a particular combination of studies that has a logic behind it and some internal coherence.

A former student we know, for example, went to a college that had majors in English, French, or Spanish. Each of these majors began with the earliest works in those languages and came up to the present. But this student liked the literature of the late nineteenth and twentieth centuries. He also liked learning about relationships between literary works, social conditions, and historical events. He did not like reading ancient works. So he went to the Dean and said, "Isn't there any way you can slice literature horizontally? Isn't there some way I can study contemporary literature in English, Spanish, and French instead of having to go from the beginning in just one of them?" The Dean knew him because he had been on probation for two semesters for poor grades and had been a disciplinary problem as well. After a minute's thought, the Dean said, "I suppose you might have a major in 'comparative literature.' We don't have a formal major like that but if the chairmen of humanities, classics, the Spanish department, and the French department will put together a set of courses for you and design your comprehensive exam, I don't see why you couldn't do that." In two days the student managed to talk with those four faculty members, and they all agreed to lay out courses and a comprehensive exam when the time came. He thinks they agreed in part because they saw a first, faint spark of intellectual interest, instead of simply "poker, parties, and girls." His whole orientation toward studies changed. From that semester on he got A's and B's, so that by graduation his record and faculty recommendations were sufficient to get him into Harvard's Master of Arts in Teaching Program. It's not too far-fetched to think that the response of that Dean and those faculty members, their willingness to create an exception and extend themselves for this heretofore problematic student, turned around his college career.

We can't guarantee that all deans and faculty members will respond to you the same way. We do know, however, that many will take seriously a clearly articulated and thoughtful request for a unique major that suits your particular interests and orientation toward the future.

It is also important to recognize that, although your major defines your academic program and the range of course electives open to you, it does not have to define your total college experience. Your interests and orientation may be clear, unified, and strong enough that you want to organize all your time and energy around your major. You may wish to choose extracurricular activities, internships, volunteer work in the community, part-time jobs, how you spend your vacations—even friendships and contacts you make—so that they all help you toward the goals that lie behind your major. But you should also feel comfortable not doing that. You can use all those other rich opportunities for learning and personal development outside the courses required for your major to achieve other purposes important to you.

Remember that a satisfying life means integrating (a) vocational plans, (b) personal interests, and (c) issues concerning values, lifestyle, and family. Remember also the critical distinction between a "vocation" and a "job," between a career and whatever you need to do in the short run to earn a living. Recognize that the communication skills, critical thinking abilities, and interpersonal competence you develop, and your capacity to manage your emotions and develop mature relationships will be the building blocks for whatever combination of career, interests, and lifestyle you aim for. Also remember that you have a long life ahead. Many persons find themselves happily employed in areas not pertinent to their major. You can change directions in the future. An off-base decision now need not be catastrophic.

Defining Your Major

When institutional expectations require a decision, you may or may not be ready. Dorothy, Amanda, Amos, and Betty were all positioned differently for their decisions. All four responded in ways that made sense to them. And their responses make sense to us. As "experts," we cannot do better than echo their advice.

1. Do what you enjoy, because then you will invest time, energy, and emotion. You will *learn*.

2. Do something you're good at. Don't force yourself into an area where you know you are weak just for some abstract future payoff.

3. If you are not clear, take your time. Take lots of different courses, reach out for lots of different experiences. The world is full of interesting things. There are majors you don't even know exist.

4. If, like Dorothy and Amanda, you are quite clear, find volunteer work, internships, or other experiences that will give you direct knowledge of what the work actually is like, day to day, week in, week out.

Of course, the trick is identifying what you will really enjoy and stick with, and clarifying how that connects with a satisfying life and career. Most of us wish to unite our avocation with our vocation, to earn a living through socially useful work that we really enjoy doing. Few of us fully achieve that combination. To do so you need to become as well informed and as clear as possible about three complex areas: (a) available institutional resources; (b) yourself; and (c) the opportunities available to you.

INSTITUTIONAL RESOURCES

The career planning and placement services are one of your most important resources. These services typically include a wide array of occupational interest inventories, value-clarification exercises, goal definition and planning exercises, and other helpful devices. They also have up-to-date information about job trends, as well as local, regional, and national employment opportunities. They usually have job fairs and a stream of on-campus visits by employers. In addition, there are experienced counselors who can help you think things through.

Faculty members whose background or expertise seem relevant to your interests are another key resource. Seek them out. Ask them questions, not only about your potential opportunities and areas of study, but also about other persons you might talk with or resources you might tap. Often, one of these faculty members will be your advisor. But at many institutions advising is not well developed or well rewarded, so you may need to find other helpful faculty members. Try not to be put off by feeling that you should not bother "busy professors" about your decision. They are paid to be available to students. So, think through the kinds of questions you have, the kinds of information you need, and then get on their calendar for an hour or so. If you are clearly motivated and reasonably well organized in advance, most faculty members will invest time and energy trying to be helpful.

This chapter is no substitute for making good use of institutional resources. And don't feel you need to wait until your junior or senior year. The best time to become acquainted with career planning services and to establish working relationships with faculty members is during your freshman and sophomore years. That's when you need to get perspective on how you can best use your college experiences in the service of purposes you value.

YOURSELF

The "Who Am I—Who Do I Want To Be?" worksheet you completed in Chapter 2 is an excellent starting point for defining your major. As you saw from the students we interviewed, clarifying what you enjoy, the skills called for by those most-enjoyable activities, and the personality characteristics associated with them are the most important considerations. If you did that exercise some time ago, and if your college experience has had any impact since then, your responses will be different now. The best approach is to do the exercise again; see how your responses differ and consider the implications of the differences. Maybe your current responses reflect some temporary conditions, and your earlier responses, based on your years of experience prior to college, are more valid. Or perhaps your current responses reflect important and lasting changes.

We can pick up Bill again, whose hypothetical responses we suggested in Chapter 2. After two years in college, Bill's responses no longer include rock climbing. But he has added ski touring, reading books about nature and wilderness experiences, and wildlife photography to his list of most-enjoyable activities. He has become skilled at winter camping, and recognizing terrain and snow conditions that pose avalanche danger. He has learned to write short stories that draw on his own experiences and those of friends, and he has become sophisticated about cameras, telephoto lenses, and darkroom procedures. He has developed the self-discipline to balance studies, active participation in the Outdoor Club, sharing leadership in Sierra Club outings, and trips to the mountains with close friends. He has developed the capacity to invest sustained time and effort to get the best pictures he can, and to write with vivid, moving details. He sees himself enjoying travel, writing, and photography as complements to his environmental work when he reaches middle adulthood. His is attracted to the possibility of doing research and policy studies for the Wilderness Society or Nature Conservancy. He figures he will be able to devote more time to those interests in writing and photography during later adulthood and retirement.

Bill's core interests and enjoyments have persisted, but there have been changes and significant additions. They have become more sharply focused and more solidly held. They provide clear priorities for time management and learning. He has clearer targets for future employment. Your responses may reflect a persistent core or may be dramatically different. However they come out, doing this exercise again will contribute useful insights as you think about your major. Exercises 5.1 through 5.4 will require separate sheets of paper.

EXERCISE 5.1

WHO AM I—WHO DO I WANT TO BE? name

Complete the worksheet for "Who Am I" up until your current age. Switch to "Who Do I Want to Be" at the appropriate interval.

	MOST ENJOYABLE ACTIVITIES	SKILLS CALLED FOR (musical, creative, good with people, mechanical ability)	PERSONALITY CHARACTERISTICS (sense of humor, cooperative, dependable, leadership, risk taking, serious, independent)
Early Childhood			
Adolescence			
Young Adulthood			
Middle Adulthood			
Later Adulthood			

It is also critical to pursue a major that takes you toward a future consistent with your values. Most students come to college with values acquired uncritically from their parents and community. College experiences usually raise questions about those values. Many students become more conscious of that built-in baggage. They open it up, look at it, and try to move toward their own definitions. Others are not so challenged. They are comfortable with what they have. Whatever your experiences have been, as you begin to define your major, it is worth completing that "Value Analysis" exercise again, and comparing your responses with those when you were moving in. Once again, you will want to reflect on the similarities and differences and think about the implications.

Bill's most important values changed a bit when he completed the exercise as part of thinking further about his major. Being out in nature was still the first one he listed. But the second one, "having a substantial income," had changed. Instead, consistent with his new interests in writing and photography, he gave high priority to his own learning and self-development. This change occurred as he realized that if he were going to make a significant contribution to wildlife management and conservation, he would have to pursue graduate studies. He also realized that most jobs addressing environmental concerns do not pay high salaries. But he had become more interested in living in a rural environment where he did not need a fancy house and expensive clothes, where he would spend most of his time outdoors and would not need the latest stereo equipment, where he could build his own darkroom and do his own developing. You may find similar value shifts, depending upon your college experiences and their impact.

EXERCISE 5.2

VALUE ANALYSIS   name

On separate sheets of paper, answer the following questions about each of your five most important values.

First value:

 What is this value?

 Where did it come from (parent, peer, culture, yourself, other)?

 Why is it important to you?

 How is it reflected in your life? If it is not reflected, explain why.

 In what ways will this value influence your life, career, and educational planning?

Now do the same for your second, third, fourth, and fifth values.

Clarifying your general goals for life is another key part of deciding on a major. How important is work or vocation to you as compared with investing in marriage and a family? How much do you want to be involved in varied kinds of social contributions through volunteer activities, community organizations, and such? How much do you want to make your particular intellectual interests, hobbies, or other activities part of your life? It's difficult to make a sound decision without answers to questions like these.

Goals can be categorized in many different ways. The "Goal Priorities Worksheet" suggests one set of alternatives. They are not all mutually exclusive, but if you emphasize some of them, you will probably not be able to emphasize others. These general goals will interact with those characteristics of your vocation and career that are most important to you.

Do you mainly want to help others directly? Do you thrive on competition, or prefer more collaborative working relationships? How important is money? Power and influence? Do you have strong interests you want to pursue? Once again, although some of these can be combined, others tend not to go together so well. This kind of dilemma is not unusual.

Ali said, "I'm an English major and women's studies is my minor. I'm involved with different rallies and activities here on campus that probably won't be part of the mainstream workplace. But I'm also thinking about going to law school. I have this big dilemma between getting my Ph.D. or going to law school. I feel as if I've either got to stay in the world of ideas, which would be the Ph.D., or get into something more utilitarian like a law degree. I'm torn. I feel as if I have to make the choice now because of financial aid. Those funds won't be there if I just take an editing job or something like that out of college and make a mediocre salary."

The "Career Priorities Worksheet" suggests some of the possibilities for a vocation that can help you think through such issues. If Ali completed the "Goal Priorities Worksheet" and the "Career Priorities Worksheet," she might find a way through her dilemma. For example, going the Ph.D. route in English takes her toward teaching, research, and writing at a university. Her salary level would be modest, but (at least, after achieving tenure) security and long-term benefits would be relatively high. She would not be exercising much power or authority unless she moved into administration. She might supervise a graduate student or two, but those would be more collegial relationships than hierarchical supervision. Depending on the culture of the particular university, working relationships might be quite collaborative or more competitive, but there would be minimal reporting relationships or accountability to a chain of command. She would be helping others directly, could seek out innovative institutions if she wished, and be involved in her own creative work. She would have a great deal of freedom and flexibility in how she managed her time, how much she worked on campus, at home, or somewhere else. She would have ample vacations and summers to use for professional work or simply for personal pleasure.

A career in law would be very different. Her salary potentials might be much greater if she developed a strong individual practice or became a partner in a successful law firm. But her security would depend entirely on her productivity in terms of billable hours; it would not be guaranteed by the organization. She would not be carrying administrative or supervisory responsibilities. She would be working in a highly competitive and adversarial field that puts a premium on individual excellence and productivity. In some types of practice, she would be working with clients and helping them directly, but in corporate law, or if she pursued advocacy work concerning women's rights, the "client" would be more abstract. Depending upon her practice, she might have unusual cases that called for creativity, but much of her bread-and-butter work would probably be repetitive. She would have much less freedom and flexibility concerning when and where she worked than she would as a university professor. To a large extent, her schedule would be determined by court schedules and the demands of particular clients and cases.

So there are great differences in career priorities between the two options Ali is considering. One way she could help get a better feel for those differences would be to do an internship or some volunteer work for a lawyer or law firm, or "shadow" a lawyer who has the kind of practice she might like. ("Shadowing" simply means that you follow the person around on the job for a period of time.

It may be a day here and there, or two or three days, or even a week if they are willing and you have the time. Shadowing will give you a real sense of what the job involves for them and what it might involve for you.) She could also talk at some length with two or three of her English professors about their careers, see if they would let her shadow them for a week or so to better understand the realities of their profession. Those first-hand experiences would help her sharpen her own career priorities and resolve her dilemma.

EXERCISE 5.3

GOAL PRIORITIES WORKSHEET   name

Most of our important goals fall into four areas: relationships, vocation, society, and avocation. Some of the important parts of each area are suggested. First, write a brief paragraph describing the part each area plays in your life. Try to clarify, as explicitly as possible, how you would actually like it to be, what would be important for you. Then discuss the relative importance of each area, how you see them complementing or conflicting with each other, and how you might manage whatever compromises and trade-offs might be necessary. It may be that one or more of these areas is not important to you at all. If so, by all means be explicit about that. There are no right or wrong answers here. There is no ideal combination. The challenge is to articulate your most important goals and how they interact with each other.

RELATIONSHIPS

This area includes plans and aspirations for getting married and having a family, for sustaining relationships with relatives and close friends, and for developing new friendships.

VOCATION

This area includes plans and aspirations for making money and financial security, for helping others through direct interactions, for exercising power and influence, for achieving status and recognition, and for making significant social contributions through paid employment.

SOCIETY

This area includes contributions outside the area of paid employment; that is, through community organizations, political participation, religious affiliations, and organizations and associations addressing various local, regional, or global concerns.

AVOCATION

This area includes such things as hobbies, intellectual or cultural pursuits, athletic activities, and travel.

ACHIEVING A RICH BALANCE

Now consider which of these seem to be most important, and how you might manage your time, energy, emotion, and financial resources to achieve the kind of balance you desire.

EXERCISE 5.4

CAREER PRIORITIES WORKSHEET   name

As with your goals, career priorities can be considered in several general areas: salary level, security, and benefits; power, authority, supervising others; working relationships; helping others directly; creativity and change; freedom and flexibility. First, write a brief paragraph about each area, clarifying what your needs seem to be. Then write a final paragraph describing how these complement or conflict with each other.

Finally, try to identify the particular vocations or career areas that seem appropriate for your personal priorities. Describe how each one seems to fit. If you think you don't know enough about different alternatives to do this, go to the career planning and placement center, to your advisor, to an appropriate faculty member, or to all three for some advice.

SALARY LEVEL, SECURITY, AND BENEFITS

This area includes the complex interactions among income level, job security, and long-term benefits in terms of retirement, health insurance, and such. Some careers combine high income with high risk and few benefits. Other careers provide lower incomes but high levels of job security and long-term benefits. Others involve not much of any of these, but great personal satisfaction or self-expression.

POWER, AUTHORITY, SUPERVISING OTHERS

This area includes various kinds of leadership and administrative roles and responsibilities. Some careers move along increasing levels of complexity, power, and responsibility. Other careers involve little or no power, authority, or supervision; instead they emphasize working alone or in collaboration with others.

WORKING RELATIONSHIPS

This area includes the kinds of relationships that characterize particular types of employment. Some employment environments are highly competitive; rewards are based on individual performance compared with others. Other environments emphasize teamwork and collaboration. Some working environments strive to minimize formal reporting relationships and chains of command; others specify clear relationships among superiors and subordinates, and systematic reporting and communication lines up and down the organization.

HELPING OTHERS DIRECTLY

This area includes the "helping professions," where practitioners work directly with clients to respond to their concerns or needs. The work is most often carried out in an institutional context like a school, college, hospital, clinic, or community agency. Much of this work is done by professionals in private practice, alone, or in association with a team of complementary colleagues.

CREATIVITY AND CHANGE

This area includes experimental or innovative organizations breaking new ground that value fresh ideas and new approaches, that support and reward individuals or teams that come up with fresh products, better processes, or improved services.

FREEDOM AND FLEXIBILITY

This area includes the degree of discretion employees exercise over their own time and work loads. Some careers have predictable workloads and regular schedules. Some require that persons are on call or heavily subject to the demands of the organization or of persons being served. Other careers provide much more room for individual variability and self-determination.

HOW DO THESE FIT TOGETHER?

These areas can be mutually reinforcing or in conflict. How do they fit together for you?

POTENTIAL VOCATIONS

Are there potential vocations or career areas that seem to fit your particular priorities?

OPPORTUNITIES

One typical strategy for clarifying potential job opportunities goes like this:

1. Identify those parts of the economy that seem to be growing fastest or have the most potential for growth in the near future.
2. Identify the occupations in those areas where demand is growing, or that are new and understaffed.
3. Pursue an educational program that will prepare you for one of those occupations.

Be careful of this approach. It can be flawed for a variety of reasons. The economy and occupational needs can change faster than you can get prepared and find employment. The demand you identify at the time you decide may be met by the time you are ready. The available opportunities may not be located where you want to live.

For example, the most promising occupations identified for the 1980s were doctors, lawyers, computer programmers, aero-astronautic engineers, dentists, systems analysts, and accountants. But by the late '80s and early '90s the health professions had changed. Doctors were still in short supply in many rural areas, but not so much in urban and suburban locations. The level of need also depended greatly on the specialization one pursued. So a premed major and a particular medical specialty might or might not have put you in high demand. Competition among lawyers became very keen. The field became crowded, largely because of the healthy influx of many more women. Today, the dramatic increase in computer use and the need for a great variety of software applications have significantly changed the demand and qualifications for computer programmers. Teachers are once again in high demand, while cutbacks in federal spending for the space program and military aircraft, together with airline industry consolidations and economic difficulties, have reduced the need for aeronautic engineers.

These occupations are all appealing to, and appropriate for, college students. The fact that things change does not mean that a particular occupation should be ignored or that information concerning economic and occupational trends is not useful. But such information should be treated cautiously. It should not be the determining factor when you decide on your major.

As our student interviews suggested, the best place to start considering opportunities is with what you like to do and what you can do well. Use as your starting point the insights and clarifications you get from the self-reflective exercises we have suggested and the additional instruments and information available from institutional resources. Then "cold canvass" like Victoria did. Go out and spend time with people who get paid to do work you think you might like. Find out how they actually spend their time. See if you can get a detailed picture of a typical week, month, or year. What is the general flow of activity? How much hands-on labor or paperwork is required? What kinds of working relationships, meetings, and other "people connections" are called for? How emotionally demanding is the work? How much flexibility do people have? What is their general lifestyle? Are their social relationships totally tied up with their colleagues at work? Do they take the job home with them, or do they walk away at five o'clock? What are the typical career patterns, the opportunities for promotion, advancement, moving to higher levels of responsibility or more interesting challenges? What are the monetary rewards and other benefits?

Depending upon where you are, it may not be easy to find these opportunities. You may have to take a long weekend or use a vacation. You may have to travel to another location. But you will find it a very worthwhile investment if you can get a good inside picture of what the work you aim for is really like.

Joan is a good example of the kind of initiative and exploration that can be very useful.

"I found a field that fascinated me. It offered a number of different elements and it's changing all the time. I talked with art history faculty members. I talked with people in the actual field, people who have been in art for a long time. I just called around. I found contacts through professors and advisors. That was really invaluable. Getting some direction. Doing the groundwork through internships. Spending some serious quality time with the people who are working. What I found was that I needed to define it for me first. Everybody calls it something different. No one has it outright. It is a combination of different things. I had to find what pieces I could grab from different organizations and pull together one in my field. So it was just a lot of searching and being very, very flexible."

Once you have narrowed your potential areas of interest through contacts and conversations, you might ask if you can shadow one or more of the persons in particularly appealing kinds of work.

Then the best thing is to try for an internship in the kind of organization you would like to work in. It might simply be volunteer work where you make a variety of contributions, or it might be a more formalized arrangement where you carry a clear set of responsibilities for a defined time period. Students consistently find internships and volunteer activities extremely useful in clarifying what they want to do. If that work setting is appealing and if you make a good contribution, you may be offered a job or find a position waiting when you graduate. Building this kind of relationship early on can be especially helpful in these days when the employment market for college graduates is tight.

Internships can also be helpful if you are heading for graduate school. Amos, for example, who chose a history major but is aiming for law school, said, "Next semester I will be looking for jobs and trying to get internships somewhere in a law firm. Something to get involved. Then when I go to law school and they ask what do you do on the side, I would already have tried working in a law firm. I could say, 'Gee I liked it. That's why I really want to go to law school.' And when I finish college I would already have been in the law area." Concrete evidence like this, which demonstrates your interest and motivation, sends a special message to graduate admission personnel.

Many persons make career choices without ever really knowing what the day-to-day work is really like. They have a general image of a nice lifestyle, or they are acquainted with someone who seems to like what they are doing. But when you get on the job, the important things are the actual work and working conditions. So take time for internships, shadowing, and other activities to get direct experience of the working realities. Investing that time pays off handsomely in the long run.

Perhaps the single most important message in clarifying *yourself* and the *opportunities* is "Take initiative!" Invest time and energy early so you can organize your program and future activities to maximize the value of your college experiences.

Three Problems

Many persons face three problems in deciding on a major: institutional timing versus personal timing, liberal education versus professional preparation, and family or parental pressures. Your decision may involve one or more of these.

INSTITUTIONAL TIMING VERSUS PERSONAL TIMING

Amos and Betty were not really ready to make a decision when the institution called for it. They compromised as best they could. Amos "rolled the dice" and Betty made a choice with great uncertainty. There is another alternative. Take some time out. There is nothing wrong or disastrous about taking off a semester, a year, or even longer. Work, travel, do some independent studying or exploring on your own. Many young persons profitably delay entering college straight from high school until they feel more ready. You can delay a decision about your major until you feel clearer about it. You can seek work, volunteer opportunities, or other experiences pertinent to your vaguely felt interests. Or you can simply put everything on ice for a while and see what emerges. See what interests or orientations arise that might position you to make better use of your college experiences. Today's knowledge-based society requires lifelong learning. You will be making career changes and combining further education with work and family responsibilities off and on throughout your life. Many persons take time out and return with much more focus, more motivation, more energy, more enjoyment. Don't be afraid to do that if you are hung up about your decision.

You should also realize that choosing the wrong major need not be fatal. You can change. You can add other courses and activities that increase your breadth and your future options. Many students don't end up working in areas closely related to their majors, and that may well be the case for you.

LIBERAL EDUCATION VERSUS PROFESSIONAL PREPARATION

Should you major in some "liberal arts" area you really like, but which does not point to a particular profession or occupation? Or should you choose something that leads more directly to employment upon graduation? Majors in English, a foreign language, sociology, psychology, anthropology, history, economics, or political science, for example, do not prepare you for a specific job after graduation. Usually you need more specialized graduate study. Often the most apparent career option is teaching in schools or universities. Amos and Dorothy both made such choices and recognized what was implied. But a major in some aspect of business—marketing, sales, accounting—typically will lead to immediate employment at reasonable starting salaries. Engineering, biology, and physics majors often find immediate employment at good pay.

The real issue underlying this choice is the relative importance to you of a good job upon graduation versus a wider range of long-term career alternatives. The problem with preparing for a specific kind of job is that 5 or 10 years later you may find yourself at a "dead end." The broad preparation of a liberal arts major, on the other hand, can position you to move among different employment settings as your interests change and as opportunities arise. Studies carried out by the American Telephone and Telegraph Company,[1] for example, found that liberal arts majors were better prepared for management roles than those with more specialized or technical degrees. Forty-six percent of humanities and social science majors had potential for middle management compared with 31 percent of the business majors and 26 percent of the engineers. Furthermore, after eight years, the management level of the humanities and social science majors was highest, with engineers far behind.

The American Society for Training and Development is the professional association for persons employed in corporate education and training. They are the business world's human resource development experts. They identify these skills for an effective American work force:[2]

■ Knowing how to learn
■ Competence in reading, writing, computation

- Skills in listening and oral communication
- Adaptability: creative thinking, problem solving
- Personal management: self-esteem, goal setting, personal and career development
- Group effectiveness: interpersonal skills, negotiating skills, teamwork
- Influence: organizational effectiveness, leadership

All of these skills can be developed through studies in any complex area. They certainly can be well tested and honed by most liberal arts majors. And, we should note, many of them can be strengthened mightily through involvement in activities beyond courses and classes that may or may not be related to your major. If you come out of your college experience with strong competence in these "generic" areas, you will be well prepared to create an effective career, to pursue a vocation that is more than just a job.

But significant development in these areas calls for hard work, for handling tough challenges. It requires heavy investments of time, energy, and emotion during your college years. That's why, as our students emphasized, the most important thing is to identify a major you enjoy and want to work in. If it is in the liberal arts, so be it. In the long run, you will be better off than if you pursue more specific occupational preparation in which you are less interested simply because there are better job prospects upon graduation.

PARENTAL EXPECTATIONS

There is an old story about the mother and her 2-year-old toddler at the beach. The toddler gets caught by a wave and is drawn out, floundering, over his head. The mother cries, "Save him, my son the doctor!!!" If that little boy is saved, he may still be struggling for air when he's 20.

Many of us come to college carrying powerful and long-standing parental expectations about future occupations and lifestyles. Sometimes parents are quite explicit about why they are making the "investment in your future." Sometimes it seems more like an investment in *their* future, in *their* status, than in yours. It can become even more complicated when parents don't agree.

Ping's comments may seem a bit extreme, but if you ask around you will probably find others with similar experiences:

"My father wanted me first to become a lawyer or a doctor. But I said that was not what I wanted. At first I did, but then I decided it was not for me. There was pressure because he wanted the prestige—my daughter is studying medicine or studying law. It was a big step for me to tell him I did not want to be a lawyer. I did not want to go to law school. It really disappointed him. So that is why I push myself even more. This is why I want to go into the major I do. I can prove myself to him, saying this is the right choice for me. I know he disagrees with me."

"How does your mother feel?"

"My father wants us, my sister and brothers and I, to study and stay in school as much as possible and gain all this education. But my mother wants us to get out as soon as we can. Get a job. Work and get some money first. So there is a conflict there. I can't satisfy them both. So I just try. I want to make them happy and proud. But I have to look at what I want to do and plan for myself."

"It had to be a big step to tell him you wanted to do something else."

"Yeah. It was. I never knew how to approach him but then I just said, 'Hey Dad, I am not going to do this.' He was disappointed."

"And it took a little while for that to settle down?"

"Yeah. I know that inside he still wants me to. He still is hoping. He still throws it out sometimes."

"What kind of communication do you have with your parents now?"

"My sister and I live up here now. She has already graduated. But ever since my brothers started college, they made us call every week. Every Sunday, actually. My brothers don't do it as much as we do, we girls. We have to call every Sunday, regardless. They will get upset if we don't. We just talk. They ask me how school is going or if there is anything new. I don't ask for advice. I just say what is going on."

"So when you are trying to come to a decision about something that is pretty important, you form it in your own head and then go to your parents. Or do you seek information from them while you are formulating?"

"I usually make my own decision before I ask them. I am thinking about participating in a co-op program. I have already planned it. Then I run it out to my parents. To present something to my parents you have to know everything beforehand. Otherwise, if they ask you something and you don't know the answer, they will go cold on you. So you have to know it. I asked them if they had ever heard about this program. And then I tell them this is what I am doing. I am volunteering. This is what I am doing outside of classes. Then I will seek their approval. So when I ran it across them about the coop they were like, 'Oh. That's good.'"

"So being well informed and having it thought through gives you power in your decision when you go to them, because they feel if you don't understand what you are doing, then you shouldn't be doing it."

"Right."

Ping has developed the strength and the strategies for coping with her parents' needs for close communication while at the same time asserting her own priorities and making her own decisions. She tries to be fully informed, and think things through as well as she can. Then she presents her decision. As long as her parents realize that she understands clearly what she is doing, they go along with it. When it comes to choosing a major that does not satisfy her father's need to be able to boast about his daughter as the future doctor or lawyer, or her mother's need for her to go right out and get work, she is able to go toward her own future. One consequence of that personal choice is that she feels she needs to work hard, to do well, to prove herself in the wisdom of her choice.

Wrap-Up

Choosing a major is a big decision. The most important thing is to take initiative in using the institutional resources available: the career planning and placement center, your advisor, other faculty members, students who are your classmates or more advanced. Use the various exercises we have suggested, and others you may find, to clarify what you enjoy, what you are good at, what your values and career priorities seem to be. Think through the trade-offs involved with varied life, career, and educational alternatives. Then go check out real working situations through visits and interviews, shadowing, internships, and such. If you are uncertain, take your time. If you feel confident of your orientation, make sure you find out what the actual work involves, the kind of preparation required, and the typical career patterns. Try to keep a long-term perspective. Recognize that your need to support yourself financially may mean taking short-term employment while you continue seeking work more consistent with your career interests.

Remember that it is *your* life you will be creating. Take seriously advice and counsel from parents, spouses, and other persons who are important to you. But in the end, make sure your decisions fit you as best you can tell. Finally, although your choices will be important, they can be changed. Data show that, on the average, persons in the United States pursue five different careers in the course of their life. Often, their career changes reflect significant shifts in values, talents, and interests. Although your decision is important, it is not set in concrete. When the reasons add up, you can make alterations to suit your changing self and the changing opportunities out there.

CHAPTER 6

Maximizing Learning from Courses and Classes

We hope that you have been able to identify some clear purposes for your college education. We hope these are important enough so there are things you really want to learn, skills and areas of competence you want to strengthen, personal characteristics you want to develop further. If you have decided on a major, we hope that decision adds fuel to the time, energy, money, and emotion you are ready to invest.

Learning, Not Grades

Your long-run payoffs depend on what you learn that lasts. They depend on progress you make in developing the knowledge, abilities, and personal characteristics you have specified. They depend on deep learning, not surface learning, and the tacit knowledge that comes from practice, practice, practice.

Those payoffs will *not* depend upon the grades you get by memorizing pages of lecture notes and highlighted textbook readings. We know that's hard to believe. Getting good grades and maintaining a high grade point average seem to be the most important reasons for studying, for spending long hours in the library, for psyching out the professor, for figuring out what is likely to be on exams and staying up all night cramming for them. It's hard to believe that grades are not important after college when parents, professors, and other students see them as critical evidence of success or failure.

But, since the 1950s there have been numerous studies correlating the relationships between grade point average and many diverse indicators of postcollege success: income level, career success, graduate school performance, happiness, personal adjustment, and mental health . . . you name it. Over the years, several persons have summarized this research. All these summaries say that grades are poor predictors of whether someone will be successful in work and living a good life. One of the most recent found, across a large sample of studies, no overall relationship between grades and adult achievement in the workplace.

If you don't believe us, you can, as they say, look it up. Refer to the report by Robert Brest, "College Grade Point Average as a Predictor of Adult Success: A Meta-Analytic Review and Some Additional Evidence," in *Public Personnel Management*, Vol. 18, No. 1, 1989, pp. 11–22.

There is one exception: If you hope to enter a highly selective graduate school immediately after graduation, then your grade point average is important. These schools, because of their large number of applicants, use GPAs as an efficient way to make a first cut. So, if that's your next step after college, you need to shoot for high grades.

Of course, if your grades are so poor you flunk out and don't complete college, it is a different story. The critical distinction is whether or not you graduate. Once you've got your degree in hand, your grades have little consequence for your long-term happiness and success.

We emphasize these points about grades because we want to help you maximize your learning and personal development, acquire knowledge, develop skills, and build personal characteristics that will serve you well throughout life, across a wide range of situations. Unfortunately, much classroom teaching and many course requirements do not result in learning that lasts. If you really want to learn, often you will need to invest time and energy in ways not required by the teacher. Or you may be required to take courses that are so badly taught you cannot learn effectively. Then the wisest choice may be to put in only the minimum amount of time and energy necessary to get by. Use the time and energy saved for other areas where the learning is important to you and leads to outcomes of lasting value.

Some experienced, thoughtful students have become clear about these trade-offs. Remember Victoria's comment, "Sure, you can work for a grade but the idea is to really learn something." And her description of her fiance who got C's and D's but who is "very successful," making a good living and happy about what he does.

Li Peng, for example, said, "Right now grades are more important to students than what they've learned. Right now you gotta get this kind of grade to make your parents happy, yourself happy, and your teachers happy. So the grades are more important than what you learned. I used to think that as long as I got a good grade I didn't really care what I learned. Because all they ever told me was, 'Just get this grade and you'll be okay.' I don't believe in that now. Now I feel successful if I understand what I've studied."

"What advice do you have for other students about getting the most out of their academic program?"

"Get your priorities straight first. If you want to be what you want to be, you are gonna have to work on it. If you're not really working on it that means you're not really into it. You don't have any motivation. So you might as well get out of it. Don't worry about your grades. Just try to learn whatever you can because a lot of people think too much about grades and not enough about what they are actually getting out of their studying."

If what we're saying, and if Victoria's and Li Peng's orientations sound like heresy, so be it. Listen to these students describe their courses and studies and you'll understand why we take this apparently extreme position.

Mike: "In class it is mostly listening to the lecture on whatever topic we happen to be considering. Just taking notes is the core of the class. We'll receive homework assignments. Lately we've been getting a lot of theory-related classes, which is a lot of homework and textbook-oriented work. You just kind of show up, make sure you get the information, and just do what you can with it. It requires a lot of reading and a lot of memorization."

Rebecca: "Generally it's a lecture course where we read and then are tested on the information. I generally hold off on the reading until three or four days before the exam. Then I will read everything, study my notes, and things like that. I think it is easier for me to remember all the information that way."

How much would you guess Rebecca has actually learned? How much will she retain three months, six months, a year later? If she gets an A in this course, how much value will that kind of learning contribute to her working knowledge later in life?

Lou Ann has a more systematic approach to assimilating the information. "Basically, what I do is take the test deadlines and say, 'Okay, I have 10 chapters for this test.' So I read all the chapters and start reviewing them. Then every time I go to class I take down what he lectures on in class and go back and study it together with the book. So I learn it in units, almost, so that when the test gets here I don't spend three days before cramming. That's how I learn. That's the learning process, memorizing. So that's that."

These comments from Mike, Rebecca, and Lou Ann are consistent with studies of college teaching. Most teaching involves heavy use of lectures. Teachers, on the average, spend about 80 percent of class time lecturing to students who are paying attention only about half the time. But the major problem is how much and how quickly students forget the content of the lectures. Within a few months, at least 50 percent of the content has evaporated. One study gave students a summary of the lecture, let them use their notes, and tested them immediately after the lecture. The students had retained only 42 percent of the content. When they were tested a week later, they retained only 17 percent.

Here again, if you are skeptical about this research, you can do your own experiment. Pull out a midterm or final exam from last semester. Sit down and take it cold. No reviewing notes or readings, no discussion with others, no preparation. See how you do. If you score more than 50 percent, your retention rate is outstanding. Or perhaps you have been using the material in other courses or other activities since then to keep it fresh. Or maybe it is an area of special interest to you where you've kept on learning. But we bet that if you retake five different exams at random, your retention will be closer to 20 percent, perhaps less.

Our basic point, and it is fundamental to this chapter, is that memorizing rarely creates learning that lasts. If you keep on using the ideas, concepts, and skills, then they will stick with you and become integrated. But if you simply memorize them to pass an exam and then go on to other courses or unrelated activities, you may have obtained a good grade—but not much else. If you really want to learn the material effectively, so it will serve you in the future, you need to do more.

Experiential Learning

To help you achieve learning that lasts, deep learning, from your courses and classes, we want to tell you more about David Kolb's "experiential learning theory."[1] In Chapter 4 we shared his experiential learning model of personal growth, which involves developing increased perceptual, affective, symbolic, and behavioral complexity. Now we want to go to his "experiential learning cycle," which underlies his model of growth.

Strictly speaking, all learning is "experiential," so it may be helpful to begin with some simple definitions. The dictionary says "learning" is to gain in knowledge, understanding, or skill by study, instruction, or experience. "Experience" is actually living through an event or events, actual enjoyment or suffering, and thus, the effect on judgment or feelings produced by personal and direct impressions. So "experiential learning" includes knowledge, understanding, and skills as well as judgment and feelings. It includes the educational processes of study and instruction as well as actually living through events. It recognizes that both joy and suffering often accompany significant learning. When the Bible says that "Abraham knew Sarah," it is not talking about memorizing abstract concepts. It is talking about full-fleshed, active, "experiential" knowing.

According to Kolb, most learning occurs through a four-stage cycle. You start with some experiences. You think about these, reflect on them, make observations about them. As these experiences accumulate in relation to particular events, activities, persons, and areas of interest, you begin to develop some concepts, maybe a hunch or a "theory," that seem to explain what is going on or why something seems to happen in recurring fashion. These concepts become the basis for how you think or how you act the next time you encounter a similar experience.

Take an obvious example. The first time you come on campus, the layout of the buildings is unclear. The location of classrooms or offices within buildings

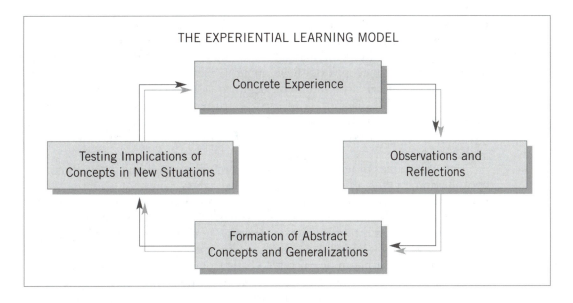

may be confusing. You are uncertain how to get from the admissions office to your advisor, to where you pay your bills, to the cafeteria, and so forth. You begin to walk around. You may look at a campus map and try to figure out what's where. You develop an initial impression of how to get from A to B to C. You try out a route, and usually, perhaps after a bit of wandering around and asking questions, you find what you're looking for. You may stop to think about where you turned wrong, what would have been a more direct route. On the basis of these reflections, you refine your own internal "map." The next time you need to get from A to B or B to C, you make fewer wrong turns. Pretty quickly you can find your way everywhere on campus. You know all the shortcuts and, down to a minute or two, how long it takes you to go from one class to another, from the student union to the library, and so forth. If for some reason you need to go to a faculty member's office, or to some particular place you've never been before, you find it much more efficiently than you would have the first day. You can do that because you have accumulated experiences and developed a rich set of concepts that help you cope with the new unknown.

Or take a more complex, more academic example. In school you had social studies courses that taught you the basics about the U. S. government, the division of powers among the executive branch, the legislature, and the judicial branch. You go to Washington, D.C., perhaps on a class trip, or with your children, and see the White House and the Capitol. Perhaps you visit your local senator or congressional representative, or attend a session of Congress. Your experiences make more vivid and clear those abstract concepts. The idea of "division of powers" takes on added reality, added richness. You won't forget it so easily.

Not all learning is conscious. The "experiential learning cycle" can apply to unconscious learning as well. You grow up living in a community where persons of certain backgrounds—who perhaps speak English poorly, or come from a different country, or have a different skin color—collect the garbage, maintain the streets, do the dirty work and manual labor. You may see similar persons sleeping in the streets. You may pick out news about robberies or violence committed by some such persons. Before long, you begin to assume that all such persons are stupid, irresponsible, dangerous, or can't be trusted. You avoid them. Your experiences get more and more selective. Your assumptions get reinforced. And you have become, without really being aware of it, prejudiced toward, biased about, such persons.

Other examples of unconscious learning involve what's called "psychomotor coordination": riding a bicycle, throwing a ball where you want, shooting a basket, stroking a tennis ball, driving a car, swimming. You usually start with experiences and observations. Sometimes you get some basic instructions. But the real learning occurs through practice, practice, practice. That's how it gets built in, how the skills get honed, how your repertoire expands.

We know from neurological research that our brain is a mass of interconnected neurons. Every sensation we receive, every move we make, every emotion we feel, every thought we think, every word we speak, involves a network of those interconnections. The fundamental thing we need to do, to achieve learning that lasts, is connect the new learning with one of those preexisting networks. Whether it is a new physical skill, a new emotional experience, a new piece of information, a new set of concepts, if it doesn't get connected it won't last long. It's like the internal map of the campus. Once we have it well developed, we can plug in new locations easily and quickly; in the future, we will remember clearly how to get there.

Kolb's experiential learning theory describes how those networks are built. Effective learning has four basic ingredients that call for four different abilities. You must be able to enter new experiences openly and fully, without bias. You must then try to stand back from those experiences, observe them with some detachment, and reflect on their significance. Next you need to develop a logic, a conceptual framework, a "hypothesis," that makes sense of your reflections and observations. Finally, you need the ability to apply these concepts, to test their implications through action, to use them to solve problems, and to try out appropriate behaviors. This testing kicks off a new, better-informed, better-skilled, more sophisticated cycle.

Note that there are some critical consequences of this approach when it is well used. First, it attaches major importance to testing ideas through action. When ideas are tested in action, their significance is greater than when they are simply memorized or left as unexamined abstractions. An idea taken as a fixed truth gives no cause for further thought; an idea as a working hypothesis must undergo continual scrutiny and modification. That, in turn, creates pressure to formulate the idea itself accurately and precisely.

Second, when an idea is tested for its soundness or its consequences, the results must be acutely observed and carefully analyzed. Activity not subject to observation and analysis may be enjoyable, but it usually doesn't add much to learning, to greater clarification, or to new ideas or improved skills. We often have the same experiences over and over, and still don't learn from them. That's because we do not take time for reflection and analysis.

Third, reflection and analysis require discrimination and synthesis. We have to make distinctions about the elements of our experience. We also need to synthesize the relationships among them. So when we talk about Kolb's experiential learning theory, we are sharing this complex set of interactions.

A good football coach uses all four elements. Players have the *concrete experience* of playing the game: missing blocks, making clean tackles, running a faulty pass pattern, getting mousetrapped, executing a perfect option play. They *reflect* between games on what worked and what didn't, reviewing video tapes and discussing how to improve. They use *abstract conceptualization* to get the plays down pat and to visualize their own moves. The next game provides the context for *active experimentation* and triggers another cycle.

When we asked Sara Jane what advice she would give students about getting the most out of their academic program, she unwittingly illustrated how part of Kolb's cycle worked for her: "Definitely attend your classes. You may get notes from someone, but when you attend classes you get a lot of examples from your teacher and she'll help you understand. Then attend any study groups you can, review what you learn each day, and be prepared for class. I find it easier, if I'm supposed to read something for class, to read it after the teacher lectures 'cause I'll understand it more rather than reading before and tuning myself out 'cause I don't understand. My mind will wander. But if they lecture about it I understand it more from them talking about it and then reading the material."

Sara Jane likes to start with the experience of her classes, even if she can get the notes from someone else. She gets a lot of examples from the teacher, which help make things concrete. Then she joins study groups where she can review the class. She likes to do the reading after the lectures because then she will understand it more and won't "tune out" of the class. So she really has described a sequence that involves the first three elements of Kolb's cycle: the concrete experiences from the lecture examples, the reflection with fellow students in the study groups, and then the basic concepts through the readings.

Our point is, the more often the full cycle of concrete experiences, reflective observations, abstract concepts, and testing in action occurs, the more powerful the learning and the greater likelihood it will remain useful in the future.

Now, to help you retain and understand Kolb's model, we want you to create an analogy that captures its basic elements and ideas. An analogy is where you use some object, attribute, or experience to describe something by likening it to something else, for example, the setting sun was like a ball of fire; loving her was like soaring through the heavens; he stood there solid as a rock; dealing with this college is a real can of worms.

Perhaps you are not used to creating analogies, so here is another example: Learning to use Kolb's experiential learning theory is like learning to be a good tennis player. Playing tennis requires serves, ground strokes, volleys, and overheads. Some players can get by with just a serve and ground strokes. Others serve and volley best. But to be really good, you need the full range of strokes. If you can't serve well, strong returns from your opponent will put you on the defensive from the beginning. If your backhand or forehand is weak, then you'll miss balls on that side. If you can't hit an overhead, then lobs will beat you. If you can't go to the net and volley, you will lose chances to capitalize on weak shots. Different situations and different opponents call for different combinations. You will only be a good player if you can put together the best combinations as the point develops.

Serves are the concrete experiences of experiential learning. They begin the action, the learning. Reflective observations are the ground strokes. They keep the action going, keep the ball in play. Often, a good ground stroke can win outright or set up a winning shot. Volleys and overheads are the abstract concepts and active testing that put the ball away and nail down the point. Then you're ready to serve again, building the next point on that learning cycle. To be a good learner, able to profit from diverse opportunities, you need a well-rounded game that uses concrete experiences, reflective observations, abstract concepts, and active testing of implications. If one of these elements is missing, then your ability to capitalize on different learning opportunities will be diminished. Over time, your ability to play life's game will be limited.

On a separate piece of paper, use Exercise 6.1, "Experiential Learning Analogy," to create your own analogy. It will help you connect Kolb's ideas to a pre-existing set of associations so you will remember them better. Your creation should follow the pattern given in the examples above. First, give the analogy. Then say how its different elements correspond to Kolb's experiential learning cycle.

EXERCISE 6.1

EXPERIENTIAL LEARNING ANALOGY   name

Describe your analogy.

Describe how it expresses Kolb's cycle and the four elements: concrete experiences, reflective observation, abstract conceptualization, and testing implications or active experimentation.

Your Preferred Learning Style

Kolb's experiential learning cycle also can be used to consider which combination of elements you prefer in your own learning. Most tennis players have some strokes they like better than others: a dynamite serve, a really powerful forehand, strong volleys. They will use those as much as they can. In learning, most of us have our preferred approaches. Our "learning style" preference has developed over the years to suit our needs and the situations we ran into. But different types of learning call for different approaches. Our learning is less effective than it would be if we adapt our approach to the type of learning called for.

Kolb introduces us to four different styles: *Divergers, Assimilators, Convergers,* and *Accommodators.*

- *Divergers* primarily use **concrete experiences and reflective observations** for learning. They are imaginative and able to see situations from diverse perspectives. They are good at generating ideas. They tend to be people oriented, tuned into their feelings, and concerned about meaning and values. As college students, they are often the ones who are interested in the arts and humanities.

- *Assimilators* primarily use **reflective observation and abstract conceptualization** for learning. They excel at inductive reasoning and integrating different observations. Their strength is in creating theoretical models. They tend to be more interested in sound concepts than in practical applications. As college students, they frequently work in basic sciences and mathematics.

- *Convergers* primarily use **abstract conceptualization and testing implications through active experimentation.** Their strength is in applying ideas to practical situations. They excel at problem solving and decision making. They are often relatively unemotional and like to deal with things. As college students, they tend to have technical interests and specialize in the physical sciences, computer sciences, engineering, and nursing.

- *Accommodators* primarily use **testing implications through active experimentation and concrete experiences** for learning. They are action oriented and good at implementing plans and doing things. They tend to solve problems by intuition and by trial and error. As college students, they are often in business, marketing, and sales.

These categories are not hard and fast. You probably won't fit neatly into any of these boxes. But they are useful as ways to begin thinking about your own preferred approaches to learning. We enjoy most, and learn best from, courses that match our preferred learning styles. When we asked Ito, our entering student with the clear interest in Japanese business, what kind of learning he liked best, he said, "I like actually knowing what's happening. For example, in computer science the books were there, but we hardly ever used them. Instead, we created programs ourselves. Then we went to the books afterwards and found out what we did. It made learning faster and it made it more fun."

"That's important for you?"

"Yes."

"Then we have what we call reflective observation. What about that?"

"I think that would be beneficial only if I was really interested in what I was learning. If I am uninterested, I probably won't pay attention and I'll worry about it later."

"What happens if you're not interested?"

"I'd probably go to sleep."

"What about abstract conceptualization?"

"That's pretty easy for me, especially if the professors give me examples."

"How about remembering it?"

"I think by studying the theories and by hands-on experiences equally."

Ito gives strong emphasis to concrete, hands-on experiences. He finds abstract concepts easy if the professor gives examples. But he thinks equal combinations of theoretical concepts and concrete experiences work best for remembering the material.

Another student, Adele, said, "I would say that concrete experiences definitely help. I am taking astronomy. There is not much you can do that is hands-on there, besides looking through the telescope. But in courses like biology, it definitely helps to do the dissections. And I learned a lot in French by practicing rather than studying. I practiced with the teachers."

"What about reflection and observation?"

"Sometimes that works for me. If I watch a play I can usually get some idea of what the author is trying to make us think about. I can usually figure out the theme or one of the themes behind the story."

"And abstract conceptualization?"

"Theories? I guess in one sense I kind of like learning that way. Taking a look at what other people think and by looking at a number of theories, developing your own theory. Because theories are generally based on facts. But I would say my best way would be hands-on. Getting to practice, like in French. Really getting to practice one-on-one or in a group."

Adele learns best, and most enjoys it, when she is actively practicing, applying, and using what she is trying to learn. Even when it comes to abstract conceptualization, it is looking at a number of theories and developing her own that works best for her.

More often than you may like, you will run into courses where the teaching is at odds with your preferred learning style. This happens to all of us, because very few teachers incorporate activities that span all four parts of the experiential learning cycle. Jessie, like Adele, finds concrete experiences and active application most effective. Her comments vividly illustrate what happens when her learning style is out of step with the way a course is taught.

"What kind of learning do you like best?"

"I like practicums and working in the field. When I can actually involve myself in the activity I learn more from it than just listening to someone talk about it or lecture on it. I prefer to learn like that. If you put me in a situation then I will get more from it than if you just tell me about the situation."

"Why do you think that is?"

"It just sticks in my brain more. Because I am actually doing it. Then, just listening to someone is kind of boring. You know, that doesn't have anything really to do with me. But when I am involved it has something to do with myself. It is something I can learn from."

"What about reflective observation?"

"It depends on the situation. If I find it interesting, a movie or play or something, then I will learn from it and be able to digest the information. But if it is not something I am particularly interested in I don't gain much from it."

"Another way to learn is through abstract conceptualization, through theories and concepts . . . You're shaking your head."

"I don't deal with those, especially theories and concepts. I am in philosophy right now. It is really giving me a hassle, to tell the truth. Because, I don't know, I am not a deep thinker I guess. Thinking, if I do this, this, and this, or breaking it down to many, many steps."

"So what do you prefer?"

"Hands-on, getting involved in a situation."

"How are you learning philosophy then?"

"I read the book. I just read it over and over until I pretty much understand what each philosopher is saying. That's the only way I can learn because from the lectures I am not getting much. I really can't understand what he is saying. So I am only learning from reading the book."

"So what happens in class?"

"I just try to take notes on what he is saying. But, most of the time, I am just wandering off looking out the window or something. I am not really paying attention. Even though it's a small class, with only 25 students, it's really boring. It's pure lecture. To tell the truth, I thought that philosophy was going to be pretty interesting. You know, everybody would have their points of view. I thought that it would be more of a discussion class rather than a pure lecture class. But I was disappointed."

"Sometimes we are faced with a teaching style that is out of synch with how we like to learn, like you just indicated for philosophy. When that happens what do you do?"

"I have to find another way for me to be able to learn. Like I said, with philosophy I just read the book. Then I just have to figure a different strategy where I will be able to digest the information."

Jessie's philosophy course is a good example of what happens when a clear learning style preference runs into content and a teacher's approach that is very different. She was interested in the subject and looking forward to the course. Because of the way it's taught, it has become boring and hard for her to learn. She even has begun to believe that she is "not a deep thinker." Jessie tries to find a strategy that will help her learn. But her strategy is limited to reading the book "over and over."

However, there are other strategies she might use that would be more consistent with her learning style. If she had been aware of these, she might have invested the time she spent in repeated reading in a more productive way. For example, she might have asked some of her friends what they thought about different philosophical concepts or orientations. Or she could have created a study group to discuss the strengths and weaknesses of various philosophical perspectives. If she wanted to be more formal, she might have suggested that she and some of her classmates each take a particular viewpoint and defend it in a debate. She could also seek out faculty members and ask them for their views on the validity of different philosophical positions. She could create a diagram or a flow chart showing the relationships among various philosophical orientations. She could also observe the behaviors and attitudes of fellow students to see how particular philosophical perspectives were reflected in action. Alternatives like these would have been more consistent with her learning style, with her preference for active involvement, than reading the book over and over. They might have helped her learn, and made the course fun instead of boring. She probably would not begin questioning her ability to be a "deep thinker."

The problem with most college teaching is that it focuses heavily on generalizations and abstract concepts. It does not provide the range of experiences and processing that creates a strong internal map. As Mike said, "We've been getting a lot of theory-related classes . . . It requires a lot of reading, a lot of memorization." Most lectures and texts do not connect their concepts with your particular prior experiences or knowledge—with the maps you already have. Most teaching does not explicitly ask you to reflect on the materials, to think about possible relationships with other ideas. Most teaching does not ask you to apply the concepts to real life issues, problems, or situations. So the concepts, the facts, the data, or the research findings are simply hanging out there, unattached to any ongoing network of associations that help enrich their meaning and increase their retention.

Obviously those generalizations don't apply to all courses and classes. There are laboratory courses that provide concrete experiences and opportunities for application. There are courses that use "practicums," field observations, volunteer experiences, and the like to flesh out and enrich the lectures and texts. There are a variety of teaching strategies and educational processes that provide for the four elements of Kolb's experiential learning model. But often, one or another element is ignored. When that is the case, if you really want to learn, you need to figure out ways to supply or create the missing elements yourself.

Here are some things you can do to strengthen your learning so you involve the full cycle.

Concrete experiences can be direct or vicarious. Both can be powerful. Films, television programs, audio tapes, live performances, and demonstrations can engage your emotions and connect with your prior experiences. A moving novel, biography, poem, or play can be a powerful experience. Direct observations, active participation, human contacts, interviews—on the campus, in the community, in natural settings—can give life to abstract ideas. Role plays, simulations, games, debates can get you actively involved.

Reflective observations can be strengthened by reviewing class notes and thinking about how they connect with other ideas or experiences. You can keep a journal where you comment on meanings that experiences, ideas, and pieces of information have for you. Discussion, study groups, computer conferencing, and teleconferencing—with other students and with faculty members who are willing—can help you share understandings, make connections. Creating visual metaphors and analogies can be especially powerful ways to capture complex sets of ideas and their interrelationships. You won't forget a good metaphor or analogy, and often it will enrich your understanding as well. We have used tennis as an analogy for experiential learning. If you have created a good analogy of your own, you won't forget the concept.

Abstract concepts come to us through print, lectures, and computer programs. A picture is worth a thousand words. Graphs, diagrams, tables, figures, and cartoons can supply rich data and clearly illustrate relationships, contrasts, and comparisons. Computer modeling, computer graphics, and flow charts can describe sequences of cause-and-effect and provide visual images of multiple interactions. Many of us have seen by now the double-helix pictures or models of the DNA molecule that carries hereditary characteristics. Or we have seen weather forecasts, on television or in the papers, that show moving cloud patterns reflecting high- and low-pressure systems or hurricanes in action. These images convey complex information and interactions clearly and economically. We understand how weather works and what is going on much better than if we simply listened to the words.

Testing the implications of concepts can occur through systematic experiments in laboratories or elsewhere. Or you can simply try out new behaviors and see what happens. You can pit the logic of one concept against the logic of competing concepts and see which seems to make most sense. You can look for settings where you can observe others trying out particular ideas or actions, and examine the consequences.

Now it's time for you to apply these ideas to your own courses and classes. First, select a course you have recently completed and complete the "Experiential Learning Course Analysis" using a separate sheet of paper.

EXERCISE 6.2

EXPERIENTIAL LEARNING COURSE ANALYSIS   name

1. List the things the teacher did and the activities required of students that fit under each of the following headings.

   Concrete Experiences

       Teacher Behaviors

       Student Requirements

   Reflective Observations

       Teacher Behaviors

       Student Requirements

   Abstract Conceptualization

       Teacher Behaviors

       Student Requirements

   Testing the Implications

       Teacher Behaviors

       Student Requirements

2. In what sequence did the various activities typically occur? For example, did the course or course units typically start with concrete experiences and then move to abstract concepts, or begin with concepts and then go to testing implications and reflection?

3. Which elements were most heavily emphasized? Which were least emphasized?

4. What student activities or products were explicitly evaluated? Which ones counted most for your grade?

5. What activities would you add that would have helped you learn and retain the material more effectively? What activities would have helped you better achieve your purposes for taking the course?

Next, using one or more courses in which you are currently enrolled, complete the "Experiential Learning Course Analysis" for the teacher and student activities that have occurred so far and which seem to be called for in the future. Then identify any additional activities you would undertake to help maximize your learning and retention. Choose courses where the learning and retention are important to you, rather than just some required course where you don't have much motivation.

Finally, this experiential learning model can also help you take your learning style into account when choosing courses. Usually, you choose courses based mainly on the content. You may also want to consider the reputation of the teacher, the time of day, how it fits with your other scheduling needs, and so on. But you probably have not thought explicitly about how it will be taught and how well it fits your own learning style preferences. Sometimes there are multiple sections offered for the same course. When that happens, there may be significant differences in how they are taught. As a final exercise in applying experiential learning theory, we suggest that you identify one or more courses you will take next semester. Make an appointment with the teacher and use our "Course Inquiry Interview Schedule" as the basis for your meeting. Don't be nervous about asking for the information you need. Most faculty members will appreciate the interest and motivation reflected in your thoughtful questions.

EXERCISE 6.3

COURSE INQUIRY INTERVIEW SCHEDULE   name

Use these questions as a basis for asking teachers about courses you are interested in or have to take. You may want to work your way through the questions explicitly, or you may feel more comfortable carrying on a more general discussion to get the information you want. Reserve half an hour or so after your appointment to jot down the information you have received. It is much more efficient and accurate to get it down immediately after your conversation. It is surprising how much you lose if you put it off, even for just an hour or two.

1. How will class time be spent? Lectures? Discussions? Visiting speakers? Films? Videos? Demonstrations? Group interactions among students, such as role playing, simulations, games, debates? Quizzes? Multiple choice exams? Essay exams?

2. What kinds of out-of-class preparation and activities will be required of students? Reading? Papers? Collaborative projects with other students? Computer conferencing? Journals?

3. Will there be laboratory activities or field experiences required as part of the course? Internships? Practicums? How will these be structured?

4. Which of the in-class and out-of-class activities will be most emphasized? Which ones will be evaluated as part of the course grade? How much will each one count toward the grade?

W rap-Up

We strongly encourage you to invest the time and effort required to do these exercises. Applying experiential learning theory will build in learning that lasts beyond the final exam. We want you to experience the advantages that come from taking or creating learning activities that suit your style and help you learn. Once you have experienced those advantages, we think you will continue such initiatives. In doing so, you will have learned how to take charge of your own learning. That ability to design and pursue learning will serve you well at work, at home, at play—in all the various roles you will assume in the years ahead.

REFERENCE

1. Kolb, D. A. (1984). *Experiential Learning: Experience as the Source of Learning and Development.* Upper Saddle River, NJ: Prentice Hall.

Maximizing Learning Beyond Courses and Classes

What advice would you give students who want to get the most out of college?"

David replied, "A good question! First of all, get involved. That is the one. I remember sitting over in the Student Union with somebody standing up on the stage preaching to me about getting involved. It went in one ear and out the other. But it is the truth. Find yourself a niche, a group, or something. *Just get involved.* You meet more people. You have more fun. You'll have something to put on your résumé that says, 'I did more in college than just go to class.' There's so many folks going out to interview that have a résumé that doesn't mean anything. You have a lot of great experiences. I remember sitting outside on a bench up by Thompson Hall thinking to myself, 'Why am I here?' But recently an interviewer said to me, 'If you could pick any brick on the wall at GMU and write something on it what would it be?' I said, 'It would be right on that corner of Thompson. It would say, ask not what GMU can do for you, but what you can do for GMU.' It's kind of corny, but it's the whole reason I consider myself successful. It's because I got out and started doing stuff with the university."

"You turned outward?"

"Oh my, yes! That's the difference. We did work with orientation programming. We did a casino. I dealt in the casino and I saw someone standing over in the corner looking just like me. I had to go and grab hold of this poor guy and drag him out there because I sat on the sidelines for a while and that isn't where it's at. You've got to get out. You've got to play. Even if you don't think you have a lot to offer, get involved. It changes your life. It really does. If I think back on a lot of the learning experiences I've had, all the friendships I've made and such, it's been through my work with different organizations. I got to do all kinds of things that Joe Schmo does not get to do as just a student."

In response to the same question, another senior, Susan, echoed David's strong response: "Do everything you can do. Don't ever think anything is going to be boring or worthless. Get involved. Don't sit back, because the organization is not going to come to you. Maybe a couple of organizations if you're lucky. But you have to go out there and sign up. Look at their tables at the beginning of the school year. Read the back of your handbook and see which organizations you are interested in or want to check into. Because if you just go to classes and never get involved in other things, it is awfully depressing. And you are not enriching what you have learned in classes with the real world, real events."

Alma describes the challenges and consequences of becoming an officer in an organization important to her. She goes on to contrast her experiences with another girl she knows.

"Yes. I hold an office in an organization. I can't just say I am not going to a meeting because I am tired, because I know it is just something you have to do even though you're tired. It is a lot more work because you have to look into different things. But it is good, I feel. Just sitting around with nothing to do makes you a lazier person. And it has made me a more committed person. It seems like I would be more tired with having a lot to do, but it made me do more, work harder. For some reason it does. Just like this past weekend, I went to a conference for my organization. I am in the National Society for Black Engineers. Just seeing other people there interested in the same thing, working for the same thing, made me like to come back to school and work even harder, knowing that there are others out there."

"Was that decision to join the organization hard or easy? Why did you do it?"

"I knew I wanted to belong to something. That particular organization goes on after school. You can be an alumni member after you move on. And you can work with undergraduates even if you are a graduate and give them some insight."

"What did the organization do for you?"

"I think it made me stronger in being more committed and getting things done. It made me more committed to my school work also."

"Do you think it is important in a college experience to become part of an organization?"

"Yes. I feel it brings a person out more. They will be more content. I know this girl who is really to herself. She is not involved in anything. She doesn't go to anything on campus. She just goes to classes. She doesn't get out to meet people. I think if she was to come out more and meet people, it would make her a whole different person. I think it would because that's what happened to a girl last year. She is like a whole different person. When you see her she is more outgoing, more happy knowing more and different people, doing more."

These are strong recommendations from three dissimilar seniors, based on their own experiences. Take them seriously. Their views coincide perfectly with research on student learning and development. The single most important factor is to what degree students are involved with all aspects of college. A student's most important teacher is usually another student. Relationships with friends made in college, together with participation in student and community activities, are primary forces for lasting change. Peer interactions typically exert more influence on personal growth than do contacts with faculty or courses and classes. Of course, this research finding occurs in large measure because significant contacts and relationships with faculty members are so rare. Most of your life and most of its significant events go on outside of academic courses, so it is not surprising that is where you experience the most powerful influences.

Your choices of organizations and activities should receive the same kind of thoughtful attention that you give to choosing courses and classes. Time is finite. There are only 24 hours in a day, 168 hours in a week. The time you invest in varied organizations and activities is time not available for other kinds of learning, for other areas of satisfaction or fulfillment. A choice to do one thing is a choice not to do many others. Juggling your varied commitments and balancing the trade-offs is one of college's significant challenges. Sometimes you learn about juggling commitments the hard way. Listen to Chung:

"Are you involved in any extracurricular activities?"

"I was until last summer. My counselor told me to drop everything."

"What were you doing before?"

"First I was president of the Filipino Club. Then I became vice president of the British Club. I was also into the Student Nursing Association. I was in a lot of clubs, but my grades were falling down because I couldn't juggle everything. I like being a leader, but you can't really be a leader if you can't really take care of yourself."

"How many credit hours were you taking?"

"Seventeen. And I was working plus the leadership things. I don't think I was ready for being a leader."

"Do you think that maybe you'll get involved again?"

"Definitely. I want to get involved and this kind of life, with nothing but studying, is not the kind of life I like. Not doing any extracurricular activities. Everyone who knows me knows that I'm the kind of guy who likes to do a lot of extracurriculars instead of the academic part. But right now I'm just concentrating on academics first. Like what my parents told me, 'It's only two more years to go. I'm sure you can sacrifice everything for two years. After two years you can do whatever you want.'"

"What were your extracurricular experiences like?"

"I was having fun. Doing those kinds of activities is fun. I've always thought that college was supposed to be that way. Not just studying. 'Cause it seems like you have all the time in the world. Boy, was I wrong!"

"What was it like when that was going on?"

"It seemed like I was gonna die. I never thought college was like this. When I was a freshman, I thought, 'Here come the parties.' Because when I was in high school, my senior year, all my older friends who went to college came back for homecoming and told me how much fun college was—going to parties, sororities, fraternities, and all that. I've always thought that college was gonna be like that. When I came here, it was a big shock. I mean, I did go to parties but my grades did go down. So when I tried studying, I said, 'Whatever happened to all those good old college movies that I've seen with parties and everything?' It wasn't like that."

"What advice would you have for other students concerning extracurricular activities?"

"I gave more time to extracurricular activities than to my academics my first two years. It's pretty sad, but I guess I was just looking for fun then. I was looking for friends. Back then, all I could think of was 'Get friends first.' 'Cause I knew that if you got friends you could always have help. I thought I could always catch up. Procrastinating all the time. I still am trying to catch up now. It's ongoing. So I did get the friends, but right now I am catching up with everything. What I would tell them is, 'Get some friends but try not to let the extracurricular activities eat you up. It's really hard to catch up.'"

Diverse Opportunities

We use the curious title for this chapter, "Maximizing Learning Beyond Courses and Classes," because we want to include the wide range of potential learnings outside the academic curriculum. So we refer not only to the "extracurricular" and "co-curricular" activities that are part of the University—clubs, programs, organizations, cultural events, residential learning activities—but also to other activities such as full- or part-time employment, volunteer work in the local community, travel, and the like. Those varied situations all provide powerful opportunities for learning.

You will have a variety of reasons for getting involved in such activities: Maybe you need the money. Or it's a good way to meet people with similar interests. Or it's a way to connect with, feel part of, contribute to the community. Maybe it's simply good fun and a nice change of pace, or a way to blow off some stress. Or it may give access to new experiences and human interactions with persons very different from yourself that you would not otherwise encounter. All these are excellent reasons for getting involved. But they don't conflict with, or preclude, learning things that will stick with you in other contexts, serve you with other groups, and help you carry other responsibilities.

Friends and the groups you identify with have the greatest impact. These relationships filter and modify the messages from faculty members and the institution. These interactions dampen and distort the forces coming from the curriculum, from teaching, from codes of conduct, or institutional expectations. The relationships built over coffee in the cafeteria, through late-night bull sessions, study groups, parties, shared cultural or athletic interests, joint academic projects, or in work settings are the labs for learning to communicate, empathize, reflect, argue. They are the anvils on which your own attitudes, values, conflicts, current problems, future plans and aspirations are hammered out. Encounters with others from different backgrounds help you develop increased tolerance and understanding as your own particular beliefs, values, and attitudes are challenged. Books you read that haven't been assigned by professors, music you listen to, films, concerts, lectures, exhibits you spend time on, all are shaped by the friendships you make and the groups you connect with.

So the wide range of human encounters, friendships, and groups are rich opportunities for learning. The other main sources are the varied roles and responsibilities you assume. Victoria strengthened her learning when she became a tutor for four classmates and when she "did internships with senators and stuff" in Washington. When Alma assumes a leadership role in the local chapter of the National Society for Black Engineers, it strengthens her commitment to her career. The added responsibilities help her learn how to "get things done," how to meet her responsibilities even though she is tired. She finds that she actually has more energy and motivation for school work despite her fatigue. It brings her out more and helps her develop interpersonal competence. She recognizes her dependence on those who are more experienced, as well as her potential contributions to budding professionals after she graduates.

Remember the larger learnings for career success and a good life we discussed in Chapter 2:

- skills in written and oral communication, critical thinking, and conceptualizing skills
- interpersonal competence
- increased clarity of purposes and values
- self-confidence
- emotional intelligence
- moving through autonomy toward interdependence
- developing integrity

You can see how the time and energy Alma invests in her organization contribute significantly to some of those learnings. There are numerous opportunities for you to do likewise. And you don't necessarily have to be in a leadership position to achieve significant learning. Every activity group and organization needs energetic contributors and workers, and thoughtful, involved followers, as well as committed leaders. The challenge is how to maximize the learning and personal development that comes from this involvement.

This kind of learning is especially important if you are a commuting student. Abundant research demonstrates that residential students typically gain much more from their college experiences than do commuters. The main reason is that they tend to be much more involved. They participate more frequently and more actively in varied campus organizations, activities, and events. They confront a wider range of students and student groups. Most importantly, perhaps, they are more disengaged from their families and from former friendships, groups, and community contexts. Many commuters, in contrast, often just come to class and go back home, perhaps with brief periods at the library. They not only are less involved, but remain more attached to prior relationships and responsibilities. These ties often supply important support, but they also can be sources of constraint. They can inhibit exploring new relationships, new ideas, new action arenas, new possibilities for self-definition and self-development.

If you are a typical adult commuting student, you already are involved in complex and ongoing relationships, activities, and organizations. You probably have a family or are in a significant relationship. You may have one or more children, at home or away. You work full- or part-time. You are involved in community organizations and in a network of social relationships. It is precisely this full, ongoing life that keeps you from spending lots of time on campus and joining the varied activities and organizations heavily populated by full-time students. Your challenge is how to capitalize on the rich possibilities for learning outside of the courses and classes that are part of your daily rounds, and how to expand or modify those to serve better the purposes driving your college education.

Applying Experiential Learning Theory

Maximizing learning by participating in varied activities outside of class is challenging. Leaders of the varied clubs, interest groups, or organizations are, not surprisingly, more oriented toward achieving the specific purposes of the group than they are toward helping group members learn from their experiences. Curiously enough, this is as true for college campuses as it is for community organizations. Naturally, organizations exist for a variety of reasons: to help people with similar interests become acquainted, to organize energy around a common concern or shared purpose, to accomplish some specific task or to make a concrete contribution, to provide recreational outlets and leisure time activities. Those are all important purposes, good reasons to create an organization. A handful of institutions around the country are attempting to create systematic relationships among "extracurricular" or "co-curricular activities" and the academic program. But usually, except for departmental clubs and associations related to majors, there is little explicit emphasis on learning. So, as is often the case in learning from courses and classes, you will need to exercise some initiative to maximize your learning from those activities.

That's where our experiential learning cycle comes in. In the preceding chapter we emphasized the usefulness of that cycle for strengthening learning from courses and classes. We recognized that often you need to add concrete experiences and active experimentation to test the implications of the abstract concepts coming from lectures and texts. For maximizing learning beyond courses and classes, you typically find yourself in the opposite situation. You are having abundant experiences. You are being challenged to apply and test your knowledge and skills in new situations. But you are seldom asked to reflect on those experiences or to formulate more sophisticated concepts that can add to your understanding and improve your performance. Indeed, you often are so caught up in the activities and so busy that it's difficult to add anything else. It is difficult to make time to keep a journal or to critique the processes with others, to give yourself a better sense of what went well and what didn't. It takes extra effort to seek out pertinent readings, to get some advice and counsel from others who have been in similar situations. So we often accumulate experiences but don't actually add much to our working knowledge. In fact, we often develop bad habits. We get used to attitudes and behaviors that help us cope with particular situations, but which are less effective than other alternatives we could learn if we were more systematic from the beginning.

Our tennis analogy provides an example. Most of us start out playing tennis without any prior instruction. Some friend invites us to play. We go out on the court and start hitting the ball back and forth. Our friend may give us some suggestions about what to do. We have fun, get ourselves a racquet, and start playing more frequently. We gradually improve our ability to get the ball back, to hit a serve so it lands in the right place, to go to the net occasionally. We decide to get more serious. We buy a book or take a lesson. Then we find that we have already developed ways of standing, or holding the racquet, or swinging at the ball that need to be changed if we are to make much progress. We get some concepts from the book or the teacher. We learn enough to analyze why some shots feel good and work well, and others don't. But we find that our prior learning has created habits that are difficult to change. When we are in a lesson or just rallying, we can remember what we're supposed to do. But when we get into a real game, when we get emotionally involved, we slip back into our earlier way of playing. Getting the new body positions and new strokes grooved and part of our regular reactions takes much more time and effort than if we had started out including the concepts and reflections from the beginning.

Take another example. You have probably been a member or leader of various committees, task forces, or work teams from time to time. Such groups often are not very skillfully led. Often, members don't recognize or know how to fill various necessary roles. The process can become very frustrating. Meetings drag on and on. The discussion wanders. The problem or task remains ambiguous. No clear sense of direction emerges. No sense of closure occurs. As the meeting is running past its deadline, a typical response is for the leader, or one or two participants, to suggest a solution or action and to volunteer to do it. Everyone else heaves a sigh of relief, and the group adjourns. The one or two people who have stepped forward do their homework, and the group reconvenes. The volunteers report. There is further discussion. The process is no more effective than the first meeting. Finally, the same persons suggest what needs to be done. The other group members agree for these formal or informal leaders to go ahead. After this cycle repeats itself two or three times, the group starts to break down. Fewer persons show up for the meetings. Pretty soon, the one or two members who have stepped forward find themselves doing all the work. There is no real group support. The whole enterprise is less effectively managed than it could have been. Throughout the experience, there has been no time given to reflecting on how the group has been functioning, why the meetings have not gone well, how they might have reached better closure or kept others more fully involved. No one has taken time to check some of the basic literature on group processes and leadership, or on functional or dysfunctional group roles. When another committee or task force comes along, many of the same behaviors are repeated by both the leaders and followers.

Our point is that using all the elements of the experiential learning cycle can help you maximize your learning from the diverse, non-course experiences and activities, just as it can from required courses and classes. David, Susan, and Alma all felt they gained a lot from getting involved, from "enriching what you have learned in classes with the real world, real events." But there was nothing in their college environment that asked them to reflect on their experiences contributing to orientation or to the casino, or taking a leadership role in the Society for Black Engineers. Nothing led them to readings or other materials that could supply concepts to enlarge their understandings of their roles and how better to fulfill them. If they had taken time to clarify what they wanted to learn from these activities, and then used the experiential learning cycle while they were involved, their long-term gains would have substantially increased.

To see how this might work for you, apply our "Experiential Learning Activity Analysis" to a club, committee, volunteer group, community or student organization. Choose one in which you currently participate, or one from the recent past. You may wish to check the previous chapter for our descriptions of some of the learning activities suggested for different elements of the cycle. Some of the items we suggested to strengthen *Reflective Observation* included keeping a journal to examine experiences and activities, discussions with others, creating metaphors or analogies that capture or evoke the experiences. Suggestions for strengthening *Abstract Conceptualization* included readings, diagrams, flow charts, figures, and computer modeling. Adding activities like these can help you profit better from the various concrete experiences and active applications as you work with various organizations, clubs, committees, and the like.

EXERCISE 7.1

EXPERIENTIAL LEARNING ACTIVITY ANALYSIS   name

Using a separate sheet of paper, complete this Experiential Learning Activity Analysis for an organization or activity in which you invested, or are investing, more than two hours each week.

Name of organization or activity?

Purposes of the organization?

Main activities of the organization?

How many participants?

What are the leadership roles?

What responsibilities does each leader carry?

What responsibilities does each participant carry?

What were/are your reasons for joining this organization or participating in this activity?

What kinds of learning or personal development did/do you want to achieve?

What is/was your role?

What responsibilities did/do you carry?

List your activities as they seem to fit under each category:

Concrete Experiences

Reflective Observation

Abstract Conceptualization

Active Experimentation

Describe additional activities you might have pursued that would have increased your learning and lasting benefits from your involvement in this organization or activity.

Concrete Experiences

Reflective Observation

Abstract Conceptualization

Active Experimentation

Victoria did "internships with senators and stuff" in Washington, D.C. Here is how she might have completed this "Experiential Learning Activity Analysis" for that program.

EXERCISE 7.1   *Victoria*

EXPERIENTIAL LEARNING ACTIVITY ANALYSIS   name

Complete this Experiential Learning Activity Analysis for an organization or activity in which you invested, or are investing, more than two hours each week.

Name of organization or activity?

    Washington D.C. Internship program.

Purposes of the organization?

    The program gives students a chance to be members of senatorial staffs and experience firsthand how Congress works.

Main activities of the organization?

> It identifies senatorial offices willing to have interns, matches interested students with available opportunities, monitors their experiences, brings participating students together monthly to share observations and reflections, reviews and reacts to participants' journals and their final reports.

How many participants?

> Twenty to thirty, depending on student interest.

What are the leadership roles?

> Program coordinator (a faculty member), student assistants, and interns.

What responsibilities does each leader carry?

> The program is coordinated by a political science faculty member. She (a) selects appropriate readings, (b) initiates contacts with senators and senatorial staff members, (c) clarifies with staff members the contributions and opportunities for the interns, and (d) reviews and reacts to student journals and their final reports. The student assistants (a) help screen and orient interested students, (b) take them to senatorial offices and introduce them to senators and staff members, and (c) serve as liaisons between participants and the faculty coordinator when problems develop. Interns participate in the program.

What responsibilities does each participant carry?

> Participants make the agreed-upon contributions and take the initiative to identify additional activities or responsibilities they would like to assume. They keep weekly journals reflecting on their experiences and the implications for the conceptual material in the readings and do a final report. They contribute to monthly sharing sessions with other participants.

What were/are your reasons for joining this organization or participating in this activity?

> I wanted to make contacts with senators and members of congress who might be helpful for future employment. I am interested in political issues and wanted to learn more about how politics actually work.

What kinds of learning or personal development did/do you want to achieve?

I wanted to learn more about the political process and about how Congress works. I wanted to learn how to get around Washington. I wanted to see if I could perform well in that kind of work. And I wanted to get a clearer sense of whether I might like to go into politics in the future.

What is/was your role?

I was an intern.

What responsibilities did/do you carry?

I composed answers to mail from constituents for review by other staff members, summarized background readings for upcoming congressional action assigned to me by the staff, and took notes on hearings I was asked to attend.

List your activities as they seem to fit under each category.

Concrete Experiences

Attended and summarized budget hearings and background material concerning proposed cuts in defense spending. Canvassed staff members for southern Democrats to find out their views. Attended congressional sessions. Participated in regular staff meetings with Senator X. Met monthly with Senator X to discuss my experiences.

Reflective Observation

Met monthly with Senator X to discuss my experiences. Wrote my monthly journal and final report. Contributed to monthly meetings with faculty coordinator and other interns.

Abstract Conceptualization

Read and outlined all the assigned materials.

Active Experimentation

Tried out some of the key concepts in the readings in working with the senator's staff. Critiqued several concepts, which seemed off-base when I wrote my final report.

Describe additional activities that might have increased your learning and lasting benefits from your involvement in this organization or activity.

Concrete Experiences

> I could have socialized more with some staff members to hear more about how they liked working and living in D.C. I could have attended more hearings and asked to meet directly with constituents.

Reflective Observation

> It would have been helpful if I had made brief notes in my journal as things came up instead of always waiting until the end of the week.

Abstract Conceptualization

> I can't think of anything more I might want to do here. There are all kinds of additional readings I could do, but I think I used the readings we had well.

Active Experimentation

> Nothing to add here.

Bill, who was interested in environmental sciences and joined the Outing Club, had a very different set of responses.

EXERCISE 7.1   Bill

EXPERIENTIAL LEARNING ACTIVITY ANALYSIS   name

Complete this Experiential Learning Activity Analysis for an organization or activity in which you invested, or are investing, more than two hours each week.

Name of organization or activity?

> Outing Club

Purposes of the organization?

> To enjoy outdoor activities, to acquire knowledge and skills, to understand and appreciate the natural world.

Main activities of the organization?

> Organizing and leading hiking, camping, canoeing, kayaking, and rock climbing trips. Sponsoring educational programs concerning plants, animals, land use, and environmental issues.

How many participants?

About 55.

What are the leadership roles?

President, vice president, secretary, treasurer, and trip leaders.

What responsibilities does each leader carry?

The president and vice president convene and lead club meetings, the secretary takes minutes of the meetings, and the treasurer collects the dues and keeps track of expenses. Trip leaders scout, plan, and lead trips.

What responsibilities does each participant carry?

Participants attend club meetings and contribute to club decisions. They help with and go on trips they are interested in.

What were/are your reasons for joining this organization or participating in this activity?

I have always liked the outdoors, camping and hiking. I became interested in rock climbing and wanted to learn about it. I wanted to make friends with others who wanted to go out into the mountains and see if I could find a girlfriend who shared my interests.

What kinds of learning or personal development did/do you want to achieve?

I wanted to become more skilled at rock climbing and more knowledgeable about getting around in the mountains away from trails and people. I wanted to learn how to be a trip leader so I might help others enjoy the mountains. I wanted to learn more about nature and environmental issues.

What is/was your role?

I started out just being a member and going on trips. Then I became a leader for high country trips. I also helped plan and organize some meetings concerning wild life photography and wild life management issues.

What responsibilities did/do you carry?

I scouted out and planned trips, managed the logistics and money. I also identified speakers and led some of the meetings.

List your activities as they seem to fit under each category.

Concrete Experiences

Went on hiking and rock climbing trips, planned and led high country trips, planned programs, recruited speakers and chaired meetings. I took pictures of deer, marmots, foxes, and a bear.

Reflective Observation

I didn't do any of this.

Abstract Conceptualization

I read a variety of books and pamphlets concerning nature and environmental issues. I wrote some short stories about some of my experiences in the mountains.

Active Experimentation

I was continually trying new moves in rock climbing with good protection. I explored lots of new territory on high country trips with a close friend.

Describe additional activities you might have pursued that would have increased your learning and lasting benefits from your involvement in this organization or activity.

Concrete Experiences

I might have tried white water canoeing, although I've never been particularly interested in that. I might run for vice president next year.

Reflective Observation

I should have kept a journal. And I should keep one now, although I don't seem to have the self-discipline. I know it would help me with my writing.

Abstract Conceptualization

I enjoyed all the reading I did. I am still on the lookout for good books and always have one I am reading.

Active Experimentation

I am exploring new approaches to high country camping under all kinds of conditions. I want to keep on doing that.

These examples for Victoria and Bill give you a sense of how to apply the "Experiential Learning Activity Analysis" to strengthen and increase your gains from those activities.

Being More Intentional

Applying the experiential learning cycle means being more intentional about why you are choosing different activities, why you are getting involved. It means becoming more clear about the knowledge, competence, or personal characteristics you want to develop by joining those groups, undertaking those activities, making those contributions. The starting points for becoming more intentional may be the general purposes you want to achieve by going to college or the more specific focus defined by your major.

In Chapter 2, "Your Purposes: You Can Learn More than You Think," we talked about the kinds of competence and personal characteristics required for career success. They include:

- skills in oral and written communication
- critical thinking and conceptualizing abilities
- interpersonal competence—the ability to "read" nonverbal behavior, accurate empathy, and a talent for strengthening others' competence and contributions
- solid motivation, resting on clear purposes that integrate vocation, avocation, values, and lifestyle concerns
- self-confidence, the sense that you can make a difference concerning things that are important to you, that you have the competence to handle complex, challenging responsibilities.

We also shared some additional characteristics required for a good life:

- emotional intelligence for self-monitoring and management
- recognizing necessary areas of interdependence and developing the capacity to give and receive direct assistance and emotional support
- developing integrity so there is internal consistency between word and word, word and deed, deed and deed

As you can see, some of these basic purposes can be one starting point for more intentional choices. As was the case with Alma, your major or occupational orientation can also provide a basis for getting involved in one or more organizations.

Another student, Monique, said, "I want to get involved with things in my major. If I can bring up my GPA a little bit more, I can apply to the honor society of psychology. One of the girls in my English class is on the honor committee, and I thought that would be interesting and helpful so I'm checking it out, too. My other friend told me that there was a peer counseling group here, and I was thinking about that, too. The girl I know who is working at that now says it is a lot of work, but she really enjoys it. So I might try to get involved in that. I also want to volunteer at the women's center and see if I can do something there."

You can see how the varied possibilities Monique pursues are related to her interest in psychology and human behavior.

Another woman, Betsy, is basing her choices on both her major and her interest in performing arts. She said, "I'm in the Accounting Club, which meets twice a month. I'm not in a leadership position, but I'm planning on running for one next semester. I enjoy the activities and speakers they have. The topics they discuss are interesting to me, to my career, and to things I want to do. I have also signed up for six performances of the Art Institute. I really enjoy that. Also, I will get credit for doing it and it doesn't cost me anything."

Any complex action arena—any organization, club, or interest group—provides opportunities to strengthen one or more dimensions of personal development. They also can be pertinent to the more specialized areas of study that may be part of your major. Colleges provide a wide range of possibilities: special interest clubs, political and social action groups, cultural and religious clubs, professional and honorary organizations, sororities and fraternities. In addition, there are typically a variety of organizations associated with different schools or departments. Your institution will have many of these.

Adult learners constantly carry responsibilities and engage in activities that can contribute to much learning and personal development. Marriage and family relationships provide ongoing challenges where, for example, concepts from psychology, child development, and the adult life span are pertinent. Novels, plays, poems, and biographies provide insights into family dynamics. Raising children involves complex kinds of teaching and learning, ranging from trying to help with homework assignments we don't understand to complex issues of self-discipline, human relationships, and societal expectations. Most of us work in organizational contexts where research and theory concerning group dynamics, leadership, organizational behavior, teamwork, and team building can help us better understand what is going on and learn to function more effectively. Volunteer activities in hospitals and social agencies, work with church programs to help the homeless and needy, or participation in various social or political action groups all provide opportunities to enrich your experiential learning. They give you circumstances where a better understanding of issues concerning health and human services, economics, sociology, social psychology, or historical dynamics can improve your awareness of underlying causes and processes and increase your effectiveness. The list goes on and on. If you are a commuting student, you may find it helpful to list some of the ongoing responsibilities at home or work, and some of the community organizations and activities that might contribute significantly to your academic learning. Then think seriously about making one or more of them part of your program.

Susan said, "Read the back of your college handbook and see which organizations you are interested in or want to check into." That's excellent advice. But we suggest that first you spell out why you want to join an organization or participate in a particular activity. Next, describe the kinds of learning or personal development you want to achieve. Then you can apply the experiential learning cycle as a way to consider how you might shape what you do. Use the "Organizational Learning Planner" as a framework for thinking through your choices. Here is how Monique might have used it to clarify whether she wants to join the peer counseling group.

EXERCISE 7.2   *Monique*
                                                                  name

ORGANIZATIONAL LEARNING PLANNER

Complete this Organizational Learning Planner for each organization or activity you contemplate joining that will require more than two hours each week.

Name of the organization or activity?

> *Peer Counselors*

Purposes of the organization?

> *The organization supplements the work of the Counseling Center by being a first point of contact for students who are having academic problems, difficulty with the university bureaucracy, or relationship problems with roommates or friends.*

Major activities of the organization?

> *It trains and supervises student volunteers, serves as a back-up resource when problems are too complicated for them to deal with, and coordinates meetings between peer counselors and students seeking assistance.*

Why do you want to join or participate in this organization or activity?

> *I am interested in psychology and human behavior. I may want to become a therapist, so I would like to have some first-hand experience. Friends often come to me to discuss personal problems, and I think it would be satisfying to be helpful to others and learn at the same time.*

From what you know about the organization now, what activities would be called for if you were to participate?

Concrete Experiences

> *Conversations with students, meetings with supervisors and other peer counselors to discuss training and to discuss problem cases.*

Reflective Observation

> *We have to keep records of our meetings with students that describe what we discussed and what decisions or outcomes, if any, occurred.*

Abstract Conceptualization

> There is a handbook that gives us guidelines and suggestions about when we should immediately refer a student to a Counseling Center staff member, such as when they are threatening suicide or talking about harming someone else or are being threatened themselves. In conferences we also discuss some general counseling principles as they come up in relation to particular situations.

Active Experimentation

> As we work with each student we try to listen openly and supportively to what they say and hear each person as a unique individual.

What are the major kinds of learning or personal development you think you might achieve by your participation?

> The main thing I want to learn is whether I would like to do counseling as a profession. I would also like to become more competent in understanding and being helpful to others by understanding their backgrounds and values and how those influence their thinking and actions.

What kinds of activities would most help you achieve these learnings in the context of this organization?

Concrete Experiences

> The direct experiences working with students and the sharing and supervision sessions with the Counseling Center coordinator will probably be most helpful. If I find the experiences satisfying I might also go visit the community mental health center and ask the coordinator to introduce me to some professionals in private practice.

Reflective Observation

> It might be helpful if I kept a separate set of notes about my own reactions to some of the cases and situations I encounter, and think about how my own background influences my thinking about them.

Abstract Conceptualization

> I don't think it would be helpful for me to do a lot of reading about abnormal psychology, counseling techniques, and such. I can go into that in depth if I decide to go to graduate school. Now, as long as I have the

Handbook, I think my own intuition, warmth and natural caring will be more helpful than trying to use some technique I don't really understand.

Active Experimentation

I think it would be helpful if I could meet with a diverse range of persons with backgrounds different from my own and who have different kinds of things they want to talk about.

What additional information do you need in order to make a sound judgment about maximizing your learning from the time and energy you invest in this organization?

How many hours are required each week? Is there a regular schedule, or are you also on call? If I feel over my head with a particular person, can I get in touch with a supervisor right away? What has happened to other peer counselors in terms of the way they are viewed by other students? How do peer counselors deal with a situation where they are strongly attracted to the person they are working with?

Who are the persons you could talk with to obtain the information you need?

Names of participants

My friend Mary Jo, who is peer counselor, and two or three other counselors she would suggest. Perhaps one or two students who have used peer counseling if I can find some.

Names of leaders

The Peer Counseling Coordinator.

Names of faculty members or other university personnel

I don't know of other university persons I might talk with.

Are there other things you could do to help you make a sound judgment? Are there meetings or activities in which you might participate before making a commitment? If so, what are they?

I might make use of the Peer Counseling services just to discuss my interest and some of my questions about a career in counseling. I could also discuss how I might be more helpful to my teenage son who just got dropped by his girlfriend. This would give me a view from the perspective of someone coming for help.

You can probably imagine some of the answers Alma, who joined the National Society for Black Engineers, might have given. Or how Betsy, who is planning to run for a leadership position in the Accounting Club, might have responded. If you take time to complete this "Planner," you will make more sound choices and learn more from your participation.

EXERCISE 7.2

ORGANIZATIONAL LEARNING PLANNER
name

Complete this Organizational Learning Planner for each organization or activity you contemplate joining that will require more than two hours each week.

Name of the organization or activity?

Purposes of the organization?

Major activities of the organization?

Why do you want to join or participate in this organization or activity?

From what you know about the organization now, what activities would be called for if you were to participate?

Concrete Experiences

Reflective Observation

Abstract Conceptualization

Active Experimentation

What are the major kinds of learning or personal development you think you might achieve by your participation?

What kinds of activities would most help you achieve these learnings in the context of this organization?

Concrete Experiences

Reflective Observation

Abstract Conceptualization

Active Experimentation

What additional information do you need in order to make a sound judgment about maximizing your learning from the time and energy you invest in this organization?

Who are the persons you could talk with to obtain the information you need?

Names of participants

Names of leaders

Names of faculty members or other university personnel

Are there other things you could do to help you make a sound judgment? Are there meetings or activities in which you might participate before making a commitment? If so, what are they?

The options available to you can be on campus and college-sponsored, they can be part of your ongoing responsibilities and activities, or they can be available in your local community. After you think through the issues in relation to various options that seem appealing, you are ready to talk with persons in leadership roles and with other participants. Find out how their plans and expectations, and their sense of the possibilities for participation match your interests and purposes. Then make the soundest choices you can based on the range of other commitments you already have.

You don't want to be playing catch-up like Chung during your junior and senior years. You want to avoid such heavy involvement in co-curricular activities that other responsibilities suffer. Moreover, if you want to maximize your learning and enjoyment from organizations and activities, you need sufficient time and energy for the activities you choose. So it is critical to make thoughtful decisions about how you invest those limited hours. Take time to think about why you want to participate. Consider how participation contributes to your purposes for being in college, or to your major. Clarify what you want to learn. Use the experiential learning cycle to identify the kinds of activities that will help you achieve lasting benefits. Then your participation will significantly enhance your college life and yield lasting payoffs.

Developmental Transcripts

A "developmental transcript" is an excellent complement to your academic transcript. It helps you plan a program that integrates your academic studies with learning from other activities. It is useful whether you are a full-time student in residence or a part-time commuting adult. It can include off-campus responsibilities and contributions at work, at home, or in the community as well as on-campus activities.

A developmental transcript provides a running record of the knowledge, competence, and personal development achieved through your varied outside activities and your courses and classes. Throughout your college career, you can use it to keep tabs on progress you are making toward your purposes and as a basis for program planning. It also contributes materially to your résumé when you apply for graduate school or seek future employment. At the beginning of this chapter, David said, "You'll have something to put on your résumé that says, 'I did more in college than just go to class.' There's so many folks going out to interview that have a résumé that doesn't mean anything." A developmental transcript means you won't be one of those "folks" that has a limited résumé.

The following materials from George Mason University illustrate a typical approach. Your institution may have a similar program. If so, we urge you to participate. If it does not have a formal program, we hope you will adapt these materials for your own use.

The George Mason program takes a "holistic approach." It suggests the following "wellness" categories as ways to organize planning and recording:

1. Physical health and well being. (Sports, stress management, drug and alcohol programs)
2. Intellectual advancement. (Academic advising, study skills, academic clubs, lectures)
3. Personal development. (Leadership skills, interpersonal skills, time management, self-esteem)
4. Spiritual growth. (Religious organizations, programs)
5. Multicultural awareness. (Diversity workshops, cultural programs)
6. Occupational education. (Career Center workshops, noncredit internships, academic/career related student organizations)
7. Aesthetic appreciation. (Concerts, dance performances, art exhibits)
8. Altruistic enrichment. (Donating time/effort to those in need such as the homeless, the elderly, children)

The "Structured Reflection" form below suggests a way to deal with each activity. It provides a framework for describing your experiences, what you hoped to gain, how it helped you achieve your goals, what you learned, and how you will use whatever you gained. It helps you decide whether you want to pursue additional opportunities for this kind of learning. It also provides for a critique of the sponsoring organization. If you are creating your own transcript, you may not want to use all these different questions or the precise language used here. But, as a minimum, you probably should include a description of the experience, the knowledge, competence, or personal development that resulted, and possible future applications.

Solid educational values result from completing the "Structured Reflection." Remember our experiential learning cycle. Reflecting on your experiences and what they mean can significantly increase your learning. If you neglect that reflection, you are less likely to build on those experiences in future, similar situations. If you have decided to assess your learning from work and life experiences as suggested in Chapter 3, "Taking Stock," "Structured Reflection" can help you identify more clearly what you gained.

As your "Structured Reflection" forms accumulate, you can summarize them in ways that seem most useful to you. The George Mason example organizes them by date. That has the advantage of giving a nice historical picture that can accompany your academic transcript, which will be organized according to a similar time frame. That may work best for applying to graduate school, or for other programs where the administration is used to dealing with college transcripts. For other purposes, like applying for a particular job, it may work better to organize your activities and "Structured Reflections" by particular areas of knowledge or competence you have achieved. That kind of organization can also integrate relevant courses or other academic experiences. This approach helps you highlight the abilities and background you have that are pertinent to the job you seek. Experienced applicants know that it is usually important to tailor your résumé to the particular program or job you are

STRUCTURED REFLECTION
(Please Print)

I.D. # _____

Name _____

Title of Experience/Activity _____

Date of Program _____

Sponsoring Department _____

Facilitator's Name _____
(When Applicable)

Format (check one)

❏ Workshop   ❏ Lecture   ❏ Conference

❏ Training   ❏ Clinic   ❏ Seminar

❏ Volunteer   ❏ Membership   ❏ Position

❏ Performance   ❏ Awards & Recognition

❏ Internship   ❏ Facilitator/Presenter

❏ Other _____
(please explain)

Please write a brief outline/description of your experience.

_____

_____

_____

_____

What were you hoping to gain from this experience? Did the experience meet
your expectations? Explain.

_____

_____

_____

_____

How does this experience help you toward achieving your goals?

_____

_____

_____

_____

GEORGE MASON UNIVERSITY
DEVELOPMENTAL TRANSCRIPT PROGRAM

NAME: Jane Doe   **ENROLLMENT DATE:** 9/97

SPRING 1999
  Clinics
    Public Speaking   2/97
  Membership
    The Outing Club   10/98–10/99
  Positions
    Treasurer, Black Student Alliance   9/98– 3/00

FALL 1999
  Conferences
    Black Student Leadership Conference   11/99
  Volunteer
    The AIDS Walk   9/99
  Membership
    The Outing Club   10/98–10/99
  Positions
    Senator, Student Government   9/99– 3/01
    Treasurer, Black Student Alliance   9/98– 3/00
    Co-Chair, Promotions Committee
      Resident Student Association   9/99–12/99

SPRING 2000
  Training
    Student Leadership Institute   6/00
  Positions
    Senator, Student Government   9/99– 3/01
    Treasurer, Black Student Alliance   9/98– 3/00
  Performances
    New York City Ballet   3/00

FALL 2000
  Workshops
    Developing Your Leadership Potential   11/00
    Time Management   10/00
  Volunteer
    Witch Watch   10/00
  Membership
    Women's Leadership Committee   11/00–4/01
    Sexual Assault Task Force   9/00–5/01
    Black Student Alliance   9/97–5/01
  Positions
    Senator, Student Government   9/99– 3/01

seeking. A well-organized set of "Structured Reflections" to accompany your academic transcript will make your special qualifications readily apparent to the people responsible for selection decisions.

Wrap-Up

Most of your significant learning, in college as in life, will occur outside of courses and classes. As David said, "Get involved." Take these diverse opportunities for learning seriously. If you are like most students, you will work full- or part-time during your college career. When possible, choose your work settings for the learning they will offer as well as for their pay or convenience. Choose carefully all the activities you pursue and organizations you join. Use them intentionally to pursue your purposes. Apply the experiential learning cycle to maximize your gains. Create a developmental transcript to help you consolidate those gains. Use that transcript as a basis for planning future priorities for learning and development, and for improving your access to future education and employment.

Developing Mature Relationships

Relationships are an essential part of growing up. They are central to your college experience. Numerous studies show that peer relationships play a significant role in student persistence and degree completion, and are major influences on learning and personal development. Several students shared the meaning and importance of relationships, what they needed, the difficulties and joys they encountered. They also pointed out that relationships with friends, faculty, and advisors influenced their successes and failures in college. Because they are so critical, we provide a framework for struggling with the joys and problems of changing, shifting relationships.

A Way to Visualize Your Relationships

You can identify differences among your relationships at college by drawing concentric circles with you at the center. The inner circle contains your closest, most intimate friends and family, who are presumably part of your life

forever. The next circle is for family, friends, and neighbors who are important in your life but not in the closest, most constant, circle. The circle
farthest away from you represents more institutional supports. Institutional
supports refer to those people you meet and work with in college, on the job,
or in community organizations, who are helpful and important to you, but
who may change with time or drop away when you leave the institution or
organization. These circles illustrate your "convoy of social support."[1] You
have a convoy all through life, but the people in it change, especially those
who are not close to you.

Mapping your supports in concentric circles helps you see how a transition
changes your relationships and interrupts or increases your support system. For
example, geographical moves can interrupt relationships between friends. Other
changes can be identified by looking at what happens to people's support systems
before and after starting college. This system of concentric circles shows how the
most important aspect of a transition may not be the change itself, but what it
does to your convoy.

Jack, a returning student, filled in the circles after he had been in school for
a year. His closest circle includes his parents and his partner. The middle circle
includes other family members, some friends from his political organization,
and two new college friends, both returning students. The outer circle includes
his teachers, a few administrators with whom he had dealings, and the athletic
director.

When Jack compared his current convoy with the year before, the major difference was in the second and third circles. Before, he had no students in either
circle. Instead, he had three coworkers in his middle circle; his boss and other
members of his work organization were in the outer circle.

Jack is basically satisfied with his current relationships and knows that as he
becomes more involved in student life, he will make more close friends. He feels
he should begin to reach out to others of all ages, not just returning students.

Ginger's circle looks very different from Jack's. She filled it out during her
second semester. The closest circle includes her mother and two sisters, her best
friend from high school, and her roommate. The middle circle includes about 10
friends from college, all first-year students. She also places her English teacher
and counselor in this circle. Her outer circle includes all the faculty she knew, her
dorm counselors, and the nurse in the health center.

Ginger's major change is the shift from a group of high school friends and
teachers to college friends and teachers. She feels badly that she has lost so
much contact with most of her high school friends, and that she has exclusive-
ly women as friends. She decided to seek friendships with men on campus. She
feels she can do that through the theater group she is joining.

How does going to college affect your relationships, your supports? To examine the relationships you now have, fill out the circles in Exercise 8.1. Put those
people closest to you in the center, and those who are part of your network, but
not that intimate, in the next circle. Put institutional supports, and others more
distant, in the outer circle.

EXERCISE 8.1

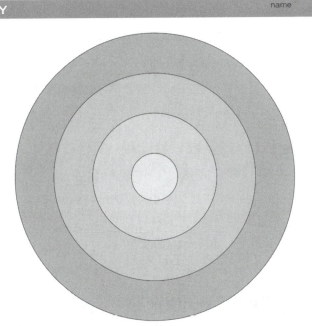

After you map your convoy, you will want to evaluate whether you have people in each circle. As you go through school, you can remap to see how the convoy has shifted. After you leave school, you might find it interesting to map your convoy once again. Completing the two exercises on your convoys will help you clarify your relationships at this time.

EXERCISE 8.2

1. How is your convoy different now from what it was in high school? What persons are present or absent now? In what circles?

2. Would you like to add persons to your closest circle?
Who and why?

3. Would you like to add persons to your middle circle?
Who and why?

4. Would you like to add persons to your outer circle?
Who and why?

5. Would you like to change the balance of men and women? How?

6. In general, how would you like your convoy to be different in the future from what it is now?

7. Can you think of ways to make your convoy look like you want it to?

Highlighting Relationships with Different Groups

As you can see from looking at the people you placed in your convoy, some are friends from college, friends from home, partners or love relationships, family, coworkers, supervisors. The students we interviewed also mentioned authority figures like faculty, staff, or administrators. What they told us might help you be more intentional about your relationships.

RELATIONSHIPS WITH FRIENDS

Friends are central to your feelings of well-being at college, yet understanding friendships is complex. "To study friendship . . . is to trip over the ambivalence, contradiction and paradox with which the subject is hedged in our society . . . Friends provide a reference outside the family against which to measure and judge ourselves, who help us during passages that require our separation and individuation, who support us as we adapt to new roles and rules. They help us in the lifelong process of self-development—transitional objects—people who join us in the journey toward maturity."[2]

Our interviews revealed the many aspects of friendship described previously. As one student said, "To me, friends are both support and release. To be able to go out with just a group of people and do the stupidest things you can think of—just to get away from everything and relax and calm down before you go back at it. Everybody needs to go out and be crazy every now and then. I have a core group of friends that I've known since freshman year, first semester. These are the people I can count on. I made most of the friends in the residence hall."

Most of the students reported making close friends at college. Almost universally they said things like, "There's some good people here that I've grown very attached to that I hope will continue into the 'real world.' When I look back on high school I remember feeling very attached. But now when I go home on vacation, I do not feel close at all. I cannot believe that will happen with my best college friends. I think they will last forever. I am sorry that some of my relationships will end when I graduate. But I know that you move on to new beginnings and I will probably make new friends through work and get attached again."

Many of our interviewees pointed to the special importance of friendships that involved shared ethnicity. One African-American woman told us, "The friends I have made here will be lifetime friends. Our relationships will be changing because when we leave we will all be going in different directions. And that will be hard . . . I have begun to get used to how female/male relationships go. At first, you feel attached and secure. At the very beginning it is exciting. But then when you separate because you have had an argument and you all split—you know, time-out—it leaves you feeling bad, depressed. Being an African-American woman places special pressure on me. I want to be friends with everyone, but I gravitate to others like me. We understand what it is like to be black in a white world."

An Asian-American woman commented, "My freshman year I did not know anybody. I would go to the dining hall and not feel welcomed. Maybe it was because of my ethnicity. It was like a double-edged sword. If you don't say hi, you are stuck-up. If you say hi, you are too aggressive. I took the initiative of reaching out to others of my own ethnicity. Eventually I founded the Asian Student Union. I did not want others to go through the struggle of feeling left out and then having to form a group to feel in."

A returning student told us that she had no time for friends at college because of demands from her family and job. Yet she felt cheated as she watched others going out for coffee and participating in study groups. She realized that not having time to build relationships in college was hindering her enjoyment and feeling of success.

Many agree on the importance of friendship, but it is an amorphous area. There are no clearly defined norms for behavior or agreed-upon sets of reciprocal rights and obligations. Even language doesn't make distinctions among types of friends. For example, there is a tremendous difference between a new acquaintance, an old friend, and a best friend, yet they are all labeled friend.

Some suggest that friendships develop in three stages, each reflecting different and more intense levels of involvement. During Phase One you have "mutual awareness," a time when two people look at each other and begin to establish contact. Phase Two is surface contact, where activities are initiated but little self-disclosure occurs. Phase Three moves from acquaintance to true friendship; self-disclosure begins, mutuality, commitment, and private norms occur.

For many college students, moving into Phase Three means having or being a best friend. When this happens there is both safety and danger. On the one hand, it is wonderful to have someone to really share with; on the other, you can be enormously hurt if the relationship does not stay as you expected and hoped for. One young woman reports, "I supposedly have a best friend, but I don't feel that anymore. I realized after several months that I was the giver and not the receiver. I was opening more doors for her than she was for me. Also, she brings out my bad qualities. It took me a while to realize what was happening. I no longer view her as my best friend."

Our interviews illustrated that it is easier to move from Phase One to Three than in the other direction. Whenever you expect that a relationship is really going to work out and it doesn't, you are usually disappointed. Unlike marriage, friendship is secured only by an emotional bond. When people engage to be married, they make a public statement; when they break an engagement, they make another statement that marks the ending of the relationship. With no social compact, no ritual moment, no pledge of loyalty and constancy to hold a friendship in place, it is fragile. There are no ceremonies when the quality of the friendship changes.

Men and women bond differently. Men's friendships are often based on shared activities and interests, and women's on self-disclosure. Any generalization is clearly an oversimplification, but there is evidence that men and women have been socialized so differently that they bring different experiences and expectations to their friendships.

LOVE RELATIONSHIPS

You can feel love, but like friendship, it is difficult to define. Clearly, the capacity to love, to commit to another and share a life, is something we all desire. It is a major concern of college students. Not having an intimate, durable relationship can lead to loneliness. Premature coupling, however, can stunt developing an inner core, a sense of self. This tug-and-pull confronts many students. George's breakup with his girlfriend illustrates this dilemma.

George and his roommate Derek became best friends. They complemented each other perfectly. George was a shy intellectual. Derek was a jock, full of fun, but not scholarly. Somehow they began trusting each other. They joined the school business club and jointly produced a calendar. The calendar lost money, but their work together cemented their relationship.

During George's junior year he met a girl and they began seeing each other regularly. George had taken a small apartment next to the campus. His girlfriend, Joan, had an apartment in the same complex. They took classes together, met each other's families, went everywhere together.

George went home for the summer; Derek lived near the campus. One night George's mother, frantically upset, called Derek. Joan had told George that she was now going with one of his other friends and planned to stop seeing him. George went into a tailspin. He went to his mother's, started vomiting, crying hysterically. George's mother asked Derek to come up. Derek left immediately for Philadelphia, and called his job the next morning to report a family emergency.

Derek gave unbelievable support to George. He stayed with George for two days, got an appointment and took him to a psychiatrist. He brought him back to his own apartment for 10 days. During that time, George cried, called his girl, begged her to take him back, cried some more, and was generally desperate.

After the 10 days, George went home. Derek called daily and made sure George kept seeing the psychiatrist. George dropped out of school for the semester and went on antidepressant drugs. The next semester he returned to college, started working out regularly in the gym, met a new girl, and began a slower, less intense relationship. George's former girlfriend called and asked to get back together. George had the strength to say no. He also had the support to look at why the breakup had been so devastating, and to begin to put it in perspective.

Clearly George's reaction was extreme. The breakup triggered some deep-seated feelings of inadequacy. To put it in psychological terminology, the breakup was a narcissistic blow; it was an assault to his very core. He felt shamed, demeaned, like a rag doll that had been thrown away.

What happened to George, and what often happens to those who are just beginning to develop love relationships, is the need to become very dependent, the need to be literally "in touch" as much as possible. In some cases, it is almost as though your own existence is in question as soon as the one you love is out of sight.

Healthy intimacy depends on each person being able to stand alone, to trust the other, to feel secure enough to let the other see behind the mask or below the surface. It requires that both partners avoid too much dependence and too much dominance. You try to see the other clearly, with all the flaws and beauty marks, weaknesses and strengths. Then you can move toward interdependence between equals where trust, loyalty, and stability last through crises and separation.

Exercise 8.3, "Friends and Love Relationships," can help you examine how you are functioning in these two areas and identify some things you might like to work on. We just talked about George, who recovered from being dropped by his girlfriend on whom he was so dependent, and who is now developing a less intense relationship with a new girlfriend. George relied heavily on Derek for support. He might have found it useful to work on 3, "I have a group of friends I can count on," on 10, "I spend at least one or two hours a day with my group of friends," and on 14, "I keep in touch with close friends." He might work on 3 and 10 by getting involved in a club related to his major or one of his intellectual interests. This might begin to broaden the range of persons from whom he could get some support. He could work on 14 by calling, writing to, or going to see some of his high school friends with whom he was particularly close, and see whether one or more of those friendships might be regenerated. See whether there are things you might like to work on. Remember that this exercise is intended to help you increase your own self-understanding so you can pursue mature relationships more intentionally. There is no need to be judgmental here. No one else has to see it. No one will grade you on it. It will be helpful only to the extent that you can be honest with yourself.

EXERCISE 8.3

FRIENDS AND LOVE RELATIONSHIPS
name

Check the appropriate column for each item.

	VERY OFTEN	OFTEN	SOMETIMES	RARELY	NEVER
1. I have friendships that provide enjoyment and security.	❏	❏	❏	❏	❏
2. I have close friends that help me grow personally.	❏	❏	❏	❏	❏
3. I have a group of friends I can count on.	❏	❏	❏	❏	❏

	VERY OFTEN	OFTEN	SOMETIMES	RARELY	NEVER
4. I let my partner or close friend know how I really feel.	❏	❏	❏	❏	❏
5. I tell my partner or close friend what I need or desire.	❏	❏	❏	❏	❏
6. My partner or close friend returns my affection in satisfying ways.	❏	❏	❏	❏	❏
7. I discuss future plans with my partner or close friend.	❏	❏	❏	❏	❏
8. I feel comfortable when my close friend spends time with someone else.	❏	❏	❏	❏	❏
9. I spend at least two or three hours a day with my close friend.	❏	❏	❏	❏	❏
10. I spend at least two or three hours a day with my group of friends.	❏	❏	❏	❏	❏
11. I anticipate what my close friend wants or needs.	❏	❏	❏	❏	❏
12. I am comfortable with my sexual relationships.	❏	❏	❏	❏	❏
13. My friend has habits that upset me.	❏	❏	❏	❏	❏
14. I keep in touch with old friends.	❏	❏	❏	❏	❏

15. Some of the most important items for me to work on are:

_____

_____

_____

_____

16. Some good ways to work on these would be:

_____

_____

_____

_____

_____

_____

_____

RELATIONSHIPS WITH FAMILY

Over and over, we heard concerns from students about how to maintain family ties and not be smothered, how to allow for separation while maintaining closeness. One student said, "My family really wanted me to stay home. Now they are used to my being away, but I know my dad worries. Sometimes he phones me in the middle of the day, prime time, just to ask what I am doing. He just wants to hear my voice and give me a little guilt trip about not coming home more. So I would have to say there is a conflict between me and my parents, but I now know I can't satisfy them both. I have to look at what I want to do, and plan. I can begin to understand where they are coming from and understand the conflict as I move into a different setting." Achieving the balance this student is striving for can be a lifelong process.

Many students expressed concern about their parents' expectations for them. Often parents expect a son or daughter to go into a certain field, to major in a certain discipline. Ping, in Chapter 5, whose father wanted her to be a doctor or lawyer but chose teaching instead, is an example. Some students feel very guilty when they choose a different major, when they began to carve an identity along a different path. You could hear Ping struggling with those feelings.

Young students, and some older ones as well, often struggle to achieve mature relationships with parents. The question is how to separate while staying connected. An essential task for becoming an adult involves developing mature relationships with parents.

RELATIONSHIPS WITH AUTHORITIES

Advisors, faculty, and administrators are there to help as you negotiate the college transition. However, they are often perceived as blocking and punitive. Two important issues are at play:

- Students project their unresolved conflicts with their parents onto authority figures.
- Students need to learn to negotiate with authorities, to assert when necessary without being torn up inside.

Working out these relationships can be important for later development. One young man told us, "One relationship that is particularly difficult since I've come to college is working with administrators who are my boss, but who are my friends. They sometimes come to me asking for my personal advice. At the same time, they are my boss. Sometimes we go out and have a beer. It is hard for me to draw the line. I am really confused about what type of relationship it is. It is hard for me to flip-flop. But it is always the boss who determines whether we are to be buddies or supervisor/supervisee."

Several of the juniors and seniors shared difficulties relating to authorities. An Asian-American male said, "I never really talk to any faculty members. I believe it is a waste of time to go to a counselor. When I see a faculty member or counselor, I feel as if I am on a conveyor belt. You know that conveyor-belt theory. You come in, you go out. The only authority figure I relate to is one of the graduate students who works as a dorm resident. She needed my help on a project relating to Asian people. I helped her. And then she would ask me, 'How's it going?' That felt pretty good."

Another student told about feeling uncomfortable. "Back at home I had my teachers, and had a lot closer relationship. Now here at the university, there are volumes of people in class and professors just can't give you the personal attention, and friendship. They come to class, give you the information and then leave. I sometimes feel that they are hostile, but I know they do not have the time."

People's Relationship Needs

The mental health service of a large university reports that one of the major needs for college students is overcoming loneliness. Robert Weiss, a sociologist who studies relationship needs, suggests that needs can be categorized as the need for being connected with a network or group, and the need for having an intimate or best friend. Weiss points out that people need to be part of a social network to avoid social isolation, and to have an intimate relationship to avoid experiencing emotional isolation. We explore both kinds of loneliness. You can evaluate what, if anything, is missing in your relationships as a prelude to doing something about it.

Social isolation results when you are not part of a community, do not have a social network. You can address social isolation by participating in clubs or religious organizations, or by getting involved in other college activities. Involvement in the community can produce feelings of belonging. Remember the student who felt marginal—not part of college life—so she started an Asian-American club. Not everyone can do that. But there are actions you can take to reduce your social isolation if those needs are not being met.

Emotional isolation results from not having a close friend with whom to share your concerns. This need for a reliable ally, for someone else who is significant to you, is central to people's sense of well-being. Remember, it takes time to form a trusting, intimate relationship where you share your inner world. Many who appear to have an intimate relationship, like George, are so intertwined and dependent that the relationship is dependent rather than mature.

You need to create and sustain mature relationships so that your social and emotional needs are met. College presents a powerful opportunity to develop the capacity to meet those needs. For all of these, it is important to learn about open communication; to give, not just take; to manage one's own anger so as not to unload inappropriately. Intimacy dissolves when you are afraid or angry. You can become defensive if you feel vulnerable.

SIX RELATIONSHIP NEEDS

Weiss suggests that to avoid social or emotional isolation, people's relationship needs must be met in different ways. Different types of relationships meet different needs. People need, therefore, to "maintain a number of different relationships to establish the conditions necessary for well-being."

On the basis of his work, he identified the following six categories of relational provisions, each associated with a particular type of relationship:[3]

■ *Attachments* lead to a sense of security through opportunities for mutual accessibility. These usually come through partnerships or best friends.

■ *Social integration* is provided by relationships in which participants share concerns with members of a social network. People in such networks are bonded because of a common concern. Clubs, residence halls, support groups, church activities, community organizations, athletic teams, and car pools are examples.

■ *Opportunities for nurturing* are provided by relationships that allow you to care for friends, family, and children. These are relationships that make you feel needed, that you matter. Many students respond to this need through volunteer activities, "Big Brother" or "Big Sister" programs, peer counseling, or community service.

■ *Reassurance of worth* is provided by relationships in the community, at work, in class, in student activities where your competence is confirmed.

■ *Sense of reliable alliance* is primarily provided by kin, whether or not there is mutual affection. These provide continuity and grounding. As we have pointed out, relationships with family, while essential to well-being, can also be very conflictual.

■ *Obtaining guidance* is provided by relationships that help you when you are in trouble. These include relationships with counselors, faculty members, mentors, administrators, student development specialists, elders.

The point is that you need a mix of relationships that provide all of the above. Weiss's framework helps you think about which of your needs are not being met. You can take specific steps to address your needs for attachment, nurturing, feelings of worth, social integration, reliable alliance, and guidance. If your basic needs for social and emotional connectedness are not being met, then you can begin to think creatively of new ways to meet these needs.

Exercise 8.4, "Meeting Your Relationship Needs," helps you take a reading on where you are and what you might like to work on. George, for example, might find it useful to work on 2, "Social Integration," and 3, "Need to Nurture." He might work on both of these by volunteering at a senior citizens center with other students, where he would share those concerns with them and have the experience of really mattering to some persons who were lonely and bored. Or he might become a Big Brother to one or more new students and help them make the transition to college and avoid some of the relationship pitfalls that he has experienced.

Here is how Jack, the returning student who shared his convoy with us earlier, completed the exercise. After he completed it he discussed it with a faculty member, who told him about a returning learner program. Jack went to a meeting. He felt a bit out of place because most of the people there were women. But there was one other man. They struck up a conversation, went out for coffee, and agreed to continue meeting with the group.

EXERCISE 8.4

Jack

name

MEETING YOUR RELATIONSHIP NEEDS

Under each need, mark parts a, b, and c, *Yes, Partially,* or *No.* Then answer each question as appropriate.

1. Your Attachment Needs

   a. I have friendships that provide enjoyment and security.

   Partially

   b. I let my partner or close friend know how I really feel.

   Yes

   c. My partner or close friend returns my affection in satisfying ways.

   Yes

   Are your attachment needs being met?

   Definitely

   If not, what can you do about it?

2. Your Social Integration Needs

   a. I have a group of friends I can count on.

   No

   b. I feel I belong to and am identified with my college, club, residence hall, or other organization.

   No

   c. I feel part of a group outside of college, like a church or community group.

   No

   Are your needs for social integration being met?

   No

   If not, what can you do about it?

   I'm pretty busy with work and family in addition to school. I like to play tennis and need to get more regular exercise. Maybe I should join the tennis club near my house.

3. Your Need to Nurture

   a. I care for family members when needed.

   Yes

   b. I am someone friends can count on when they are in trouble.

   Yes

   c. I volunteer to help others through an organized activity.

   No

Are your needs to nurture others being met?

   Yes, although I do not give my family as much time as I would like.

If not, what can you do about it?

   I feel so pushed I don't think I can take on anything more.

4. Your Need to Be Assured of Your Worth

   a. Faculty members help me feel I can succeed, even when I am having difficulty.

   Partially

   b. The college authorities treat me with respect.

   Partially

   c. My college friends help me feel competent.

   Yes

Are your needs to be assured of your worth being met?

   Partially. Younger students look up to me. Authorities treat me nicely when they notice me. I could use more reassurance from my professors.

If not, what can you do about it?

   I could make appointments to meet with my professors. Basically I think I am doing well but having them give me their views would be reassuring I think. At least I hope so!

5. Your Need for Reliable Allies

   a. Significant persons in my life, like parents, partner, spouse, or children, support my college work.

   Yes

   b. Aunts, uncles, or other relatives are on my side as I pursue college.

   Yes

   c. College policies and services help me when I need it.

   No

Are your needs for reliable allies being met?

   Partially

If not, what can you do about it?

   Call attention to college policies and practices that don't serve adult students like me well.

6. Your Need for Guidance

    a. College professionals, like advisors, administrators, and counselors, give me good guidance.

    Yes

    b. My partner and close friends share their reactions to my plans and problems.

    Yes

    c. Members of my family give me good guidance.

    Yes

    Are your needs for guidance being met?

    Yes

    If not, what can you do about it?

7. In general, how do you feel about your relationship needs? In what ways are they being met? What kinds of things can you do that would be helpful?

    My personal needs for intimacy are being met. I have a marriage relationship that has lasted ten years and still feels good. I am also very close to my parents and children. But I am not part of a group and don't feel very connected to the college. For awhile I belonged to a study group of other adult students but that petered out this semester. Maybe I should try to get another one going. The tennis club idea also seems worth pursuing.

Now work your way through it to see how you stand and whether there are things you might do.

EXERCISE 8.4

MEETING YOUR RELATIONSHIP NEEDS   name

Under each need, mark parts a, b, and c, *Yes, Partially,* or *No.* Then answer each question as appropriate. Use a separate piece of paper for this exercise.

1. Your Attachment Needs

    a. I have friendships that provide enjoyment and security.

    b. I let my partner or close friend know how I really feel.

    c. My partner or close friend returns my affection in satisfying ways.

    Are your attachment needs being met?

    If not, what can you do about it?

2. Your Social Integration Needs

   a. I have a group of friends I can count on.

   b. I belong to and am identified with my college, club, residence hall, or other organization.

   c. I feel part of a group outside of college, like a church or community group.

   Are your needs for social integration being met?

   If not, what can you do about it?

3. Your Need to Nurture

   a. I care for family members when needed.

   b. I am someone friends can count on when they are in trouble.

   c. I volunteer to help others through an organized activity.

   Are your needs to nurture others being met?

   If not, what can you do about it?

4. Your Need to Be Assured of Your Worth

   a. Faculty members help me feel I can succeed, even when I am having difficulty.

   b. The college authorities treat me with respect.

   c. My college friends help me feel competent.

   Are your needs to be assured of your worth being met?

   If not, what can you do about it?

5. Your Need for Reliable Allies

   a. Significant persons in my life, like parents, partner, spouse, or children, support my college work.

   b. Aunts, uncles, or other relatives are on my side as I pursue college.

   c. College policies and services help me when I need it.

   Are your needs for reliable allies being met?

   If not, what can you do about it?

6. Your Need for Guidance

   a. College professionals, like advisors, administrators, and counselors, give me good guidance.

   b. My partner and close friends share their reactions to my plans and problems.

   c. Members of my family give me good guidance.

   Are your needs for guidance being met?

   If not, what can you do about it?

7. In general, how do you feel about your relationship needs? In what ways are they being met? What kinds of things can you do that would be helpful?

Mature Relationships and Cultural Diversity[4]

Developing mature relationships also means being comfortable with and open to persons different from yourself. You need to respond to individuals in their own right, not as members of some group. You need to recognize your stereotypes and prejudices and learn to suspend judgments.

We all, no matter what our color, ethnic background, or national origin, grew up in a small community of persons like us. We learned what was good and bad, right or wrong, acceptable or unacceptable. We learned appropriate dress, manners, and language. We learned how close or how far apart to stand when talking to a stranger, friend, or relative. We learned to hug each other when meeting, or to kiss each other on both cheeks, or simply to shake hands. In short, we have built into ourselves from childhood the attitudes, expectations, and behaviors with which we feel comfortable. We think of these as "normal." When somebody behaves differently, that's not normal. We can be upset, frightened, or insulted by actions that, for another person, are completely normal and expected. And we can be frightening, upsetting, or insulting to others when we violate their cultural expectations about standing near, giving direct eye contact, or touching.

When these differences are not recognized, there can be powerful consequences. There is a big difference in the speech patterns of Athapaskan Indians ("Eskimos") and white "Anglos" from the "Lower 48." The Athapaskans speak slowly. There often will be a 5- to 10-second pause between sentences or phrases. Anglos speak more rapidly. If there is a two- or three-second pause, it usually means they have finished what they are saying. This simple difference in the length of that pause has led to major misunderstandings. In meetings, or when teachers are dealing with students in school, the Anglos get the impression that the Athapaskans don't know what they want to say. They are dumb. They never finish a sentence or a thought. From the point of view of the Athapaskans, the Anglos are pushy, aggressive, rude, not interested in what the Athapaskans think. Some very unfortunate relationships and attitudes get established because of that simple cultural difference. But once that difference is openly recognized, both parties can find ways to hear each other, communicate more effectively, develop relationships of respect, and engage in productive problem solving and learning.

Use the "Enjoying and Respecting Differences Inventory" to take a reading on where you are in this area and what you might like to work on. This exercise might be helpful to the African-American woman we mentioned earlier, who said, "I want to be friends with everyone but I gravitate to others like me." She might work on 5, "I strike up conversations with persons who are different from me," and 6, "I try to learn about how persons from different backgrounds live." She could work on these by taking a bit of risk in the student union or a campus eating area, sitting down and chatting with someone of a different race or national origin. They could be from southeast Asia or the Middle East instead of the United States, if that would make her more comfortable. She could begin reaching out to others who were different. Or she could join some kind of multiracial or multinational political action or interest group that would give her a chance to meet persons from different backgrounds. As with the "Friends and Love Relationships" and "Meeting Your Relationship Needs" exercises, this will be useful only to the extent that you can be honest with yourself when you respond.

EXERCISE 8.5

ENJOYING AND RESPECTING DIFFERENCES INVENTORY   name

Check the appropriate column for each item.

	VERY OFTEN	OFTEN	SOMETIMES	RARELY	NEVER
1. I am aware of stereotypes when I see them in films or on TV.	❏	❏	❏	❏	❏
2. I am put off by the way people dress or look.	❏	❏	❏	❏	❏
3. I am fearful or nervous with some kinds of persons.	❏	❏	❏	❏	❏
4. I actively try to understand things from another person's point of view.	❏	❏	❏	❏	❏
5. I strike up conversations with persons who are different from me.	❏	❏	❏	❏	❏
6. I try to learn about how persons from different backgrounds live.	❏	❏	❏	❏	❏
7. I have become friends with persons of another race or nationality.	❏	❏	❏	❏	❏
8. I have dated persons of another race or nationality.	❏	❏	❏	❏	❏
9. I participate in discussions where different values and backgrounds are expressed.	❏	❏	❏	❏	❏
10. I defend others who differ from me if they are criticized.	❏	❏	❏	❏	❏
11. I attend cultural events or other activities that portray a different culture or lifestyle.	❏	❏	❏	❏	❏
12. I raise a question when prejudices or stereotypes are expressed as the "truth."	❏	❏	❏	❏	❏

13. Some of the most important items for me to work on are:

_____

_____

_____

_____

14. Some courses, classes, extracurricular activities, or other opportunities to work on enjoying and respecting differences would be:

_____

_____

_____

_____

_____

_____

_____

_____

_____

Wrap-Up

Relationships with others are often our major concern. College is a period when relationships are formed, dissolved, and reformed. The opportunities to get close, define boundaries, trust, and move away set the stage for developing healthy relationships.

We asked some senior students what they had learned about relationships during college. They had learned a great deal, but the dominant theme was embracing diversity. Amos, whom we met earlier, aiming for law school but deciding on history for his major, explains his relationships this way: "They are expensive, time-consuming. They take a lot of energy out of you. They are beautiful because it is like every person is a little fingerprint. They are all different. Everyone comes from a different background and they have their own story to tell. And that's what makes it so beautiful when you interrelate with all these people and bring all these different experiences together."

Another student confirms this view when he says, "The most important thing I have learned in college that will impact my future is acceptance of different people. When I first came here, I was in a house with eight other people I had never met before. I was 18, just fresh out of high school, and I had a guy living with me who was 26 years old. Whether you like to believe it or not, high school is a pretty homogeneous place. So, accepting different people of different ages, from all over the country, different religions, different races is something I did not expect."

Over and over, this theme was repeated. Another senior said, "I have become more open-minded. I've seen myself become more friendly. Now that I know more people, I accept more people. I have learned to respect people, and not just white or black, but people from Pakistan and Iran and all over the place. College has done this for me."

Many seniors were still concerned about relationships with friends, faculty, or families. Relationships are never static. Working out ways to become more independent from, or interdependent with, their families and to be more assertive with faculty, more balanced in their relationships with friends, more trusting and intimate with a select few, will continue for many years. You can be intentional about developing a network of friends and some intimate relationships. You can be aware of the need to avoid social and emotional isolation by examining your "convoy," seeing what you need, and then deliberately setting out to develop and maintain healthy relationships. The connections between your relationships and your college experience are clearly central to your feelings of well-being and success. In Chapter 10, "Taking Control and Keeping It," we review some strategies that you can apply to increasing or modifying your relationships.

REFERENCES

1. We acknowledge the work of R. L. Kahn and T. C. Antonucci for their work on the convoy of social support.

2. Rubin, Lillian B. (1985). *Just Friends*. New York: Harper & Row, pp. 11–12.

3. Weiss, R. S. (1968). "Materials for a Theory of Social Relationships." In Warren G. Bennes et al. (Eds.), *Interpersonal Dynamics*, 2nd edition. Homewood, IL: Dorsey, pp.154–163.

4. The title for this chapter, *Developing Mature Relationships*, and material concerning *Mature Relationships and Cultural Diversity* are borrowed from Chickering, A. W. and Reisser, Linda, *Education and Identity*, 2nd edition, San Francisco: Jossey Bass. 1993.

CHAPTER 9

Time Management, Learning, and Test Taking

The preceding chapters supply quotations, concepts, and exercises to help you make an effective transition into college and maximize your learning.

- We describe a 4 S system: Situation, Supports, Self, and Strategies, for making the transition into college.
- We emphasize the importance of being clear about your purposes and interests, and intentional about managing your own learning to achieve them.
- We help you take stock as you begin and plan your college career.
- We help you learn about learning and understand how to maximize your own.
- We stress the critical importance of defining a major you really want to learn about.
- We underscore taking initiative, taking charge, and working for learning that lasts, not just grades.

- We introduce you to experiential learning theory and learning style differences so you can gain more from courses, classes, and other activities.
- We suggest ways to create mature relationships and respond to the diverse types of persons you will meet.

But all these conceptual frameworks and understandings, all these self-assessments and planning, all these initiatives and self-direction won't amount to much if you don't manage time effectively, don't learn well, and don't deal with tests so you succeed and learn.

By the same token, constructive time management, effective test taking, and all the learning skills in the world won't help if you feel negative about what you are learning. They won't help if you are hung up in the transition, unclear about why you are in college, uninvolved in learning and personal development beyond courses and class, or tangled up in relationships that consume all your energy and emotion. Getting the most out of college requires both the general perspectives we have suggested so far and the nuts and bolts behaviors we address here.

Time Management

A number of junior students described a typical week. Practically all of them had clear, well-planned schedules, but their patterns differed. Barbara, the track team member we heard from earlier, shared one pattern.

"Monday I get up about 8:00 and go jogging. Then I come back around 9:30, take a shower, eat, watch TV until it is time for my 11:30 class. After that I go to my 12:30 class. Then I come back and either go to the library and do a bit of studying before my 2:30 class, or go back to my room, get a snack, and then go to class. My 2:30 class ends at 3:30 and I go to practice. I come back from practice around 6:00 and eat from 6:00 to 7:00. About 7:30 I study in the library with some friends until about 11:00, and then come back and get ready for the next day. Tuesday class starts at 9:00. I get up at 8:30, take a shower and all that stuff. My clothes and little backpack are all ready for class. Class ends at 10:15. I go to practice at 10:30 and come back around 12:30. I eat lunch, study, and go to my 4:30 class, which ends at 7:10. I eat dinner and go to the library and study. Sometimes I might study in my room. Or if I don't have anything that needs to be done right then for the next day, I might take a night off from studying."

"How about Wednesday?"

"Wednesday is like Monday. Thursday is different. We don't start studying until about 9:00 because we have to watch the TV shows. Actually Thursday is an off night for people on this campus. We don't usually study that much, maybe from 9:00 until 11:00. Then we just kind of chill out unless we have a test or something. Friday is real easy unless we have a test on Monday."

"Your courses and practice on Friday are the same as on Monday?"

"Yeah."

"How about Saturday?"

"Saturday is our chill day. We get up later. Do our house work, because I live in student apartments. Do some studying. Mostly on Saturdays and Sundays we do our sorority stuff. If I have a track meet, we usually go on Friday. Sunday we are either coming back from a meet or we go to church on Sunday morning. Then take a short nap and study. Monday it's back to the same routine."

Jim differs from Barbara. He works best late at night.

"Monday I have four classes. I start at 10:30 and have an hour break between 1:30 and 2:30. I go eat lunch. We just came out of history class, so during lunch we go over the notes to see if we missed anything. My last history class is over at 3:30. I might goof off for a while, go see some friends, or whatever. I study better real late, from around 11:00 or 12:00 p.m. until 4:00 or 5:00 a.m. For some reason I seem to work better during those hours. I am more focused. Tuesday I only have one class. I go to class and after that I study for a few hours or do whatever I have to do. Then I go to work."

"How about Wednesday?"

"Wednesday I follow the Monday routine and Thursday is the same as Tuesday. I can work on Friday nights or usually I like goofing off or hanging out with friends. Saturday, if I'm not working, I try to get up around 11:30 or 12:00 and put in a few hours studying because I like to go out Saturday night. Sundays, if I'm not working, I will do the same thing. Sometimes I end up studying the whole day."

"About how many hours a week do you study?"

"I try to do 25 to 30 hours."

"How do you reward yourself for your studying?"

"How do I reward myself? I don't necessarily call it 'rewarding.' I feel like, 'It's been a long week. It's time to go out and forget about school.' Basically that's my best reward. I just don't want to think about it. If somebody brings up, 'I have this teacher . . . ' I say, 'I don't want to hear about it. I had my own teachers this week.' At the end of the semester I reward myself, like after this semester I plan to go skiing."

So different folks have different patterns that depend on their class schedules, involvement in other activities, work, and personal preferences. The important thing is to create the schedule that works well for you. You need sufficient time for academics and other commitments. You need time to hang out with friends, and for important relationships. You need enough rest and relaxation so you don't burn out. Learning to manage time effectively, to balance different demands, responsibilities, temptations, and enticements can be one of the most important outcomes from your college experience. It's a key requirement for many complex work situations and for a satisfying life.

These examples illustrate some important points about managing your time:

■ Each person has his or her own combination of interests and requirements. Some persons have lots of different interests, acquaintances, and obligations, each of which only takes a little time. Others have a few consuming interests, one or two close friends, and responsibilities that take major chunks of time.

- Some persons can function independently and flexibly, others are tied into obligations and responsibilities that require great regularity.
- Some persons need a lot of sleep and a fixed eating pattern, others don't. We all have different times when our energy and creativity are high and when they are low.
- Some persons can study productively for three hours straight, others need to take a break every hour or so. We all have different endurance levels for different kinds of tasks.
- Some persons are extroverts who need more time for human contact. Some are introverts who need to protect themselves from interruptions.

The crucial thing is to establish your own pattern—but there are external considerations you need to recognize. How you allocate time for learning depends on what you're trying to learn. Some kinds of learning are best achieved by frequent, short time investments. To learn a foreign language, an hour a day in the language lab or speaking with others is much more effective than two three-hour time blocks, or six hours once a week. But a science problem, a philosophical principle, a work of art, or an essay or paper may only be well addressed with a minimum of two or three hours' work. A key to efficient, productive time management is allocating the right amount of time to the right things. Most experienced professionals or executives have "to-do lists." They know which things they can do in 10 minutes, which in 30, and which require an hour or more. They know what things to work on if they are apt to be interrupted, and what requires sustained privacy. Victoria said, "I've gotten a feel for how long it takes me to read something and how long it takes me to understand something." You need to develop the same capacity, not only for reading and understanding, but for many other parts of your life.

Finally, if you are pressed for time, be alert for opportunities to do two things at once. There are lots of ways to use commuting time or just-waiting-around time. You can work on many of the approaches and activities we discuss in the section of this chapter called "Forgetting and Remembering."

- listening to tapes of notes or classes
- rehearsing
- visualizing an outline or mind map
- thinking up metaphors, analogies, pictures, diagrams
- making up songs or rhymes

Cooking, cleaning, doing the dishes, mowing the lawn, walking to work or class, riding on a train or bus, all can be combined with various ways to increase understanding and retention.

You can also use time with your children or spouse to do things related to your learning. Ask them what they think about various facts or concepts you are trying to grasp or remember. Have them be an audience for drafts of papers you are writing, and give you critical reactions to your language or ideas. Their attention spans will vary. If you don't exceed them, it can be a nice way to be together, to share some of your learning and excitement, to involve them in your studies. Take advantage of such possibilities when you can. You will be surprised how much you increase your learning time and effectiveness.

BASIC STRATEGIES

How to actually manage your time, that is the question. At one level, the answer is simple. As one student put it, "Use a daily planner. That's the best answer. I don't think you will see anybody without a daily planner. I also manage my time. I always try to set priorities. Always school first. I have been one of those persons who can't say no if someone asks me to do something. But I am learning to say 'no' now, to say, 'Sorry, I can't do it.' Or to say, 'I can do it in 10 minutes, or half an hour, after I finish this work.'"

A daily planner simply lists hours of the day and days of the week, and leaves space to fill things in. Busy executives and professionals are never without their date books or palm computers so they can immediately assess their other commitments when something comes up. Use a large-size desk calendar with blocks for each hour, carry a pocket-size version, or post sheets on the wall. You may need to experiment to find which works best for you. Whatever you choose, the most important thing is to have it readily accessible. Whether you keep it in your pocket or purse, stick it on the refrigerator or on the wall of your dormitory room, set it up on your desk—or a combination of these locations—you need to keep it always handy so you can use it for deciding about what you are going to do, when. You are continually making decisions about how much time you are going to spend on study, recreation, friendships, work, volunteer activities, committee meetings, your favorite TV programs, eating, and sleeping—all the things that are competing for those 24 hours of each day, 168 hours of each week, 672 hours of each month. This simple device helps you maintain the balance that best meets your priorities and preferences. Keeping it in front of you makes clear the realities of prior commitments and the trade offs if you add something more.

PRIORITIES AND PLANNING

There are so many interesting and enjoyable things out there that most of us have difficulty saying no. Thus, the most difficult part of time management is setting priorities, making hard-nosed, realistic decisions about how much time you are going to allocate to all these possibilities during what parts of the day or week. Your priorities will rest on three things: your basic obligations, responsibilities, and commitments; your values; and your interests or things you do for relaxation and enjoyment.

Most of us have responsibilities and commitments to meet while going to college. You may work full- or part-time. You may have kids to get to or from school, meals only you can prepare, shopping only you can do. You may need to spend at least one weekend a month with parents. You may be committed to church or community activities.

Your values lie behind many of these commitments, but they also influence your priorities for using discretionary time. Every choice, every act, every dollar you spend is a value statement. Most adults returning to college have experienced value conflicts in choosing between studying, spending time with friends, partner or children, and doing something for their own pleasure. Most residential students experience value conflicts in choosing between time with friends, getting heavily involved in extracurricular activities, and studying. In Chapter 2 you completed a "Value Analysis." You may find it useful to go back to that exercise so that you have it in mind as you set priorities for using your time.

You also want to build in time for relaxation and recovery. All work and no play burns out the best of us. You need time just to relax. You need activities that drain off tension and vent frustration. You need to have fun with others and enjoy those relationships. Chapter 2 asked you to identify your most enjoyable activities, starting back in early childhood, coming up to the present, and projecting into the future. You identified the skills and personality characteristics called for by these activities. It would be helpful to refer to these as you create your "planner" and learn to manage your time. You may find that many of these activities can contribute to things you want to learn and characteristics you want to develop, and be fun at the same time.

If you are not already using a calendar or a planner, there is a basic strategy that works well for many persons for getting started and translating priorities into behavior:

- List all the things you have to do and want to do.
- Beside each item put the amount of time you require or want to give to it.
- Give each item a score from 1 to 5, with 1 standing for the things most important to you, or the things you just have to do, and 5 the least.
- On a month-by-month calendar, work your way down the list. First block out the times required by certain recurring commitments, like classes, a job, athletics, helping kids with homework, commuting. Then put in the other activities at the times that seem to work best for you. Begin with the 1s and end with the 5s.
- Now enter all the deadlines you have for future products or performances: the dates when exams will be given or when papers are due, when some major task where you work needs to be completed, when you have to have the house ready for a party or for guests. Then put in the appropriate amounts of lead time so these important items don't get shortchanged because they've crept up on you.

A monthly time frame is useful because there are important things you want to do that don't happen every week: going to visit parents or having guests come to you; and special events like concerts, conferences, parties, children's performances, athletic events, and such. You need to keep this calendar on a rolling basis, writing in future events or activities that are high priorities for you. Then you can anticipate them and change your weekly schedule accordingly. The present week and the week coming up will be the fullest and most detailed. Future weeks will probably have some windows of time here and there. It's a good idea to protect those blank spaces as long as possible to leave room for unexpected things you either want to do or absolutely must do.

If you are lucky, you may find all the time you need for your commitments and other things you want to do. Most of us are not so lucky. We have to either eliminate some activities or reduce the time given to them. Thus, you will probably need to take the next step.

- Starting with your 5s, reduce or eliminate the time given to them until you have a schedule that, given the finite number of hours available, best fits your priorities. Note: You may be able to satisfy some 5s by doing them only once or twice a month instead of every week.

These steps require an analytical, linear, rational approach. However, there is another way to identify your priorities and develop your calendar for more intentional planning that may work better for you. This approach helps if you already keep a calendar. It goes like this:

- Create a detailed time log for the last week or two. The further back you can go accurately, the better. Include every hour of the day, or break it into half-hours. Record as precisely as you can how all those hours were spent.
- List each activity and rank it from 1 to 5 according to its importance to you.
- Add the amount of time spent on each activity.
- Examine the fit between your priority rankings and the amount of time you are investing, and identify those where there are big discrepancies.
- Modify your schedule for the next week or two to minimize the discrepancies and improve the fit between your considered priorities and your actual behavior.

Whichever approach you use, it is critical to treat this calendar as a living document. Which it is: It's your life. These are your priorities, whether they are expressed simply through the way you behave or expressed more consciously through explicit attention. These priorities will undoubtedly change with experience, and as new interests, friendships, activities, obligations arise. In fact, one of the most useful things you can do is examine your priorities and schedule from time to time, perhaps at midterm, the end of the semester, or when some serious or meaningful change presents itself.

In the work world, urgent items can often override important ones. You get very busy putting out fires or reacting to pressing short-term, perhaps trivial, needs. Vital areas that have long-term significance, but which are not so compelling, are neglected until they become crises. The workaholic who is driven by the immediate needs of the job, who neglects a spouse and children and wakes up divorced or alienated, is a classic case. Research projects, term papers, or building relationships with faculty members or fellow students can be similarly neglected if time is not specifically reserved for them.

Learning

Allocating appropriate time for study and learning is the starting point. But how much you learn, how efficiently you learn, and how long the learning lasts depends upon how you go about it. Many people talk and write about "study skills." Many colleges have "study skills centers." They can be very helpful. Don't hesitate to use them.

We like the word *learning* for two reasons:

- We are interested in long-term gains more than in short-term results.
- You can spend lots of time studying, following some of the best suggestions, and not come out with learning that lasts.

We want you to keep your eye on learning, not simply on studying.

EXPERIENTIAL LEARNING

Kolb's experiential learning theory, which we shared in Chapter 6, "Maximizing Learning from Courses and Classes," and applied further in Chapter 7, "Maximizing Learning Beyond Courses and Classes," provides the foundation for your learning. We suggested diverse activities to amplify each aspect of the experiential learning cycle: "Concrete Experiences," "Reflective Observations," "Abstract Conceptualization," and "Active Experimentation." The most important thing is to master all those different approaches and apply them to whatever you are trying to learn, wherever you are trying to learn it—in a course or class, a work setting or volunteer activity, a club or an organization. As with the different tennis strokes we used as an analogy, you need to use that full repertoire flexibly, depending upon the learning game you're playing.

WORKING WITH PRINT

You'll spend most of your study time with printed materials. This may not be the case in courses with a strong emphasis on laboratory work, practicums, field experiences, and the like. And it won't be true for activities beyond courses and classes. But, for better or worse, most of your course assignments will involve printed materials *of one kind or another.* That last phrase makes a key point about dealing with printed materials. Verbal and numerical symbols will come at you in lots of different forms for lots of different purposes.

The material you encounter in newspapers and news magazines is straightforward prose. It aims primarily to inform or to express opinions. It uses basic English. It emphasizes *telling.* The messages are clear and simple. They use a standard format, the who, what, when, where, and why. Newspaper articles typically start with a headline. The first sentence or two gives you the basic information or idea. The rest of the article supplies details. News magazines use a similar structure, although the greater length available for the articles permits more elaboration. They capture and maintain your interest through provocative headlines and lead sentences, together with sharply selected details.

You read newspapers and news magazines to find out what's going on in sports, politics, business, international affairs, whatever, according to your interests. Experienced newspaper readers—and you may be among them—can go through *The New York Times* in 20 minutes or half an hour. That's because they mostly catch the headlines and lead sentences. They skip sections they are not interested in. If they are interested in a particular item, they skim for more details.

Novels, short stories, and plays take almost the exact opposite approach. They aim primarily to entertain, to share experiences, to express personal realities. They try to grab you by the lapel at the beginning and keep you absorbed and turning pages. They don't give you headlines or the main point first. They may supply some clues about how the plot works out to keep you guessing. They emphasize *showing*. A good novel or short story does not *tell* you what the plot is, it *shows* you by using dialogue; by describing what characters look like; by creating complex human relationships, specific settings and situations, concrete behaviors, and action sequences related to a larger story line. They capture and maintain your attention because you get involved with the story. You identify with the persons, you recognize the situations, you want to know what happens next, and how it all comes out. If you stop to look, most chapter endings will leave you in suspense so you will go on to the next.

Although you may learn interesting things along the way, you don't read novels, short stories, and plays for information, and you don't usually stop to analyze them. You don't ask yourself how the different characters are created, how the plot is developed, how future events are "planted" so they don't strike you as incongruous when they occur. In literature courses, you read differently. You examine carefully how the characters of the protagonist and other key persons are revealed by their dress, language, past backgrounds, reactions to each other and to different situations. You may underline key phrases or sentences that express each person's essence. You may trace how the plot is introduced, develops complexity, reaches a climax, has its denouement. So, you will read differently from simply reading for recreation.

Textbooks, which will comprise the bulk of your reading (especially for introductory courses), are dramatically different. They aim to instruct, to educate. Their purpose is to help you understand and assimilate basic information and concepts. Most textbook authors don't try to be entertaining. Unless you are very interested in the subject, most texts will not grab you by the lapel and carry you along. You work with a textbook to recognize and understand the important material, and to digest it so it increases your ongoing knowledge and understanding. To achieve lasting learning from a text requires more than simply "reading." That's why we titled this section "Working with Print," and talk about "working" with a text. Working implies an active, systematic approach. The worst way to tackle a text is to just sit down and start reading. You will not learn much by being a passive receptacle, drinking in or gulping down one chapter after another.

Think of a text as a tree. The "tree of knowledge" is an old metaphor. The kind of tree your text represents will vary with the subject matter. Some subjects may be like a Christmas tree: The content will be orderly, hierarchical, going from large, broad branches close to the ground to smaller, more delicate branches toward the apex. The general shape is symmetrical and pointed. Other subjects may be more like an oak or maple, with a sturdy trunk that has several major branches going off at different intervals, some of which are intertwined and overlapping. The crown is well rounded and evenly balanced. Still other subjects may be like an elm: The long, straight trunk has few interruptions, and the top branches are overarching, forming a fan that opens outward, reaching for more light.

Your task is to learn the tree. First you need to comprehend the trunk, then you need to grasp the principal branches. Each branch will have its limbs and off-shoots; offshoots will have twigs and leaves. How many of these limbs, offshoots, and leaves you need to know will depend upon your interest in the subject, the requirements of the course, and the orientation of the teacher.

What does our tree metaphor imply about how you work with a text? Treating the text as a tree to be understood makes your approach obvious. You don't learn about a tree one leaf at a time or one branch at a time. You begin by looking at the whole. The same with a text. Think about the title and read the table of contents. Though this book is not written specifically to be a text, you can use it as an example. The title, *Getting the Most Out of College*, describes our major topic. The three major parts, "Moving In," "Moving Through," and "Moving On," give you the basic structure. They signal that you need to attend to how you enter and how you leave, as well as how you function while enrolled. The chapter titles in the table of contents indicate the most important elements for maximizing your gains. Within each chapter you see the key points and get a sense of our general orientation.

After getting a good grasp of the table of contents, tackle each branch the same way. If the text has major sections, go to each one. They may give you an overview, or explain what the section contains and why. Get a sense of what makes each part a section, and what each section's leading elements are.

When you have a sense of the whole and its significant parts, then you are ready to address a chapter. Most texts assume you will start at the beginning. Most often that does make the most sense—but you don't have to be rigid about it. If you are especially interested in a section or a chapter, it may be best to begin there. When you have mastered that material, when it has become connected to your interests and other knowledge, then you may more easily and productively pursue the other material and see how it relates to your major interest. Remember our basic neurological functioning. For learning that lasts, we need to get new information and concepts attached to preexisting networks. A *logical* order used by an author may not fit the *psychological* order that works best for you.

Again, use this book as an example. We have a logical order. We begin with making the transition to college, then talk about dealing with different aspects of your experience while there, and close with making the transition to your next phase. Whether you have never been to college, are returning, or are already enrolled, you may be more concerned about deciding on your major, or getting the most out of courses and classes, or developing mature relationships, than making the entry transition. So it may work better for you to go to those chapters first instead of simply conforming to our logic.

For each chapter you should use the same approach as you do for the table of contents and major sections. Get a picture of the whole. Many texts use headings, subheads, and chapter summaries. Examine those. Read the summary. Look at pictures and illustrations. See what kinds of exercises, experiments, or activities are suggested. Looking at the headings and exercises in each of our chapters gives you a good sense of the major points.

Now—and this may seem like it has been a long time coming—you are ready to read the text. But even now you don't necessarily want to just sit back and read word by word. Textbook writers will often start subsections with brief overviews. They will use topic sentences to begin each paragraph. Reading the overviews and topic sentences may give you all the understanding you need. If the concepts or principles are not sufficiently clear, then you will want to read enough of the details to make sure you understand. Don't be too cavalier about skipping details. It's easy to kid yourself about how much or how well you understand. And often a striking detail can help you nail down and remember the basic concept.

The point we are trying to emphasize here is *read actively*. It is not easy, relaxing, or entertaining. It's hard work. But a half-hour or an hour spent working with a text in this way, in figuring out the special shape and structure of this particular tree of knowledge, in capturing the essence of each chapter, will be much more productive than spending twice that length of time passively reading page by page.

A number of strategies help to make the text efficiently accessible for future review. You undoubtedly already use some of them. Underline or highlight summaries, topic sentences, and key words. Turn down the page corners of key sections so you can find them quickly. Fold in upon themselves pages that have the most important points. Write key words or your own brief summaries in the margins to express the essence of what's being said. Use you own special marks—stars, exclamation points, question marks, smiling or scowling faces, whatever suits you—to remind you, when you go back another time, of your reactions.

When you get through working, your text it should look well used. Some people try to keep a book pristine and unmarked so they can resell it for a good price. That's a terrible waste of money—a bad way to economize. You are paying high tuition, and you are investing a major portion of your finite time and energy. Although texts can be very expensive, they are by far the least costly part of any course or class. So use them thoroughly in whatever way maximizes your learning.

WORKING WITH CLASSES

Use the same active approach for class sessions as for texts. Be actively involved. This does not mean having your hand up all the time in response to the teacher's questions, interrupting a lecture every time something is not clear, or talking during discussion sessions. In fact, while you are thinking about your own contributions or formulating your own questions, you may be missing important points or contributions by others—even though it does mean your mind is in gear.

Having your mind in gear means being well prepared beforehand. Victoria said, "Usually I'm about two or three chapters ahead of the class. One reason I get good grades . . . is that I'm ahead." If you are not prepared, you won't understand the lectures well; you won't be able to contribute to or learn from discussions; you won't be able to participate in subgroup exercises or activities. In some highly interactive classes, if you are not prepared, your time will be better spent doing the preparation than going to the class.

During class you want to capture the main ideas. If the lecture is well organized or the discussion well led, then those ideas will be quite apparent. The teacher will emphasize key points orally or on the board. There will be transition statements that let you know a new topic is coming up. Discussions will be summarized from time to time, and new questions asked or new positions taken. You can record these points in simple outline form. You also can use "mind mapping." A "mind map" puts the principal concept at the center and subsidiary points or supporting evidence around it at various distances; lines connect different parts to show internal relationships.

Another strategy is to draw a line down your note-taking paper, splitting off about two-thirds on one side and one-third on another. Use the two-thirds for your notes and leave the other space for your own key words, summary phrases, or questions. You may note some of these during class as they occur to you. A good feature of this format is that after class, you can actively review your notes and then enter your summaries, questions, illustrations, and such. If you find you need more space for your own reactions, get a loose-leaf notebook and use one page for notes and the facing page for your own additions.

What you do after class is just as important as thorough preparation and having your mind in gear during class. During lunch after history class, Jim goes over notes with friends. Try to arrange your schedule so you don't have commitments right after each class ends. There may be times when you cannot have that desirable space. Sometimes it is hard enough just to get the classes you want without spacing them apart neatly. Institutions use computer scheduling that may give you back-to-back classes. When that happens, see if you can find another section that is taught equally well. Try to design your schedule to protect time after class as often as you can.

This time after can be used in several important ways. The most obvious is catching the teacher if there are things you don't understand or need to talk about. Don't be bashful. Teachers are paid to help you learn. Most of them will appreciate your interest and concern. If your problems are more complex than can be handled in a brief sidewalk conversation, make a date to pursue them further.

You also need time to review your notes; add any points you did not have time to enter; note things you need to clarify; write in your own summary phrases, or key words; and create or refine your outline or mind map. Doing this immediately after class is much more efficient, and makes a much better contribution to learning, than putting it off. Psychologists use a term called "interference." It denotes what happens as new or different experiences accumulate after a particular event. As interference occurs, the details and meaning of a particular event or activity are obscured, drop away, recede from consciousness. It takes time and effort to recover them later, and you are much less accurate. You will save time and increase learning by getting things down in your own words right after class.

The best thing is to meet with some other students, if only for 15 minutes or a half-hour. Talk about the key points, share your summaries, identify different interpretations or understandings and resolve them if you can. If there is still confusion about a concept or problem, flag it to be clarified by reading, by the teacher, or by future study group meetings. During those conversations you can amplify and sharpen your own notes instead of simply doing it alone.

WORKING WITH COMMUNICATION AND INFORMATION TECHNOLOGIES

If you are not already adept with a computer, email, Web search, and associated technological resources, you need to become so. Just using word processing software will save you huge amounts of time, money, and frustration. Here are some areas in which computer use will dramatically increase your efficiency:

- writing and revising papers
- keeping and reviewing notes
- searching for and getting access to library materials and other resources
- communicating with faculty members
- communicating with fellow students
- working with study groups

Institutions vary in their facilities and resources for emerging communication and information technologies. Many colleges and universities have an infrastructure and resources that link student rooms in dormitories, faculty and administrative offices, libraries, student unions, and all other facilities. Off-campus students with their own computers and modems can access this system from home telephones. Labs provide instruction on computer use and equipment for doing your own work. Some institutions require that you own a computer, and make them available for purchase at low cost.

You will take courses that use computerized learning resources. Some of these are relatively simple, straightforward, didactic programs that replace lectures and books as sources of information. Others are more complex, interactive, instructional programs that combine (a) information and concepts, communicated and illustrated with visuals and graphics as well as print; (b) exercises, "laboratory" experiments, and problem sets; and (c) integrated evaluation and feedback that lets you know how you are doing, and points you to special help sections if you need them. Courses using these resources tend to be more frequent in engineering and the sciences rather than in arts and humanities, although computerized learning resources are becoming widely used for language learning. Rapid progress is occurring throughout education, both to increase the power of the technology and to increase the range and effectiveness of the instructional programs available.

In this first decade of the twenty-first century, you will not only have access from your own home to most institutional resources—faculty, facilities, fellow students, administration—but also to many different courses, classes, and instructional materials. In addition, you will have access to an enormous pool of resources beyond the university. University hook-ups to the Internet already link to resources such as the Library of Congress, the Smithsonian Institution, and networks of professional expertise. Furthermore, many such resources are currently available internationally. Future study groups and research projects will include people in many countries, not just your own. These connections are growing quickly. Access is becoming cheaper, easier, and more efficient.

The quality and efficiency of your learning will be greatly strengthened if you develop expertise in using these technologies. They can provide some of your most important opportunities for learning.

FORGETTING AND REMEMBERING

There is copious research on forgetting. Recall of memorized nonsense syllables—disconnected items in no meaningful relationship—drops to 40 percent in 24 hours and 25 percent in five days. Memorized passages of simple prose drop to 50 percent in 24 hours, to 40 percent in five days, and to 28 percent in 30 days. Chapter 6 shared findings concerning retention from lectures, which dropped to the 15- to 25-percent range soon after the lectures were over. Forgetting is easy. It comes naturally from the interference we mentioned previously; it incorporates survival value so we can separate wheat from chaff, important from trivial, essential from frivolous.

Remembering takes work. It is not easy to get a text from between the covers to between your ears. It is not easy to digest and metabolize all those class notes, reactions, and observations to nourish your working knowledge. After you have done your laboratory exercises, completed field observations, and participated in various activities beyond courses and classes, you still need to get the learning from those experiences into your system so it stays with you.

In Chapter 4 we discussed the differences between surface learning and deep learning. We talked about the difference between mindful learning and being on auto pilot. You might find it useful to go back and review those sections. Deep and mindful learning are critical for learning that lasts.

You can forestall forgetting and make new information, insights, and experiences an enduring part of yourself in many ways. These range from simple and obvious to more complex and demanding. Many of these you already do.

■ Create a standard outline that integrates materials from texts, classes, exercises, experiential activities, and such. Here you are creating your own resource book. Use your own language and phrases for the main ideas instead of simply lifting quotes. That will help you understand the material and remember it better.

- Draw a picture or make a diagram. You can create your own tree with the trunk, branches, limbs, and key offshoots clearly labeled. Or you can use some other figure that may work better for you or for the content: a house, car, garden, horse and buggy, spider web, road map.

- Create a verbal metaphor or analogy that captures the major ideas and their interactions. We have already illustrated those on occasion in this book.

- Make up rhymes or poems. The rhymes and rhythms are internal cues that carry the material. Remember, "I before E except after C, or when sounded like A as in neighbor and weigh"? Or "Thirty days hath September, April, June, and November"? Once you learn these, you don't forget the concepts or information.

- Make up a song or create lyrics to a tune you already know, which will carry the basic ideas. The melody provides cues that help you remember. Notice that if you haven't sung a song for a long time, usually the tune comes back first, then the words gradually return. You're literally tuning up that neglected cerebral network so it works again.

- Reflect on other things you know and can do that are strengthened or complemented by this new learning.

- Reflect on prior learning or preexisting attitudes and values that run counter to the new knowledge, skills, and value orientations you encounter.

Creating these outlines, pictures, diagrams, metaphors, analogies, rhymes, and songs helps you assimilate these materials so they become available in the future. These activities will also reveal what you don't clearly understand and highlight complexities you might have missed.

After having done these various things, you need to *rehearse, rehearse, rehearse*. The most important key to retaining complex concepts, information, and sets of facts is "rehearsal." That's the way actors learn whole plays. They say them over and over to themselves, preferably aloud. Talk through your outline. Review your visual and verbal images, recite your rhymes, and sing your songs.

So, to *learn* you need to:

- Use the repertoire of different approaches associated with Kolb's experiential learning cycle.

- Read actively, first getting a sense of the whole tree, then its principal branches, and finally the important limbs and offshoots.

- Go to class prepared, keep your mind in gear, and follow up as soon as possible afterwards.

- Become adept with new technologies and exploit institutional resources for using them.

- Use the full range of strategies for remembering and rehearse, rehearse, rehearse.

If you learn this way you will be thoroughly prepared for tests. Examinations, no matter what kind, will be enjoyable challenges, opportunities to consolidate what you know and can do, instead of threats and obstacles to be overcome.

Test Taking

We are a credentialing society. Tests and examinations sort and sift entry applicants for education and work. They certify competence and provide quality assurance for activities as diverse as giving you a haircut or manicure, driving an automobile or flying an airplane, replacing your heart or defending you in court. Many tests and exams are flawed; few assess the full range of knowledge and competence required. But they are here to stay. Their efficiency and objectivity, relative to other forms of evaluation, make them useful tools for many decisions involving human competence.

LEARN FROM EXAMS

Tests can be significant opportunities for learning. They provide deadlines and contexts for assimilating and integrating prior learning. Thoughtful scrutiny of results yields information about gaps and confusions, which can guide further learning. Thus, our fundamental point about tests is to use them for learning opportunities, for consolidating prior preparation, for diagnostic purposes when the results are available. If you have learned in the ways we suggested previously, preparation will be easy. Learning from test results requires additional effort.

INTERPRETING RESULTS

After the exam is over, don't just find out your score and let it go at that. Spend time looking at what went right and what went wrong. On essay exams, some teachers may give a grade without clearly articulating their criteria or the basis for the judgment. When that happens, go ask. Get the teacher's first-hand report of the strengths and weaknesses of your responses. On multiple-choice exams, look carefully at the items you missed. Try to understand why you chose the wrong response and why you missed the right one. Then pull those observations together as a basis for reviewing your learning materials and remedying the deficiency.

Examinations are scored in two basic ways. Some scores are based on "norms," others are based on explicit criteria. When scores are based on norms, your "grade" depends upon how well you do compared with other people who have taken the test. The subject matter achievement tests and the Scholastic Aptitude Tests for college entrance are good examples. Your score reflects the percent of randomly selected students it exceeds. On other tests, your score depends on how well you meet the specified criteria. It doesn't matter how well or poorly everybody else does. Your driving license examination is a good example. You have to meet minimum criteria on the eye exam, you have to get the correct number of answers on the written test concerning the rules of the road, and you have to drive the streets in ways that meet specific standards. The fact that most people get good scores on the test does not affect your score. If you meet the criteria, you get your license.

When college professors "grade on a curve"—distributing A's, B's, C's, D's, and F's according to some rough percentages they have determined in advance—whether they realize it or not, they are using norms as a basis for your grade. Most professors are not very skilled at establishing clear criteria for performance and then creating tests based on them. They think that if they assign numbers to different exam questions they have created criteria. They will give an exam with one essay question worth 40 percent, another worth 25 percent, a multiple-choice section worth 20 percent, and a matching section worth 15 percent. Those percentages tell you how much each question contributes to your total grade, but they don't tell you anything about (a) the criteria used for grading your responses on the essay questions; (b) the criteria used for selecting the items on the multiple-choice and matching sections; or (c) the criteria underlying the percentages allocated for the different parts.

It can be very frustrating to feel you know the materials well, have answered most of the questions correctly, and still end up with a B or a C simply because your classmates were also well prepared. To really learn from the test, to understand what it says about your strengths and weaknesses, ask teachers to describe the criteria used for scoring each question and for assigning your final grade. If your teachers can give you clear answers, you will know a lot more about your performance. If not, then you will at least have been a force for improving their thinking about their exams.

The most important basis for interpreting the results is your own frame of reference. Results based on norms that show how you stack up against others are helpful. Results that show how well you meet specific criteria are more useful. But it is the *gains* in knowledge or competence you have achieved, relative to where you started, that are most important. If you started out totally ignorant, you may have made great strides and still not perform very well on the exam, whether it is graded by norms or on specific criteria. For example, if you spend a summer or long vacation in a foreign country, you may go from total ignorance of the language to being able to order food, understand basic directions, and carry on simple conversations. You might not do well on an exam, but you will certainly have made major progress with the language. You have a level of competence, developed the ability to function and to get around that you feel good about and that works for you. That may be as much as you want or need at the time. So, the most important thing is what we call "self-referenced" evaluation. When you get feedback from the exam, how do *you* assess your learning? It is your learning and your standards that are critical for you, not the professor's, not the test maker's. That should be the basis for your final interpretation.

TEST-TAKING STRATEGIES

There are things to know and skills to develop concerning test taking. These skills are no substitute for thorough preparation, but they will help you perform in ways that accurately reflect your knowledge and competence rather than short changing it.

Essay Exams

When you are answering an essay question, follow these basic steps:

Make sure you understand the question. Most of us teachers are surprised how often students simply misread the question. When asked to critique an argument, or contrast different theories or concepts, or evaluate the evidence for an assertion, they will simply describe the ideas. When asked to list, they will explain. When asked to outline, they will narrate or summarize. If you misunderstand the question, there is no way to do well.

Exercise 9.1 lists key words that often are used for part of essay questions. Look up each one and write your own definition. Then review the list before you go into an essay exam. When you get the exam, underline the key words in the question to make sure you understand.

EXERCISE 9.1

KEY WORDS FOR ESSAY EXAMS   name

Look up and write down the dictionary definitions for each of these words. When it is helpful, add your own language. The groupings include words with fine distinctions. Keep the results to review before each exam that will include essay questions.

1. Analyze, Criticize, Critique, Evaluate, Justify, Prove.
2. Describe, Discuss, Explain, Interpret, Relate, Trace.
3. Compare, Contrast.
4. Define, Enumerate, Label, List.
5. Narrate, Outline, Review, Summarize, Trace.
6. Diagram, Illustrate.

Brainstorm. Write down key words or abbreviations for all the ideas that come to mind as potential responses. Brainstorming can be especially important if you feel a bit shaky about how much you know. Once you get into it, you will find other relevant information coming to mind.

Plan your answer. Some persons find it helpful to create a brief outline. A mind map may work better for you—or simply jotting down key words or phrases that signal ideas you want include. You don't necessarily have to get down everything you might want to say. Just try to get a good structure.

Get clear about how much time you have for the question. Think through how much detail or how many illustrations you can include for each major point.

Be brief and to the point. Your purpose is to reveal how much you know. If the teacher and exam permit, you may find it most effective to use telegraphic language and an outline rather than full sentences. You can cover more territory that way. If you like that approach, clarify whether it is okay before the exam.

Leave lots of space as you write. If you are given an exam booklet, use just the right or left page and leave the other blank. As you move through your answer, you often will remember content that should have been included earlier. Leaving space between your key sections or on the opposite page makes room for these insertions. They will be easy for the teacher to read and to recognize where they go.

If time permits, reread your completed response. Often that rereading will identify things that need to be clarified, or additional points you want to make.

Multiple-Choice and True-False Exams

Multiple-choice and true-false exams, especially those composed by teachers who are not experts in test making, often contain internal clues that help you eliminate wrong responses and identify right ones. They will also contain questions you immediately know and others where you are uncertain. The most important thing is to go through and first answer every question you are sure of. Answer each question in your head before looking at the options. If you can do that, you are likely to choose the correct response.

Then you need to know whether you will be penalized for incorrect answers. To protect against guessing, test scoring often deducts 20 or 25 percent of your wrong answers from your right ones. When that is the case, you have to be more calculating about guessing on the basis of clues other than your own sure knowledge. You need to eliminate alternatives so that your chances are one out of two instead of one out of four or five. But if there is no penalty, don't hesitate to make your best guesses. Here are some internal clues you may find helpful:

- Be alert for answers suggested by other questions. A concept, fact, or piece of information may be supplied or implied elsewhere in the test.
- Options that use absolute words like always, never, all, none, only, and the like are rarely correct.
- If the answer offers sentence completions, eliminate options that don't result in grammatically correct sentences.
- Eliminate options with incorrect details.
- If two options are similar, choose one; if two options contain similar quantities, choose one.

Matching Exams

Matching exams are a bit more difficult than simple multiple-choice or true-false exams. They don't lend themselves to guessing unless you accurately eliminate most of the alternatives. Do all the match-ups you are sure of first. Cross out both parts if the exam format permits. Then you can clearly distinguish the remaining alternatives.

TEST ANXIETY

No one is immune to performance anxiety. Actors, athletes, public speakers, and such all have reactions ranging from mild butterflies to cold sweats. It's normal and healthy to feel nervous or uptight before an exam. The tension helps you be alert, sharpens your reflexes, gets your juices running. It can also lead to panic, confusion, and mental blocks.

The best moderator of test anxiety, of course, is thorough, ongoing learning beforehand. But there are others things you can do to be ready.

- Get your normal amount of sleep.
- Do some aerobic exercises to burn off a bit of that extra energy.
- Play a game you enjoy, or do something else—just for fun.
- Have some water and a bit of fruit before you go in.
- Do some deep breathing and relaxation exercises.
- Tense and relax muscle sets: feet, legs, hands, arms, neck, torso.
- If you are getting some strong physical reactions, visualize their location in your body and describe them to yourself.
- Do some creative visualization, seeing yourself at the beach, in the mountains, soaking in the tub.

When you get the exam, look it all over. Identify the questions you know well and those that will take more hard thinking. Calculate the approximate amount of time you need for each question. Develop a general strategy for completing the exam. Begin with those questions you know best or can handle easiest. Save the toughest for last. If you feel blocked on some questions, set them aside. Once you get into other questions, the block may disappear. If there are some questions that are totally beyond you, don't try to fake them. Simply say what little you know, or indicate you can't respond, and concentrate on doing your best on the rest.

Wrap-Up

Effective time management is as critical to success and satisfaction in college as it is in the rest of life. Knowing how to learn, how to invest your finite time and energy to get lasting results, is also critical, not only for college, but for our knowledge society. You will encounter various kinds of tests and examinations not only in educational institutions, but in other parts of your life as well. Mastering these three basics will help you get the most out of college and help you toward career success and a good life.

Taking Control and Keeping It

Moving into college, moving through, and moving on present a variety of challenges. Each challenge is a significant opportunity for learning. We learn when we respond to situations, requirements, or conditions for which we are not prepared, conditions that call for knowledge, competence, or personal characteristics that are not already well developed. Courses and classes requiring new ways of thinking and new knowledge present such challenges. Joining a new club or activity, providing leadership for an organization, or taking a new job often demands new skills and perspective. New friendships, or working relationships with persons different from ourselves, can challenge preexisting assumptions about human behavior and the wisdom of some of our own attitudes and values. Even the challenges involved in coping with a frustrating institutional bureaucracy can help us learn how organizations work and how to deal with them more effectively.

Sometimes you cope successfully. Other times you fail or just muddle through. But however it comes out, you usually learn something important about yourself, the challenging situation, and new strategies for coping. Your knowledge base expands. You learn new skills and develop new abilities. How much you learn and profit from the various challenges you encounter depends on how you respond. The Chinese symbol for crisis also is a symbol for opportunity. That's the spirit you need to keep in mind.

Profiting From Challenge

Rosalynn and Jimmy Carter seemed bitter after his defeat in the presidential campaign. However, they have turned that defeat into a positive life contributing to the well-being of others. Arthur Ashe, a tennis star, faced the cruel fate of someone with AIDS, and turned his tragedy into an inspirational story for others. Betty Ford turned her drug addiction into a mission to help others by founding the Betty Ford Center. Of course, not everyone can turn defeat into success. We see many instances where people give up instead of thinking how they might take control.

People of all ages who manage challenges well share several characteristics: diverse options, informed understanding, and feeling in control.

The trio—options, understanding, and control—does not guarantee a fairy-tale ending to a challenge. But more options, and an increased understanding of what is really going on, leads to more control of your life.

INCREASING YOUR OPTIONS

Each time you bump into a roadblock, examine your internal and external options. Take the example of those living in rural areas where no college exists, who want a college degree but can't pay to move away from home. They face some real roadblocks. For Bertha, who lived in a small town, the option of attending college was unavailable. Then the telephone company she worked for cooperated with the state university to offer extension classes locally for telephone employees. The minute these classes became available, Bertha exercised her option and enrolled.

But how could Bertha have created her own options? She might have gone to her personnel department and asked about alternatives. They might have told her about correspondence courses or special workshops that would carry credit with them. They might have described ways she could develop a portfolio to document the learning she has achieved through work and life experiences; later, this portfolio could be transformed into college credits.

Sometimes we do not exercise choices because there are no external or tangible opportunities; other times we just don't see the possibilities. One way to overcome this myopia is by "Taking Stock," which helps you pinpoint which of your coping resources are low (see Chapter 3). Then you can begin "Taking Charge" by generating new options for improving your "Situation, Self, Supports, and Strategies."

INFORMED UNDERSTANDING

Many students said, in effect, "If only I had known my first year what I know now." However, there is no way to write a map for the college years since there is such variety in each new class—some people are young, others old; many have disabilities. Each one is unique; some are part of a minority group, but being a Native American is clearly different from being an African American. There is no "typical college student," therefore, there is no typical college experience. Thus, we cannot tell you exactly what to expect as you move in, through, and out of college.

Students differ about when and how they face certain underlying issues, but sometime during college they face the following questions:

- Who am I?
- Do I belong?
- Do I feel I matter to others, that others appreciate me?
- Am I competent to handle the academic and social tasks involved with college?
- Can I achieve and maintain relationships?

These questions arise not only during college, but through life. As you enter college for the first time, whether as a traditional-age student or an older student, you may wonder, "Will I fit in? Am I competent to do the work? Will I make friends?" As you continue in college, no matter what your age, ethnicity, or family background, you may be one of the many people who have trouble maintaining and sustaining their involvement and commitment. As people leave, they begin thinking about next steps and evaluating. . . . "Has it been worth it?"

TAKING CONTROL

People can take control by learning new strategies and knowing that:

- Reactions change over time.
- Adjustment depends on the degree to which your roles, routines, relationships, and assumptions have been challenged and changed.
- A system exists for understanding change. You can "Take Stock" of your resources (as you did in Chapter 3) and then apply the coping skills and strategies to "Take Charge," described later in this chapter.

Everyone's college experience will be unique. Yet the structure for examining your challenges, so that you can understand them more fully, remains stable. You can get the most out of college by taking control and keeping it.

Challenge and Support: The Right Mix

We asked Angela if she had ever experienced a situation that made her feel uncomfortable. After a long silence, she started talking:

"Well, I told one of my professors that I was working a lot. I was always late to class. I went in to talk to her and explained that I worked and had to do my homework late at night. I did not want her to think I was being a bad, irresponsible student. She asked, 'Well, are you a waitress?' I said, 'No'. I was really offended. Why would she think I'm a waitress just because I said I worked a lot?

"Why do you think people make assumptions?"

"Well, she was white and I'm black."

Angela described herself as "very sensitive" and unable to handle situations that she assumed were a result of racial bias. However, she told us, "I've gotten stronger. A lot stronger. I was helped by the new counselor in the Black Peer Counseling program. He knows a lot about black history. He brings in movies and books and talks a whole lot about what we've done and things about Africa. Everybody loves him."

Wanda suffered all through high school because of a learning disability. She went to a low-key school, and graduated without knowing how to organize material for papers or how to plan ahead so assignments could be handed in on time. After high school she worked as a receptionist in a doctor's office. She complained about the constant pressure and felt inadequate because she often misspelled patient's names and made errors when calling in prescriptions. The office manager constantly criticized Wanda, who continually felt miserable. Her low self-image went even lower.

With help from a career counselor, she began exploring what she should and could do. After a number of sessions and extensive testing it became clear that working as a secretary exacerbated her problem. She resigned from her job and entered a small liberal arts college where she spent six years, much of it in turmoil.

The college did not provide the kind of support needed by someone with a learning disability. The head of the college's learning center knew very little about disabilities and labeled Wanda "lazy." She made Wanda retake the same English class five times. She would not allow Wanda to take English in another institution. At first Wanda was devastated. However, she hung in by hiring her own tutor, finding a counselor who helped her learn negotiation skills with her faculty. Wanda made the Dean's List her final semester, and graduated with a B.A. in History and a minor in Art. Her advisor thought her senior thesis was good enough to be published.

When we asked Wanda what accounted for her eventual success, she attributed it to her own determination, the support of a History advisor, her tutor, and counselor. She felt sabotaged by the Learning Center personnel, but the combination of support and self-determination enabled her to succeed. She evaluated the total experience as one with more pain than pleasure, but admitted that the challenge of having to produce papers, engage in original research, and meet college standards helped improve her self-image from that of an academic loser to an academic winner.

This case powerfully illustrates the point that college can foster new competencies, new self-assumptions. Many students feel the need to control their worlds. Wanda, with assistance, got control. She recently told us that she will always have problems with judging how long it takes to complete an assignment, with focusing her energies on the task at hand, with prioritizing, and with short-term memory. However, she now has techniques for handling her deficits. When she does forget, she no longer tortures herself by defining herself as a failure.

Wanda has successfully tackled and completed college. She still has more challenges, but she has developed strategies for coping. We will look at strategies other students use to cope with their challenges, then we will return to you and how you might increase your coping repertoire.

Appraising Your Challenge— The First Step

Wanda and Angela experienced different problems as they encountered challenges in college. Both became stronger. You will face a myriad of problems, failures, and successes during college. The question is, how do you handle these inevitable ups and downs? Can you creatively manage your life?

To cope, you need to appraise both the situation you are facing and your resources for dealing with it. A famous line from Shakespeare's *Hamlet* is illuminating: "There is nothing either good or bad, but thinking makes it so." To one student, a failing grade can be a challenge; to another, it might be a catastrophe that triggers dropping our of school. Wanda initially appraised her learning disability as overwhelming. After four years of college, she appraises it as a mixture of challenging and overwhelming.

Several psychologists developed an "appraisal training" system. They found that people often appraise a negative situation in such dramatic ways that the negative is multiplied and becomes totally overwhelming. Appraisal training teaches people to break down the challenge into smaller parts. Instead of saying, "I am learning disabled, I'll never succeed, I'll never get my college degree," you can take the negative condition—being learning disabled—and break it down into smaller parts. For example, you might say, "I have difficulty getting papers in on time," or "I spell terribly," or "I forget appointments." In other words, the global assessment, especially if it is negative, is broken down, thereby becoming less daunting. It is much easier to deal with "I spell terribly" than "I'm learning disabled."

Take a moment now and think about some issue, either academic or personal, that is challenging you. The following list of barriers identified by students at one university might help you identify your challenge:

- lack of study skills
- difficulty managing time
- difficulty understanding course material
- no clear goal; unsure of major
- difficult classes; hard schedule
- financial problems
- physical illness or health problems
- alcohol or drug issues

- adjustment to America
- trouble making friends
- feeling pressured
- test anxiety; difficulty with test taking
- general adjustment to college
- separation from home, family, friends
- lack of motivation
- loneliness; lack of emotional support
- housing or roommate issues
- disability
- transportation
- computer error

This chapter encourages you to try new strategies to apply to your current challenges, whatever they may be, and provides a long-range approach to take with you after college.

APPRAISING YOUR RESOURCES

Psychologist Richard Lazarus contends that individuals constantly ask two sets of questions:

1. "Is the transition or challenge good, bad, or neutral?"
2. "Whether or not I evaluate it as good, bad, or neutral, do I have enough resources to cope with the challenge?"[1]

An easy way to think about your resources is to return to your 4 S's, which we discussed in Chapter 3. The 4 S's—Situation, Supports, Self, and Strategies—refer to your potential resources for coping with any eventuality. Wanda at first evaluated her learning disability as overwhelming. She simultaneously evaluated her resources for coping with it. She saw her Situation as mixed. She felt "off-time" about returning to school because her classmates from high school were finishing their sophomore year as she was beginning. She felt her Situation was somewhat out of her control, because no matter how she tried she could not get rid of her problem. Her Supports were also mixed. At the beginning, she had the support and concern of her parents as well as her fiancé. However, she felt no support at the school—the place she really needed it. Over time, that changed. She uncovered supports at school. She found a counselor who was very supportive, and was retested so she could identify her problems and begin to master them. Her mother, who worked as a housekeeper, saved enough money so that Wanda could hire her own tutor, a person who was trained to work with learning-disabled adults. As she developed new Supports and increased her Strategies, she reappraised her ability to deal with her disability. Instead of seeing it as totally overwhelming, she began to feel more confident about her ability to cope.

The way you handle a challenge depends largely on the way you appraise it. The evaluation includes appraising the challenge and your resources for coping with it.

It might be helpful to return to Kathleen, who reviewed her Situation, Supports, Self, and Strategies in the "Taking Stock" chapter. Remember, she was the first in her family to go to college. She did not have a lot of emotional or financial support from her family, although she did have support in college from a mentor and from two other first-generation students. She was feeling very pushed by all her school work. Her major strategy for coping with the challenges she faced was to work very hard and keep busy despite her emotional difficulties with her parents. But now she has successfully completed her first two years with about a B average. Her parents have become more accustomed to her being in college, and she has found a part-time job to help support herself. Here's how she now appraises her challenge and resources.

EXERCISE 10.1

Kathleen

APPRAISING YOUR CHALLENGE AND RESOURCES   name

What was your challenge?

The main challenge was keeping up with my school work. The lack of support from my parents was another challenge.

1. Did you appraise the challenge as:

   Overwhelming? Neutral? Challenging? Mixture?

   I appraised the challenge of keeping up with studying as pretty overwhelming.

2. Now evaluate your resources for coping—your 4 S's

   Your Situation—Do you see it as:

   Positive or negative? At a good or bad time in your life? In or out of your control? Explain.

   My Situation has become much more positive during the past two years. I got help from the study skills center. I can handle my school work more easily now although I still don't do as well as I would like. I have made some friends and enjoy singing in the college glee club and the choir of the nearby church.

   Your Supports—Do you see them as:

   Helpful or not helpful? Enough or not enough? What would have helped? Explain.

My mentor has been wonderful. She helped me decide on a music major and introduced me to the priest in the church near college. He has been helpful with my parents and they now feel better about my being in college. He also helped me get a job house- and baby-sitting for a nice family. I am still good friends with Sophia, one of my first two friends from my mentor. Prof. X in the music department thinks I have a good voice and is encouraging me to take private lessons as soon as I can find the time and money.

Your Self—Do you see your Self as:

Someone who can handle challenges or not? As optimistic or pessimistic? Explain.

I think I have handled the challenges I faced when I entered quite well, all things considered. I am optimistic now that I will complete college.

Your Strategies—Do you use:

A variety of Strategies or just rely on one or two? Would you benefit from learning new strategies?

Explain:

Working hard and long is still my main strategy. But I have learned to be more clear and direct with my parents about my needs and future plans. I've learned to manage my time and set priorities better. I often play volley ball with a gang of men and women after supper, before I hit the books. I imagine there are more strategies I could learn.

3. Overall, as you look at your challenge, do you see the problem as being with the challenge or with your resources for coping with it?

I think the challenges with studying and with my parents were pretty real. But I also relied too much on just working hard. Now I think I have better resources. My situation is better and so are my supports. I still feel optimistic and confident. I think increasing my strategies for coping would be the most useful thing.

Let's return to the challenge you have selected to work on in this chapter and examine your appraisal of it.

EXERCISE 10.1
_____

APPRAISING YOUR CHALLENGE AND RESOURCES   name

Use a separate piece of paper to respond to this exercise.

What was your challenge?

1. Did you appraise the challenge as: Overwhelming? Neutral? Challenging? Mixture?

2. Now evaluate your resources for coping—your 4 S's:

   Your Situation—Do you see it as:

   Positive or negative? At a good or bad time in your life? In or out of your control?
   Explain.

   Your Supports—Do you see them as:

   Helpful or not helpful? Enough or not enough? What would have helped?
   Explain.

   Your Self—Do you see your Self as:

   Someone who can handle challenges or not? As optimistic or pessimistic?
   Explain.

   Your Strategies—Do you use:

   A variety of Strategies or just rely on one or two? Would you benefit from learning new strategies?
   Explain.

3. Overall, as you look at your challenge, do you see the problem as being with the challenge or with your resources for coping with it?

Increasing Your Coping Strategies—The Second Step

Now for the most important question: What can you do about your particular challenge? You have appraised your challenge and your resources for coping. You have identified your strengths. You now can identify the areas that need strengthening. The "Coping Strategies Worksheet" is based on the results of thousands of interviews that enabled two sociologists to identify numerous coping strategies that people employed as they faced life's ups and downs. They discovered the obvious—there is no magic coping strategy. The effective coper is the person who can retrieve coping strategies, use new ones, even invent some as needed.[2] Most coping is intended either to:

1. Take action to change or modify the transition, challenge, or issue by:

- negoitiating (compromising, talking things through)
- taking optimistic action (mobilizing yourself and your resources; making a plan and carrying it out
- seeking advice (asking others for guidance)
- asserting yourself (standing up for yourself)
- brainstorming a new plan (generate all possible suggestions or solutions)
- taking legal action (if needed)

2. Change the meaning of the transition, challenge, or issue by:
   - applying knowledge of the transition process (recognizing that all change requires adaptation and time to adjust to the new situation)
   - rehearsing (practicing in your mind for a future occurrence)
   - developing rituals (creating a rite to add meaning to your transition)
   - making positive comparisons (counting your blessings; comparing your situation to those less fortunate)
   - rearranging priorities (reemphasizing other areas of your life as more important)
   - relabeling or reframing (redefining the transition in a more positive way)
   - selectively ignoring (playing down bad parts and playing up good ones)
   - using denial (delaying facing the facts for a short time)
   - using humor (improving your laugh life)
   - having faith (reflecting through prayer, meditation, or solitude)

3. Manage reactions to stress by:
   - playing (allowing the child within to emerge and have fun)
   - using relaxation skills (controlling physical reactions to stressful situations through relaxation tapes, biofeedback, muscle relaxation, or imaging)
   - expressing emotions (letting off steam through crying, yelling, or vigorous physical activity)
   - doing physical activity (walking, running, tennis, exercise of any kind)
   - participating in counseling, therapy, or support groups (working with a professional to help you manage stress; joining a support group with people experiencing a similar situation)
   - reading (to provide guidance, instruction and inspiration, or distraction)

4. Do nothing (consciously deciding to take no action—just sitting tight to see what happens)

5. Use other strategies (employing a range of strategies) knowing there is not one magic strategy but several that may help you cope

Milt, a junior, used a variety of strategies. He *took action* by creating a club called The Political Independents. He said, "I get a real charge out of doing something new. I like to help make things happen. This was a big change from freshman year when I was trying to find my way. I became active and really got involved in politics.

We asked how he managed life as a student. Milt asserted himself and learned how to get around the bureaucracy. "Well, let me give you a clue. I've already done my registration for spring. The earlier it gets done, the more time I have to fix it. If you don't want to stand in a line for five hours, find out everything you have to about the class." In other words, Milt *sought advice.*

He also learned to prioritize and *change the meaning* of his challenge. He told us that ". . . last year is the first year I ever worked and went to school. I never had to accept responsibility. My parents were masterminding everything."

Milt summarized his coping strategies by pointing out that when he transferred to his present college, he began to take control of his life by paying bills and taking responsibility for himself.

Milt also *managed his reactions to stress* through basketball. "I found that basketball was fun and exciting. I also realized I could impact my environment."

We talked with April about her resources for dealing with college. When we discussed her 4 S's—her Situation, Supports, Self, Strategies—she said openly that the major stumbling block was herself. Her inadequacies were highlighted each time she bumped up against the bureaucracy and failed. At the Financial Aid Office she felt like a number, as if someone were telling her, "Here's your money, now get out." Then at work she imagined people thinking, "Here she is, the gofer, the work-study student." She felt unappreciated.

April told us that she was sometimes overly sensitive and always ready to think the worst. However, she clearly saw a difference in the way she perceived things when comparing herself now, as a junior, with herself as a first-year student. Now she tells herself, "Oh you could have done this differently. Wait a minute, CALM DOWN, and think rationally. Start going over what happened, pulling it apart." April concluded, "I have begun to see what is out of my control, and what I can control. I try to figure out my role in it. I am getting better through practice."

Over her three years at college, April changed the way she explained life. Instead of being pessimistic and seeing herself as a failure, she no longer generalizes, assuming that every failure is her fault. She told us, "I think I've become a more outspoken, responsible, independent person—more sure of myself—than when I started out."

We asked April to explain how this change had occurred. First, she read an article in her psychology class about ways to think differently about failure. Her professor lectured on the subject, giving examples of how people can change their outlook from pessimistic to optimistic. In addition, she observed how her peers dealt with inevitable failures.

She volunteered the following: "There is something else. I made up my mind in my second year to become more involved. I got active in politics and student government. I took on a part-time job. I think involvement is key."

Matti described herself as quiet, independent, closed. As a first-year student, the hardest thing she had to deal with was meeting people. At first she wanted to transfer. She would call her mother and say, "Mom, it's not right, it's not right." Matti's life improved, however, when a sorority rushed her during her sophomore year. "I knew that joining a sorority for a black person would be real important and provide a close bond, something to last your throughout life." Although Matti is still quiet in groups and with unfamiliar people, she finds the sorority supportive.

As a junior, Matti still has a major problem—fear about poor grades. She feels tremendous pressure. "It's like you are always thinking I gotta get a B, I gotta get a B. Or I have to get an A to balance my C." To cope, Matti prays and talks with her mother. "As long as I can contact my mother, I'm fine."

Matti was not interested in getting to know people with disabilities or people from other cultures. She reports, "It is hard to become friendly with someone different. You do not have something common. You listen to different music, you like to do different things."

We asked Matti if she sought help from the counseling center or from the Minority Student Services. Matti is not interested in soul searching and analyzing herself. In fact, she told us that she did not want to answer personal questions. She feels she is the same person she was when she came to college. If she can have time alone to breathe, go out sometimes and have fun, stay in her sorority, and talk with her mom, she will be okay.

Matti has grown at college, but not as much as she could have if she had expanded her coping repertoire. She was a junior when we interviewed her, and she still was not ready to do that. People have different times in life when they are open to learning more about themselves, and learning new strategies.

Exercise 10.2, "Your Coping Strategies," can help you be more intentional about expanding the range of things you can do to respond to challenging situations. By the time Kathleen had weathered the first two years of college, she probably would have expanded her repertoire. Here is how Kathleen might handle this exercise now.

EXERCISE 10.2   *Kathleen*

YOUR COPING STRATEGIES   name

1. Identify the *Coping Strategies* you use now and want to learn to use.

COPING STRATEGIES	USING NOW	WANT TO
a. Taking action to change or modify the transition:		
Negotiating	❏	✔
Taking optimistic action	✔	❏
Seeking advice	✔	❏
Asserting yourself	✔	❏
Brainstorming a new plan	❏	❏
Taking legal action if needed	❏	❏

COPING STRATEGIES	USING NOW	WANT TO
b. Changing the meaning of the transition:		
Applying knowledge of the transition process	☐	☑
Rehearsing	☐	☐
Developing rituals	☐	☐
Making positive comparisons	☐	☐
Rearranging priorities	☑	☐
Relabeling or reframing	☐	☐
Selectively ignoring	☑	☐
Using denial	☐	☐
Using humor	☑	☐
Having faith	☐	☐
c. Managing reactions to stress:		
Playing	☑	☐
Using relaxation skills	☐	☑
Expressing emotions	☐	☑
Doing physical activity	☐	☐
Participating in counseling, therapy, or support groups	☐	☐
Reading	☐	☐

d. Doing nothing

e. Other strategies:

Can't think of any.

2. Can you think of ways to develop the strategies you want to use?

There is a course in conflict resolution and the student activities program offers a workshop on mediation skills. Maybe I could use those to learn to negotiate better. If I had more time I could join the Big Sister program to work with new students, and that might help me understand how to make transitions better. The health center offers relaxation training and I probably should take advantage of that. I don't like the idea of counseling or therapy either alone or in a group.

Let's see what strategies you are using for your challenge and which ones you would like to develop that will help you take charge. Remember there is no magic strategy and the effective coper is one who can use lots of strategies flexibly. We suggest that you select one coping strategy from each cluster that you have never used before. Begin thinking about ways you might incorporate them into your coping repertoire.

EXERCISE 10.2

YOUR COPING STRATEGIES   name

1. Identify the *Coping Strategies* you use now and want to learn to use.

COPING STRATEGIES	USING NOW	WANT TO
a. Taking action to change or modify the transition:		
Negotiating	❏	❏
Taking optimistic action	❏	❏
Seeking advice	❏	❏
Asserting yourself	❏	❏
Brainstorming a new plan	❏	❏
Taking legal action if needed	❏	❏
b. Changing the meaning of the transition:		
Applying knowledge of the transition process	❏	❏
Rehearsing	❏	❏
Developing rituals	❏	❏
Making positive comparisons	❏	❏
Rearranging priorities	❏	❏
Relabeling or reframing	❏	❏
Selectively ignoring	❏	❏
Using denial	❏	❏
Using humor	❏	❏
Having faith	❏	❏
c. Managing reactions to stress:		
Playing	❏	❏
Using relaxation skills	❏	❏
Expressing emotions	❏	❏
Doing physical activity	❏	❏
Participating in counseling, therapy, or support groups	❏	❏
Reading	❏	❏

d. Doing nothing

e. Other strategies:

_____

_____

_____

_____

2. Can you think of ways to develop the strategies you want to use?

_____

_____

_____

_____

_____

_____

Taking Charge

We have seen how some of the students we interviewed handle their stress. Now let's see if you can think of new ways to face your challenges.

You have already identified and appraised your challenge. Is your Situation working to your advantage? What about your Supports? What about your Self? And do you use lots of Strategies flexibly? As you think about your 4 S's, you can see which ones are working for you and which need strengthening.

Once you identify the S or S's that need help, you can then decide on the appropriate strategies to use. To make this decision, you can ask four questions about the S you will be targeting:

- Do I want to change my S? If so, I need to consider lots of possible strategies, including negotiation, optimistic action, seeking advice, asserting myself, and brainstorming.
- Do I want to change the way I see my S? If so, I need to consider lots of possible strategies, including applying knowledge of the transition process, rehearsing, rituals, positive comparisons, rearranging priorities, relabeling or reframing, selectively ignoring, denial, humor, and faith.
- Do I want to change the way I manage my S, even if I can't change it or change the way I see it? If so, I need to consider strategies like playing, relaxation skills, expressing emotions, physical activity, counseling, support groups, and reading.
- Do I want to do nothing and let sleeping dogs lie?

The following exercise, "Your Own Action Plan—Taking Charge," helps you realize that you can take charge of your life, that you can manage more effectively. There is no such thing as a perfect life, but each person can cope more creatively and make decisions about how to proceed. Taking charge involves first taking stock of your resources and identifying which ones need strengthening, and second, using new coping strategies.

The following exercise shows how Kathleen might have done it.

EXERCISE 10.3   *Kathleen*

name

1. Identify the resources you need to strengthen from the exercise where you appraised your challenges and resources.

   The main resources I think I need to strengthen are my coping strategies.

2. Now ask yourself the following:

   Do I want to take action by changing the designated S? If yes, check one of the following. Give specific examples.

   ☑ negotiation   ❑ optimistic action
   ❑ seeking advice   ❑ asserting yourself
   ❑ brainstorming   ❑ other

   I checked negotiation in the exercise before this one. I would like to learn how to negotiate better with my parents. It would also be helpful in future jobs.

3. Now ask yourself:

   Do I want to change the way I see the designated S? If so, which of these will I use? Give specific examples.

   ☑ applying knowledge of the transition   ❑ having faith
   ❑ rehearsing   ❑ developing rituals
   ❑ making positive comparisons   ❑ rearranging priorities
   ❑ relabeling or reframing   ❑ selectively ignoring
   ❑ using denial   ☑ using humor

   I would like to learn to use this one better. I will be making the transition from college, and there will be future transitions concerning work, marriage, and so forth.

   I would like to learn to use humor more. Sometimes there are situations where a bit of humor can help get things in perspective. So far I seem to take everything pretty seriously, and it's hard for me to see the lighter side.

4. Now ask yourself:

Do I want to manage my reactions to the designated S? If so, which of these will I use? Give specific examples.

- ❏ playing
- ☑ expressing emotions
- ❏ participating in counseling, therapy, or support groups
- ☑ using relaxation skills
- ❏ doing physical activity
- ❏ reading

I think relaxation skills will be useful throughout my life. I enjoy singing and am a music major. I get butterflies before performances. Learning to relax will help me deal with those better.

I don't express my feelings very easily. I am more of a stoic. Then sometimes I just burst out or leave a situation or begin to cry. I'd like to be able to just say, more easily, how I am feeling but I don't seem able to do that.

5. Now ask yourself: Do I want to do nothing about my designated S? If so, explain why.

I want to increase my coping strategies in the ways I described because it will help me in college and in the future.

By doing this exercise you should be able to decide specifically what you want to do to meet your challenge.

EXERCISE 10.3

YOUR OWN ACTION PLAN—TAKING CHARGE   name

Use a separate sheet of paper to respond to this exercise.

1. Identify the resources you need to strengthen from the exercise where you appraised your challenges and resources.

2. Now ask yourself the following:

Do I want to take action by changing the designated S? If yes, check one of the following. Give specific examples.

- ❏ negotiation
- ❏ seeking advice
- ❏ brainstorming
- ❏ optimistic action
- ❏ asserting yourself
- ❏ other

3. Now ask yourself:

Do I want to change the way I see the designated S? If so, which of these will I use? Give specific examples.

- ❏ applying knowledge of the transition
- ❏ rehearsing
- ❏ making positive comparisons
- ❏ relabeling or reframing
- ❏ using denial

- ❏ having faith
- ❏ developing rituals
- ❏ rearranging priorities
- ❏ selectively ignoring
- ❏ using humor

4. Now ask yourself:

Do I want to manage my reactions to the designated S? If so, which of these will I use? Give specific examples.

- ❏ playing
- ❏ expressing emotions
- ❏ participating in counseling, therapy, or support groups

- ❏ using relaxation skills
- ❏ doing physical activity
- ❏ reading

5. Now ask yourself: Do I want to do nothing about my designated S? If so, explain why.

W rap-Up

Kathleen, Milt, April, and Matti each identified different challenges. Kathleen's major challenges were the lack of support from her parents and her difficulties keeping up with the academic work load. Milt's challenge was to "grow up" and take responsibility for himself; April's task was to turn herself into an optimistic person; Matti's concern was her shyness.

Kathleen got help on her study skills and support from her friends and her mentor. She increased her range of coping strategies, got a part-time job, and used her singing talent to get involved with the college glee club and a church choir.

Milt went back to his 4 S's, realizing he needed to use a variety of strategies. In fact, he used "Take Action" strategies, began managing his reactions to stress, and changed the way he saw his challenge.

April's major stumbling block was herself. She often saw the glass as half empty. She purposely challenged her way of thinking about herself and took action by becoming more involved.

Matti forced herself to take action by joining clubs, thinking differently about herself, and entering a counseling relationship.

As you see, everyone is different, but the structure for growing remains the same. Many times in life you will not feel up to managing the challenge before you. We hope, however, that you have learned how to turn low resources into ones that work for you. Our conceptual map and exercises aim to help you do so. If you continue to use them you can face challenges with enthusiasm and optimism. You can see them as opportunities rather than as crises. You can use them for significant learning and personal development.

REFERENCES

1. Lazarus, R. S., and Folkman, S. (1999). *Stress and Emotions: A New Synthesis*. New York: Springer.
2. Pearlin, L. I., and Schooler, C. (1978). "The Structure of Coping," *Journal of Health and Social Behavior*, 19, 2–21.

Seven Principles for Doing Your Best

So far in Part II, "Moving Through," we have talked about using different aspects of your college experience to achieve learning that lasts. We used Kolb's experiential learning cycle as a way to analyze and improve learning through courses and involvement in diverse organizations and activities. Various exercises helped you plan and carry out learning activities that suit your purposes and your style. We provided conceptual frameworks and practical suggestions for developing mature relationships, and for taking control of your college experience by creating appropriate combinations of challenge and support. We gave concrete suggestions about time management, learning, and test taking. We suggested ways to respond to challenges and take charge of your college experiences.

Now, in concluding Part II, we supply seven "Principles for Doing Your Best." These principles apply across the full range of your college experiences and activities. They apply whether you are coming fresh from high school or returning as an "adult learner," a resident or commuter. If you act on these, we guarantee you will get much more out of college than if you ignore them. The principles are:

1. Build relationships with faculty members.
2. Work collaboratively with other students.

3. Learn actively.

4. Get prompt feedback.

5. Emphasize time on task.

6. Set high expectations.

7. Respect diverse talents and ways of learning.

Let's take these one at a time and see what they mean to how you actually operate.

Build Relationships with Faculty Members

Maintaining frequent contact with faculty members is the single most important thing you can do to enhance your college education. Faculty can give good help when there are things you don't understand in their courses. When you get to know a few faculty members well, they can provide more general help and support when the going gets rough. Conversations with them can help you better understand how to cope with your whole college experience, and help you clarify your values and future plans. They can help you become more realistic and knowledgeable about career or graduate school possibilities. Sometimes they can even help you think through personal problems with friends and family.

Mary, an entering student we met in Chapter 2, said, "The professors are really nice. All my high school teachers said, 'Your professors are going to be mean and everything.' But professors are nice to me. And they say, 'If you have questions, my office hours are this, or you can call and make an appointment when it's convenient for you.' They're nice about everything. I thought they would be, 'Here's the materials, you're on your own.' But if you don't understand they are there to help."

Carmen's experiences during her first semester are a good example:

"When I had problems with my math, I had Dr. M., and anytime I needed help he would help me. I had Professor E. for English. She stayed late with me and worked on our papers with us in the computer center. The teachers really helped a lot. If you needed help they were there and you didn't have any problems about them."

"So you felt they were very caring?"

"I felt, yeah, they did care, because if you don't understand things and go after class they will go into more detail so they don't take up class time."

"You found that satisfying?"

"It helped a lot."

Barbara, our track team member, said, "We have research papers. After class I might stay back and ask her questions when I don't understand what she wants us to study for, or the papers we have to do. And if I'm not going to be there, I will talk with her about when I can turn it in."

"Is that because of the conflict with the track meets?"

"Most of the time they want you to turn it in earlier, so that puts a little pressure on me. But most of the time they understand so I may turn it in after the class."

Some students saw very specific advantages in getting to know faculty members. Juanita, for example, said, "I would encourage students to get as involved as they can with the professor. Because if you know the professor and the professor knows that you've been trying, if it comes down to a question in the end of the kind of grade, or anything like that, as long as the professor knows you've been trying, it helps a lot."

"Did you know that in your freshman year?"

"No, no."

"When did it click in?"

"I think when the classes started getting a little bit smaller. During my second semester I took public speaking with a grad student, and the class was really homey and warm. Everyone was nervous. Everyone had to get up and talk in front of the class. But she made everyone feel comfortable. People could talk to her. I started to realize that the professors aren't as intimidating as they seem."

We asked Ahmed, "What else do you do to achieve your goals other than just study?"

He replied, "I try to contact the professors and get to know them. I had a class with Professor A., who is a very good teacher. He invited us to call him anytime at home. We did and had study sessions at his house. He's easy to get along with. He was more like a student with us."

"So it's important to you to get to know faculty members?"

"Yeah, it is. If they get to know you, one aspect is, if you're close to a grade, they're more likely to give that two points or whatever to throw you over to the B or the A. The other aspect is that they are always there to help you. If they recognize you and that you tried, they're more likely to help you."

Hong found a faculty member who has become a helpful friend: "Whenever I need someone I usually go to Dr. L. She's a pretty nice lady up in the nursing office. She's not really my counselor. She's not even a counselor for undergraduates. She's a graduate counselor. I became friends with her when she needed help on her project for the Asian minority people. I've tried to use that friendship if I need some confirmation."

"You have befriended faculty on campus that you can go to?"

"Yeah, whenever I'm in big trouble that's who I go to, but if I believe I don't really need them, I just go to friends and see what they would do in my position."

"Did any of them ever follow up?"

"Dr. L. did. Whenever she'd see me she'd ask me, 'How's it going?' It felt pretty nice, actually."

A senior student got a real boost in self-confidence from her faculty contacts. "My English professors really influenced me. I had very low self-confidence, but then I started taking courses in my major. I got acceptance from quite a few of my professors. They liked my work and gave me good feedback about it. I felt so good about that. Not that I had necessarily mastered it, but that I was into something. I could sink my claws into something I could do well. It was very empowering. And you know, it goes beyond the classroom. A lot of my professors are like 'Hey, did you read that new article that's out?' So it's not just doing classwork and that's the end of it. It's a constant discourse. So that's been a source of strength and has led to other more tangible achievements."

Ellen has not found all faculty members as welcoming and generous as the students we have just quoted.

"I do see, you know, a few faculty members. I'm having trouble in my Decision Science class with some of the problems. Believe it or not, I have found that if you spend enough time in the professor's office you get to know them and they get to know you and take a personal interest in you. Because I'm in there like once a week, we carry on a conversation that goes beyond class. We talk about personal things. I've been to see my history teacher about a couple of questions in the reading, and after a while he was telling me about his daughter, and his son that just went to college. So I think it's good to get to know your professors. I feel more comfortable in class and I feel real comfortable asking questions. I don't feel stupid if I ask a question. Now I've got some professors that don't like it when you come to see them at all. One professor made me feel like, 'Why don't you know this?' When you asked him a question he was like, 'You shouldn't be in this class if you don't know the answer.' So I did not appreciate that at all. He made me feel stupid. He made me feel I was not worthy to be in his classroom. But generally speaking I've had very good rapport with my professors here."

"How do you know when a professor really doesn't want you in there?"

"If they don't answer your question. Or if you say, 'I still don't understand,' and they'll like whisper 'Oh God.' It's probably more body language. Some professors are into their own research. It's their own personal time. Some professors don't want to dedicate as much time to students as others do. But I've had lots that really do genuinely care about education and their students. If you're really interested in their course, they will generally take an interest in you."

Ellen has sought out faculty members to get help with questions concerning her courses and to make connections with them. She has learned that not all faculty members welcome that out-of-class follow-up, but that most do. And she not only gets specific help, but also a chance to share personal concerns. You can't expect all faculty members to welcome you with open arms, but most often you will get a helpful reception. When you don't, simply write that one off and put your energies elsewhere. Don't take it personally. Recognize that the problem is with the faculty member, not with you.

We share these quotes to illustrate some of the ways building relationships with faculty members can be helpful. We can't emphasize too much the importance of this first principle. Use our exercise, "Building Faculty Relationships," to see whether there are things you would like to work on in this area.

EXERCISE 11.1

BUILDING FACULTY RELATIONSHIPS   name

Check the appropriate column for each item.

	VERY OFTEN	OFTEN	SOMETIMES	RARELY	NEVER
1. I look for opportunities to develop relationships with one or more of my professors.	❏	❏	❏	❏	❏
2. I seek feedback from my professors about my work.	❏	❏	❏	❏	❏
3. I question my professor when I disagree with what is said.	❏	❏	❏	❏	❏
4. I talk with my professors outside of class about my courses and other things.	❏	❏	❏	❏	❏
5. I find out about my professors—what else they teach, areas of expertise, and other areas of interest.	❏	❏	❏	❏	❏
6. I attend events in which some of my professors are involved.	❏	❏	❏	❏	❏
7. I give my professors both positive and negative feedback about the courses in which I am enrolled.	❏	❏	❏	❏	❏

As I look at my responses to the exercise, I could improve my functioning for this principle by doing the following:

_____

_____

_____

_____

_____

Work Collaboratively with Other Students

You learn better when you treat it more like a team effort than a solo performance. Good learning, like good work, is collaborative and social, not competitive and isolated. Working with others increases your involvement and motivation. Sharing your ideas and responding to others' reactions deepens your understanding and strengthens your critical thinking ability.

We asked Carmen what advice she would give new freshmen coming in. "I would tell them, 'Don't expect to be able to stay out all night. Come in, study, and go to class.' And be friendly, because in college you really need friends. You need someone who will walk with you to the library. You need someone who will help you on a paper. You need a tutor for math or something. Just be friendly. Don't be mean all the time. Ask for help if you need it, because if you don't ask for help you won't succeed."

We asked Joan, "Can you tell us about yourself and other students in relation to your academic work?"

"Yeah. For most of the tests I have someone else I will study with the night before. We'll all study individually the week before. Then that last night before, we'll sit down for a few hours and study together. What one doesn't know the other one will, so you can figure things out. One time it was with papers. My roommate and I were both taking the same class, so we just exchanged papers and got everybody together. Then we got the other viewpoints on it to see what could be done."

"Do you find study groups helpful? Did you use them in your freshman and sophomore year, or have you just started?"

"I used them my sophomore year with some classes and it does help, because things I don't understand or don't remember, somebody else will reinforce how to do it."

"What do you think encourages persons to use study groups?"

"A lot of times teachers will tell you to study with others or to work with others because the course work is hard. In high school, you don't usually study with others. It's too hard to get together, or whatever. So you carry that into your freshman year. And usually, first-level courses aren't that hard, so you don't need to study as much. But once you get into higher level courses, you really need other people to help you understand what's really going on."

Harry told us about other students in relation to his academic work: "Most of my classwork lately has been group work. In my economics class we have a group of five that write papers and study together. I had a communication class where we did the same thing. Now I'm in harder classes. I had a philosophy class that was very difficult, and we had an eight-person study group that met almost daily."

"How did it work?"

"We taped all our classes. Then we took questions we thought the professor might ask and discussed them at length. One of our group meetings lasted almost six hours."

"Was it just males or mixed?"

"It was mixed, almost 50/50."

"And that got you through the course?"

"Oh yeah. That got us an 'A'."

One problem with working collaboratively is that it's tempting to just socialize and not really work. One student, for example, said, "I don't necessarily like to study with my friends because we end up talking about clothes and everything else rather than studying." Another said, "My friends will come over to study with me just to get out of their room or something. We'll go over to the library together, but usually it ends up we don't study. We just socialize. It's hard."

Another problem is studying with someone when you're in a dating relationship. When we asked Martin if he had any joint projects this year he said, "Yes. I've got a couple right now. Actually I'm going out with a girl that I'm doing a project with, and we don't really work on it. We haven't even got halfway through it and it's due in less than a month. Can you believe that? I probably might do it all by myself another time, because it's a distraction if you like each other. She's nice, but you gotta start thinking about studying before the friendship and all that. I don't want to get her mad or anything. I told her I had done my part of the project by myself. She didn't even give me a chance to apologize. In fact she's still a little bit angry. She told me I'm gonna have to trash what I solved and do it again with her. It's kinda hard. She doesn't have that much time, and whenever she has the time, we go out. We don't really get to the project. It's hard."

So, working collaboratively with others requires self-discipline. Joint projects can get complicated when someone does not do their share in a timely fashion, especially if the person is a good friend. But working collaboratively greatly improves learning. Moreover, most important work in "real life" is done collaboratively, so learning how to work that way is an important skill to develop in its own right. Use our exercise on "Working Collaboratively with Other Students" to see if there are ways you can improve that part of your college experience.

EXERCISE 11.2

WORKING COLLABORATIVELY WITH OTHER STUDENTS

name

Check the appropriate column for each item.

	VERY OFTEN	OFTEN	SOMETIMES	RARELY	NEVER
1. I find out about the backgrounds and interests of my classmates.	❏	❏	❏	❏	❏
2. I work with other students in informal study groups.	❏	❏	❏	❏	❏
3. I assist other students when they ask me for help.	❏	❏	❏	❏	❏
4. I tell other students when I think they have done good work.	❏	❏	❏	❏	❏
5. I discuss issues with students whose background and viewpoints differ from mine.	❏	❏	❏	❏	❏
6. I offer to serve as tutor, advisor, or resource person when I am knowledgeable and can share my skills with others.	❏	❏	❏	❏	❏

	VERY OFTEN	OFTEN	SOMETIMES	RARELY	NEVER
7. I work to reduce competition in my courses.	❏	❏	❏	❏	❏

As I look at my responses to the exercise, I could improve my functioning for this principle by doing the following:

_____

_____

_____

_____

_____

Learn Actively

Learning is not a spectator sport. You don't learn much from just sitting in classes, listening to teachers, memorizing prepackaged assignments, and spitting out the answers. You have to talk about what you're learning, write about it, relate it to past experiences, and apply it to your daily life. You have to make what you learn part of yourself.

Our conversations with students reinforced the importance of learning actively. We asked Ellen, "How do you determine whether or not a professor is inadequate?"

"They don't challenge me. They say, 'Buy this textbook,' and then lecture on what's in the text. You could very easily not go to class and still do well. I think a professor should cover some of the material that's in the book but go beyond that to challenge the student. I had a very good psychology professor. She was very interactive, asking questions of the class, not just standing up there, screech, screech, screech on the board. That is poor learning for me. I need more interaction."

In Chapters 6 and 7, "Maximizing Learning from Courses and Classes," and "Maximizing Learning Beyond Courses and Classes," we used Kolb's experiential learning cycle as a way to think more systematically about active learning. Ito gave us a good example of active learning when he and his fellow computer science students first created programs and then went to the books. Adele talked about learning a lot in French by practicing rather than just studying the books, and about looking at a number of different theories and developing your own. Jessie liked practicums and working in the field, actually involving herself in the activity instead of just listening to someone talk about it. She talked about trying to find ways to learn better when her philosophy professor just lectured. Applying the experiential learning cycle and using all four elements—Concrete Experiences, Reflective Observations, Abstract Conceptualizations, Active Experimentation—is the most important key to active learning.

Use our exercise on "Learn Actively" to check how you're doing concerning this principle.

EXERCISE 11.3

LEARN ACTIVELY   name

Check the appropriate column for each item.

	VERY OFTEN	OFTEN	SOMETIMES	RARELY	NEVER
1. I speak up when I don't understand class material.	❏	❏	❏	❏	❏
2. I question the assumptions of the materials in my courses.	❏	❏	❏	❏	❏
3. I try to relate outside events or activities to the subjects covered in my courses.	❏	❏	❏	❏	❏
4. I seek real-world experiences to supplement my courses.	❏	❏	❏	❏	❏
5. I list questions that I have from classes or readings, and follow them up by consulting with my peers, my professors, or on my own.	❏	❏	❏	❏	❏
6. I seek out new readings or research projects related to my courses.	❏	❏	❏	❏	❏
7. I take careful notes or tape and review my classes.	❏	❏	❏	❏	❏

As I look at my responses to the exercise, I could improve my functioning for this principle by doing the following:

_____

_____

_____

_____

_____

Get Prompt Feedback

Knowing what you know and what you don't know helps focus your learning. To really benefit from a course and use your study time effectively, you need prompt and frequent feedback on your performance. You need opportunities to show what you know or demonstrate your skills, and to get helpful suggestions about how to improve. One reason learning different sports is fun, and one reason why you can often improve rapidly, is that you get immediate and clear feedback about how you're doing. When you time yourself jogging or running, when you strike out or get a hit, when a ball goes in or out of the hoop or the court, when your skis take you neatly down through the moguls or flying off into the woods, there is little question about your competence and knowledge.

If you think about it, evaluation and feedback are a necessary part of human functioning. When we stand up and walk out the door, our direction, balance, and muscular sequences are guided by a continuous stream of perceptual feedback. We can't ride a bike, drive a car, write a word, or give someone a kiss without that constant interplay of action, perception, and reaction. The reason drinking and driving don't go well together is that alcohol disrupts that intricate process. Strong emotions can do the same.

Teaching and learning in college typically suffer because we are unsophisticated about evaluation and underestimate the importance of frequent and thoughtful feedback. Students often recognize the problem. Sherry, for example, said, "The courses I like least are the ones where there is a midterm and a final, and that's it. I don't think those are fair. In psychology this semester the only test I've had is multiple choice. I'm not happy with that. I don't think it shows what a student is doing. Some people are better than other people at testing on half a semester's worth of work. I like classes where there is a lot of work and a lot of homework, things that show how you're doing in the course. I had an English course with a lot of writing. It was very demanding, but I always did the homework because it helped my grade and I learned better. The professor let us turn in our papers. We got them back with a grade and comments. Then we could rewrite them for another grade if we wanted. We had to have other students critique our paper before we turned it in, and make any necessary changes from what they said. I liked it. He was very difficult, but every student in there really tried. And it's nice to have someone on your level telling you, 'I don't understand this,' or, 'I think you got it right.'"

Another student, Bob, said, "I'm having trouble with my business law course because it's all true-false. There's a lot of information, but I don't know how to study for the class. You get no information about why your answer is right or wrong. They just throw it at you. On my last test I had 15 chapters of material. I mean I knew it! I studied my you-know-what off and I only got a 70. It was hard to know how to interpret lots of the questions. I could almost have just gone down and randomly colored in true-false and gotten graded without knowing the information."

When you run into courses and teachers who don't give you prompt and thoughtful feedback themselves, or who don't provide other ways to get it, you need to take initiative yourself. Set up a study group with other students. Those groups are helpful mainly because you can check your understanding and progress with others. Go to the teacher and ask for comments on how well you are doing and how you might do better. Or ask for criteria and guidelines that you can use to evaluate yourself. Kolb's experiential learning cycle makes for powerful learning because through active experimentation and application, you test and get feedback on how well your concepts and skills actually handle the situations you are facing. You can use our exercise on getting prompt feedback for other ideas and to see how you are doing in this area.

EXERCISE 11.4

GET PROMPT FEEDBACK

name

Check the appropriate column for each item.

	VERY OFTEN	OFTEN	SOMETIMES	RARELY	NEVER
1. When I get feedback from my professors on exams, papers, or other classwork, I review their responses to assess my strengths and weaknesses.	❑	❑	❑	❑	❑
2. I talk over feedback with my professors as soon as possible if anything is not clear.	❑	❑	❑	❑	❑
3. I redraft my papers and seek feedback from the teacher in doing so.	❑	❑	❑	❑	❑
4. I carefully assess my preparation and background for the courses I take.	❑	❑	❑	❑	❑
5. I consider feedback from peers and consciously decide how to act on it.	❑	❑	❑	❑	❑
6. I keep a journal in which I reflect on what I am learning.	❑	❑	❑	❑	❑
7. I think about what I am learning in my courses and discuss it with my professors after the course has ended.	❑	❑	❑	❑	❑

As I look at my responses to the exercise, I could improve my functioning for this principle by doing the following:

_____

_____

_____

_____

_____

Emphasize Time on Task

No matter how well you may act on the first four principles, if you don't emphasize "time on task" you won't learn much. Time plus energy equals learning. Learning to use your time well is critical. It is another skill, and personal quality, that will serve you well the rest of your life. Allocating realistic amounts of time to the varied demands of course and noncourse learning, and giving yourself time for recreation, relaxation, and renewal requires careful planning and self-discipline. Remember Chung, who fell behind during his first two years when he got overcommitted to extracurricular activities and did a lot of partying? Allocating realistic amounts of time also requires creative juggling when unanticipated problems or opportunities come up.

Here's what one student we interviewed had to say:

"I just have a set schedule of times I am going to study. I keep pretty much to those. I set a time that I go to bed every night regardless of when my classes are so I have the right amount of sleep. And if I have a report or something, I try not to procrastinate any more. I was a big procrastinator in high school. Now I just tell myself I've got to get started on this. I make myself sit down and do it, just to make sure I get the things done that I need to. Because if you don't have a schedule, then you're just like, 'Okay, I'm not going to do it right now. I'll do it an hour later.' Now I say, 'From this time to this time I will do some studying.' No matter what and I just go on with my studying. Just get it out of the way."

"How about if you can't keep to your schedule? What does that feel like?"

"It kind of makes me feel bad inside. If something gets in the way or I don't get back to my room on time, it makes me feel I have let myself down for some reason. I don't know why. It just does."

"How do you cope with that, that sort of self-stress?"

"I study a little bit longer past the time I was supposed to study. Whatever time I start, I will finish an hour later. I'll take a little break and then study for another hour."

In Chapter 9, we emphasized managing time effectively and suggested some strategies for keeping organized and for setting priorities. Our "Emphasize Time on Task" exercise can help you check how you're are doing in this area.

EXERCISE 11.5

EMPHASIZE TIME ON TASK name

Check the appropriate column for each item.

	VERY OFTEN	OFTEN	SOMETIMES	RARELY	NEVER
1. I complete my assignments promptly.	❑	❑	❑	❑	❑
2. I proofread and review my work before handing in assignments.	❑	❑	❑	❑	❑

	VERY OFTEN	OFTEN	SOMETIMES	RARELY	NEVER
3. I practice presentations before giving them in class.	❏	❏	❏	❏	❏
4. I maintain a regular study schedule to keep up with my classes.	❏	❏	❏	❏	❏
5. I attend classes on a regular basis.	❏	❏	❏	❏	❏
6. I confer with my professor if I am concerned about keeping up with a particular class.	❏	❏	❏	❏	❏
7. I identify areas where I am weak and seek extra help to strengthen them.	❏	❏	❏	❏	❏

As I look at my responses to the exercise, I could improve my functioning for this principle by doing the following:

Set High Expectations

How much you emphasize time on task will depend greatly on the standards and expectations you set for yourself. Expect more from yourself and you will get it. High expectations are important for everyone, for the well prepared and unprepared, for the bright and motivated as well as those who don't want to exert themselves. When teachers and institutions set high standards for themselves and for students, everyone learns more. When you set challenging goals for yourself, your learning and personal development get a strong boost.

Antonio gave us a picture of how teachers' expectations, how he uses his time, and his own standards, have interacted.

"What challenges you to go further than you've gone before?"

"My professors. The course work they give is a lot harder than it was in high school, and it gets harder and harder every year. Although I'm not getting the grades I want, it's because the professors want more out of me, want me to strive even harder."

"What's that like?"

"I like it. I like the fact that they want me to strive harder. I'm not slacking off. Every class and every semester I'm trying harder. I'm giving more time. My freshman and sophomore year I just played around. I was either talking with friends or watching TV."

"Because of that first semester you're playing catch-up. Is that true?"

"Right. I have to catch up now because of my incompetency beforehand. I mean the impact of that has really been great. My failure then is still with me now, grade-wise. I'm putting the failure behind me but I still have the grade from that failure I'm having to work with."

"What would you share now as a junior with a freshman coming in?"

"Take your freshman year seriously. Take every year seriously. Adjust to the pressures as best you can. You don't have to become a study hog or whatever. My attitude was, 'It's my first year. I don't have to do well this year because I've got three more years.' But if you mess up, it takes the three years to dig yourself out."

Sherry, who liked the English class where she had a chance to rewrite papers, described her standards and how she achieves them:

"I think the standards I set for myself, academically at school, are very, very high. I've always been that way. My first semester here was difficult. I lived at home and was so overwhelmed by everything. I met my boyfriend then and I kinda let things go. I didn't do as well. I'm really making up for it now, hopefully. I just push myself. I'll sit down and spend 10 hours on a paper to get it done the way I want it. I will go home at five o'clock in the morning if I have to in order to type the paper. Some of my friends look at me and tell me I'm crazy. A few of my other friends who don't go to school tell me that if that's what it takes, then they don't want to go. But if it gets me where I want to go, I am willing to put up with it as long as I have to."

Bob, who had trouble with the true-false tests in his business law course said, "I personally set very high standards for myself. My downfall is that I expect the same from everybody else, which is wrong."

"Tell me about that. What do you mean?"

"Well, in a work situation I try to do my best, and I expect my coworkers to work just as hard, to put as much pride into their work as I do. I strive to do well. I believe in learning. I like learning new things and I like being challenged."

"Anything else on standards?"

"When I don't do well I'm disappointed in myself. I feel that my peers are disappointed in me. I feel like everybody is disappointed in me, although my parents could probably never be more proud of me. You asked how I achieve them. I set goals and I work toward them. Like in my school work, I'm going to do this by this day and I do it."

"What happens when you don't meet your goals?"

"The business law course would be an example. I spent my whole fall break—I went home and I haven't been home since school started—and I spent my whole break studying. I didn't sleep, I didn't do anything. I hardly had any time to see my girlfriend. I know I learned the information and that I did the very best I could, but I'm still disappointed with myself and that grade."

You may not want to push yourself the way Bob seems to, but setting high expectations will make a great difference in how much you get out of college. Use our "Set High Expectations" exercise to see what you might like to work on in this area.

EXERCISE 11.6

Check the appropriate column for each item.

	VERY OFTEN	OFTEN	SOMETIMES	RARELY	NEVER
1. I set personal goals for learning in each of my courses.	❏	❏	❏	❏	❏
2. I try to get clear information about my teacher's goals.	❏	❏	❏	❏	❏
3. I keep an open mind about material even if it is not directly related to my major or career interest.	❏	❏	❏	❏	❏
4. I do additional unassigned work in order to reach my learning goals.	❏	❏	❏	❏	❏
5. I consciously think about the trade-offs between the things I do to really learn and the things I do to maximize my grade.	❏	❏	❏	❏	❏
6. I try to achieve my best in every class.	❏	❏	❏	❏	❏
7. I use all the resources on campus that are pertinent to my courses.	❏	❏	❏	❏	❏

As I look at my responses to the exercise, I could improve my functioning for this principle by doing the following:

_____

_____

_____

_____

_____

_____

Respect Diverse Talents and Ways of Learning

People bring different talents, ways of learning, and personal backgrounds to college. You will encounter wide-ranging differences in age, race, ethnicity, and national origin. These differences can make your college experience much more rich and powerful than if everyone shared your particular background and orientation. Respecting that diversity, being open to relationships with others, and going toward persons who bring different perspectives instead of away from them, will help you learn things about yourself and about the rest of the world that are otherwise inaccessible.

In interviewing David we asked, "Is it hard to become friendly with someone from a different country, a different lifestyle, or with a disability?"

"Oh boy. Is it hard? I would say it's difficult. Yeah. Where I work, about half the people are from the Middle East, and, um, I mean, I'm nice to them. We talk or whatever, but sometimes if you want to ask someone to do something and they don't understand you, it makes it more difficult."

"Because of the language differences?"

"Yeah, and the cultural differences. They're used to doing something one way and you do it another."

"How about here on campus, with other students?"

"It's the same thing. Any time someone has a different background than yours, it's a little harder to make a connection with them."

"How do your parents feel about friendships with people different from yourself, in appearance, values, religion?"

"They don't concern themselves with that. I had an Australian friend for a while and my parents were like, 'That's perfectly fine.' Of course, he spoke English. It wasn't this big difference. I think my father really liked him because he had been to Australia in the military when he was younger. So they would talk a lot."

"What is it like to deal with people who are different from you?"

"Well, it's frustrating. It can be a learning experience as well. I mean you learn things about other cultures and things like that. I know more stuff about Ethiopia than I ever did just from work. It's educational, even though it gets a little frustrating at times. It's a bit more difficult to get into a close, personal relationship with people of different backgrounds. It can be done. I have done it, but it's more difficult."

"You have done it?"

"Yeah. With that group of friends I was talking about. Various people from different backgrounds have come in and out."

"Once there is a relationship with someone who is different from you, what is the value in it, if there is a value?"

"Well, it's just sort of a learning thing. It helps you become more tolerant of people."

"Is it something that just happens for you or something you seek?"

"It normally just happens. Like I said before, people generally tend to come to me, for whatever reason. So, it just sort of happens. I'm pretty open-minded. I'm into trying different things. But we live in a very paranoid society. I think some people are just basically scared. Anytime they see anything that is outside their little framework that they are happy with, they get nervous. I could write a paper on that!"

David was open to new relationships, new experiences. His open-mindedness meant that diverse persons tended to come to him. He was part of a group where people of different backgrounds came in and out. He recognized the frustrations and difficulties that sometimes arose in working with or relating to people who do things differently, but he values the learning and increased breadth these relationships give him. He thinks it's unfortunate that persons get paranoid about encountering "anything that is outside their little framework." He will get a lot more from his college experiences than people who shy away from contacts with others who, at the outset, may be a bit difficult or make them nervous.

So it is important for your learning and personal development to stretch yourself and take advantage of the diversity that exists in a college environment. Chapter 8, "Developing Mature Relationships," gave you some practical perspectives on dealing with diversity. Use our exercise, "Respecting Diverse Talents," to see if there are additional things you might do in relation to this principle.

EXERCISE 11.7

RESPECTING DIVERSE TALENTS

name

Check the appropriate column for each item.

	VERY OFTEN	OFTEN	SOMETIMES	RARELY	NEVER
1. I try not to embarrass other students.	❏	❏	❏	❏	❏
2. I consciously adjust my learning styles to accommodate the teaching practices of my professors.	❏	❏	❏	❏	❏
3. I share information about myself and how I learn most effectively.	❏	❏	❏	❏	❏
4. I support professors who respect and respond to students with different backgrounds and levels of learning.	❏	❏	❏	❏	❏
5. I support professors when they include in the content of their courses the contributions or interests of underrepresented populations.	❏	❏	❏	❏	❏
6. I try to make others aware when I see or hear sexist, racist, or otherwise offensive language or behavior.	❏	❏	❏	❏	❏
7. I am open to considering ideas that are different from my own.	❏	❏	❏	❏	❏

As I look at my responses to the exercise, I could improve my functioning for this principle by doing the following:

_____

_____

_____

_____

Wrap-Up

You've reviewed our seven principles for maximizing the gains from your total college experiences. By using the exercises you have identified one or more things you might do to help you act in ways more consistent with each principle. Use Exercise 11.8, "Maximizing Your Gains," to review the things you have identified for each principle and identify which of those would be most important for you to act on now. Set some priorities to actually start changing your day-to-day behavior so that you will get the most you can out of your college experiences.

EXERCISE 11.8

MAXIMIZING YOUR GAINS	name

For each principle, list the things you identified that would improve your functioning for that principle. Respond to this exercise on a separate piece of paper.

1. Build relationships with faculty members
2. Work collaboratively with other students
3. Learn actively
4. Get prompt feedback
5. Emphasize time on task
6. Set high expectations
7. Respect diverse talents and ways of learning

Now list, in order of importance to you, the three principles that would be most important for you to address to maximize your gains and the specific things you can do.

The most important principle

The second most important principle

The third most important principle

III

moving on

Where Are You Going From Here?

The Doonesbury cartoon by Garry Trudeau says it all! A father, talking to his son, says: "Mark, son, have you given any thought to the sort of job you want when you graduate?" Mark answers, "Oh, sure . . . I know that it will have to be creative—a position of responsibility, but not one that restricts personal freedom. It must pay fairly well—the atmosphere relaxed, informal; my colleagues interesting, mellow, and not too concerned with a structured working situation." Father responds, "In short, you have no intention of getting a job." Mark argues, "I didn't say that."

Some about-to-be graduates, like Mark, feel entitled to special treatment. Others, those with no sense of direction, are wondering where to go next, and how to get there. Whatever the scenario, there is probably a mixture of excitement about completing a major task—getting the college degree—and uncertainty about the future. This chapter highlights some special aspects of this transition, and some important learnings and concerns as you prepare to move on to the next part of your journey.

Voices of Students: What They Felt

We talked with several students six months after graduation, and a number of seniors as they were contemplating next steps. Their voices highlight many concerns, fears, and joys students experience as they move toward the future.

THE COLLEGE GRADUATES

We basically asked the graduates how the past months had gone, and what insights they could give us.

One of the group, Abe, was thrilled. If we had interviewed him the week, or even the month, after graduation, he would have seemed depressed and scared. Depressed because there was no structure in his life. He found himself living at home again, reporting to his parents his plans for dinner. Scared, because he was worried that he might never find a job and that the college education had been a waste of time. However, after four months of intense job hunting, he landed an ideal job in the advertising division of a large company about two hours from home. He had a job with benefits, and an apartment he could afford. He was far enough away from home to feel independent, but close enough to go home for chicken soup when needed. The outcome was ideal. Wouldn't it be wonderful if we could assure everyone of a happy ending if they would only hang in there for four months?

Abe's twin sister, Susan, landed a job about a month after college—but she hated it. She felt her job was menial, that all she did was sit at a reception desk and answer the phone. She had been a college leader and expected that her first job would continue to build on what she had learned in college. She was unprepared for the realities of first jobs.

Janice worked so hard in college that she never saw beyond it. After graduation she had two wonderful weeks feeling great—free at last. After two weeks she began job hunting, but with no clear goal direction. Some places would not interview her until all her references were in, others interviewed her but never called back, most places wouldn't even see her. She simply could not find a job. She complained, felt sorry for herself, and blamed the school. Eventually, she faced the facts. She realized that to move ahead she would need further training. She enrolled in some classes and is working as a part-time file clerk. She feels comfortable with her role and setting. She realizes she'll eventually have to work full time, but feels she needs focus and with graduate training she will have that.

Lee, on the other hand, enjoyed a month of getting himself together after graduation. Unable to find a responsible job, he volunteered in a hospital where he eventually wanted to be a doctor. His plan to work as a volunteer while looking for a "real" job was short-circuited, his volunteer job turned into a paid job. Delighted and proud, Lee used this time to take premedical courses. After two months, he realized medicine was not for him. He knows that he must face decisions about what to do with his future. Should he go to graduate school? Should he look for a job with benefits like health coverage?

Talal graduated, moved home to his affluent parents, and worked out at the health club. His parents did not pressure him to move on, get a job, and begin to take responsibility for himself. However, Talal became embarrassed when his friends continually asked what he was doing. As they began finding their niches, he became conscious that his behavior was inappropriate. He took a job working at the health club where he worked out.

Nick knew exactly where he was going—to medical school. He had planned this for years. He was right on track.

COLLEGE SENIORS CONTEMPLATING THE FUTURE

Every senior we interviewed had a great deal to say about what's next. Some used the phrase "moving into the real world" as they discussed their excitement and fears about the future. For the first time, many of these students will not be in a school environment.

One senior said that within six months she hoped to be starting a job, getting settled in a place to live, staying in touch with college friends, but beginning to make a new set of friends. "One year from graduation I hope I will be adjusted in my job, and that everything is running smoothly and I am doing what I want." Another student voiced real concern about how to get a job, what strategies to use, and who would help. Others, with families and already working, had plenty of experience with the "real world." They discussed fears about money, about being self-supporting and independent.

Everyone expressed concern. There were wide variations about the degree to which they had concrete plans. There were those without plans, with definite plans, with ambiguous plans, with short-range plans, or with long-range plans but no immediate plans. Many felt they had to become more concrete. For some students, not having plans created anxiety. As one senior said: "I kind of feel bad, a little bit distressed that I do not know exactly what I am going to do once I graduate. I am a little bit disappointed that I don't have enough experience to get a job."

This contrasted with the senior who said, "I do not have long-range plans. I don't feel I have to make them. My ideas have changed during these years and will keep changing. So I don't feel pressured or obligated to make these decisions. I am still young, still exploring and not afraid of that. In the short run, I will get a job so that I can start paying back student loans. So for me, I want to go into the world on my own, live without Mom, pay back loans, and explore options."

Another senior is clear about immediate plans, but not set for the long haul. "I hope to get in the Peace Corps. I plan to take three months to tie things up by seeing my friends and my boyfriend. I want to go to Latin America because I speak Spanish. Whatever happens, I feel competent because I put myself through school. What I am really afraid of is failure down the road in parenting. If I get into the Peace Corps, I won't have to worry about getting a real job or going to graduate school. I can put that off. Everything can be delayed."

And yet another senior said, "I am excited about getting on with my life. Somehow during the last 20 years something has been tying me down. Now I can go off and explore the world if I want. I don't know what I will be doing, but in college I had two different internships and can start networking. I intend to go about my job search by first talking to people I interned with. Eventually I will probably go to graduate school, but I will think about that later. Of course, there is some fear about the real torture of life—staying up on your bills, paying for a house, a car, gas. Until now my parents have paid for almost everything, and facing that is scary."

One woman said, "I have a very strong idea of what I want to do with my life, but the job is not there. It is a thing that I need to create. I want a research position that has to do with following art transactions, following the ethics of buying, selling, loaning. I am interested in the problems of legal transfer of cultural property. But I don't know how to study that, how to get into that. Maybe I'll set up an internship after I graduate."

As our interviews illustrate, many about-to-be-graduates have questions about how to get from here to there. It is no wonder that Dr. Seuss's book, *Oh, The Places You'll Go*, is a best seller.[1] It really is written for this group. Some have long-range goals, but don't know how to get there; others don't want to deal with the long range yet, but need help in getting a job and thinking about how they want to be in this world.

Underlying Issues

Many are struggling to connect with the world of work. Young students are establishing their identities and older students are reexamining theirs.

MAKING YOUR CAREER CONNECTION

A recent study of the work experiences of university graduates found that:

- University personnel had not prepared students for the realities of the work world.
- The initial period after leaving college was often one of euphoria, what they labeled the "vacation period."
- The next phase was the "downward trend," which produces feelings of discouragement.

Of course many students know exactly where they are going, but often it is a time of ambiguity.

Perhaps this is the place to tell you about Nancy's experience after she graduated from Barnard many years ago. Nancy's role model was the president of Barnard, who was married and the mother of five, a woman who could do it all easily. Nancy had the idea that women could do it all, and furthermore, that graduating from Barnard was a ticket to success. Wrong! Nancy pounded the pavements for four months, and only then landed a job as a salesperson in a book store. It was December. She was stationed by the door. She was very cold. She mentioned to her supervisor that perhaps the store should invest in a storm door. He responded sarcastically, "Go tell that to the boss." She did not hear the sarcasm, and went immediately to the president's office. He said, with a smirk, "Well, you had better dress more warmly." Nancy did just that, wearing ski clothes to work the next day. She was fired.

Nancy's next job was even a worse fit for her. She became a file clerk in a huge company. That lasted 10 days.

Nancy remembers walking up and down the streets of New York wondering if, when, and how she would ever fit into the world of work.

Nancy could have been helped by this book. She would have realized that:

- Transitions can be difficult.
- The way you feel when you are leaving a secure place and moving into an uncertain world can be very unsettling.
- The way you feel today is not the way you will feel forever.
- Each person has potential resources to deal with transitions.

This sounds very much like what we wrote in Chapter 1 about moving into college. A similar process is involved when moving out of college into a period of limbo while trying to get one's bearings. Many students find it difficult to leave the structured world of school and move into a world with no organized plan, no admissions directors, no counselors, no student development educators. As one student told us, "I am trying to decide whether I will live at home and get a job, or whether I will move out of the house for good, then get a job. It sure would be nice to graduate from college and have a serious relationship and not have to worry about going out and trying to find somebody out there." Another student said she was sad and scared about " . . . leaving behind the involvement with the university, the organizations, the faculty." Another said, "I'll be leaving behind all the people who gave me support—the entire university, my friends, my fraternity." And yet another senior reports, "I feel like I am leaving behind a safe haven to continue to experiment and grow. Once I get out, there will be a smaller margin of error."

College is promoted as the route to success. Clearly, college graduates do much better in the world of work than those who do not go to college. But most college graduates are not helped to set realistic expectations about the next steps. Yet realistic expectations are essential for this next phase of life.

Realistic expectations include knowing that life is full of discontinuities. Mary Catherine Bateson, in *Composing a Life*, described the discontinuities in the lives of five adult women. This view of adult development contrasts with the popular model of a successful life, the early commitment that launches one on a single rising trajectory. She points out that a recurring issue for adults is the need to leave a structured, safe environment for the unknown. In fact, every time we make a change, that is what happens.[2]

Realistic expectations also include realizing that there might be a temporary period of *downward mobility*. Many young college students, especially those who have assumed leadership roles, have had access to power. If they want to become powerful, by and large they can, by participating in student activities and student government. Once into the "real world," that is no longer true. They start at the bottom again. The lack of congruence between what they had and what they expected can be discouraging. It feels like downward mobility; they have fewer resources, less access, less power.

One senior said that she felt badly, in fact distressed, that she did not know exactly what she is going to do once she graduates. She is afraid about the immediate future—getting the next job and a career direction. This sentiment was echoed by others. As one young man said, "I'm sure on my abstract goals. I want to get a job that I feel comfortable with. But I'm mixed up about what that's actually going to be. I'll probably be waiting tables after college because I am so unsure of my career direction."

The job search is a search to connect with, or change your relation to, the world of work. Realizing that it takes time to find the right niche for yourself, that there are periods of downward mobility and discontinuities, helps ease this period between the relatively secure world of college and the ambiguous world of work.

SEARCHING FOR YOUR NEWER IDENTITY

Daniel Levinson's book, *The Seasons of a Man's Life*, describes the early adult transition for men. This process of entering adulthood takes many years. It is the time where the young man is "creating a basis for adult life without being fully within it. . . . His tasks are now to explore the possibilities of this world, to test some initial choices, and to build a first, provisional life structure." Levinson continues: "The primary, overriding task . . . is to make a place for oneself in the adult world and to create a life structure that will be viable."[3]

Despite the fact that Levinson and his colleagues concentrated on men, his description of the tasks of this period apply also to women. Both women and men are concerned about their emerging identities, how to build a life that will enable them to work at the level they want and in an area that interests them, and how to establish a meaningful relationship.

There are two main tasks of this period. One deals with separating from the family of origin. This requires more independence, more autonomy. If, because of special circumstances, the young person still lives at home, he or she can, according to Levinson, work on separating and differentiating from his parents and siblings. Of course, separation from parents is a lifelong process. There is always an attachment, but as Levinson points out, this attachment changes. To summarize: "During the Early Adult Transition, he has to separate from the family in a new way. He must remove the family from the center of his life and begin a process of change that will lead to a new home base for living as a young adult in an adult world."

Several students specifically mentioned the psychological and financial separation from family. Arthur said, "I will be moving. I don't know where. Hopefully, I will be moving to what I consider home. I know I have to establish a life without my parents. I have always lived with them. I will be leaving my family, in a way. I will be establishing new work. I am excited about proving to myself that I can survive on my own. I have always been protected by my parents. It is time to prove to myself that I can do everything that I have done before and take on additional roles." Another senior said, "With leaving, I will be taking on more responsibility for being independent. I will be leaving the life of being dependent on parents."

The second major task, according to Levinson, is beginning to fashion a life structure that shifts "the center of gravity of . . . life from the position of child

. . . to the position of novice adult. This is a period of exploring options, changing courses, and making something of his life. He is beginning to get grounded occupationally and often in a permanent relationship. This task really has two contradictory parts to it. On the one hand, the young man is exploring possibilities. On the other hand, he is trying to make commitments to a life structure of permanence."[4]

This contradiction was reflected in comments that dealt with fear of the unknown future, the desire to have closure, and at the same time being afraid to close options prematurely. The senior quoted earlier said, "I am looking at joining the Peace Corps. It is a different learning experience than college, and I can still go off from it and get a job. I want to keep open different options and opportunities. Maybe later I will go to graduate school. Now I can go off and explore the world. But maybe I'm wrong. I read marketplace surveys, which predict that if you don't get involved or get a job immediately or have something that is directed towards your education, they will start questioning whether you are ready to deal with life. I am ready to deal with life. But the marketplace won't comprehend that I want to delay committing to a career. I want to spend this period discovering the world."

Maggie, a senior, said she felt no pressure to make either a career or relationship commitment: "I am still thinking about do I want to teach or do I want to work in an office or whatever. I feel I can still explore different options. I am excited about going into the world on my own, living without mom. Now I won't have to go back home on breaks. My only fear is not getting a job or not making it. I want to be happy and successful. Coming to college was the hardest thing I ever had to do. Now I am ready to leave. I only wish my advisors had given me more insight into different jobs."

Another young woman told us: "My roommate wants to travel. Her boyfriend, probably her fiancé by Christmas, hates traveling. He despises going any place more than an hour from his home. I wonder why she is limiting herself. She has the rest of her life to be married. But she does not see that. She will marry him and maybe in 15 years regret it. It is going to be hard for me to tell my roommate I'm so happy for her when she gets engaged. In a way I am happy for her, but I'm scared she is limiting herself and will regret it. I sure don't want to limit myself, either in work or love, too early."

Arthur talked about this also. When asked what he feared about leaving college, he answered, "Not finding a job. Maybe I should go to graduate school, but I want to keep my alternatives open."

HIS WORLD, HER WORLD

It is important to point out that although both women and men deal with the two issues Levinson identified—separating from the family of origin and fashioning a life structure—they go about it in different ways.

Dreams influence the unfolding of one's life structure. For many men, their dreams are primarily vocational; women are seen as helpmates. In contrast, many women have "split dreams" that include career and relationships. These dreams play out differently.

In a longitudinal study of 34 women, Josselson (1987) concluded that the different pathways women follow in identity development tell more about women than looking at their roles. In other words, what is relevant is not whether a woman is a mother, a worker, a single parent, or childless, but rather the way in which the woman separates from family and anchors or commits to the adult world. Although there is no pure type, Josselson identifies four general categories of women:

- *Foreclosures* are those women who stick with their family's expectations. These women often adopt their parents' standards and follow their career directions.
- *Identity achievers* are those who have tested new waters, are forging their own identities, and keep focusing on the future. These women are more concerned with their own view of themselves than the foreclosures who are more concerned with their parents' expectations.
- *Moratoriums* are those who struggle to make commitments but have not found the right niche. While open to choice, they fear too many options. They are struggling to find their own identities.
- *Identity diffusions* are those who are drifting and avoiding an identity. This group has the most difficulty forming stable relationships. They are the most troubled.[5]

Although Josselson was writing about and for women, we think these categories are also applicable to men. Everyone is struggling with identity issues. Some will stick close to home, others will go in new directions. There are many ways to live out a life. We are reminded of a young man who wanted to write, who wanted to create. When he graduated from college, he resisted pressure to enter the family insurance business. In fact, he broke with his parents. He worked for an advertising company as a copywriter. Then he met a young woman with aspirations for money and community status. She pushed him to return to his family. He entered the business and became very successful. In his 50s, he began volunteering with a local community theater group, never giving up his role as president of the insurance company. When he reached 60, he had built the community theater into a major force in the city, was president of that board, and remained in the insurance company.

Another young man who wanted to be a writer turned out differently. He married a woman who encouraged him in that direction. His wife went to work and earned the money. He wrote. At age 40 he is now witnessing the production of two of his plays.

Many women have ideas and dreams of what they want and are either subverted or encouraged by their partners. Your choice of a partner will clearly influence the direction your identity takes, how much your dreams are encouraged or subverted. In general, women's dreams have been subsumed, taking second place to men's dreams.

Carolyn Heilbrun, alias Amanda Cross, points out in *Writing a Woman's Life* that to be a woman in previous generations was to put a man at the center of one's life. "If he notices me, if I marry him, if I get into college, if I get this work accepted, if I get that job, then I will know who I am. There always seems to loom the possibility of something being over, settled, sweeping clear the way for contentment. This is the delusion of a passive life."[6] Although this book was written for and about women, the need to define oneself by a relationship or by a job and the need for closure applies to both genders among those we interviewed. This need can lead to the panic some felt when leaving a structured environment.

In a recent speech to graduating senior women at Scripps College, Naomi Wolf, author of *The Beauty Myth*, provided a survival kit for women. Her messages included:

1. Refuse to have your scholarship and gender pitted against each other.
2. Don't be afraid to ask for money for your work.
3. Never cook for or sleep with anyone who routinely puts you down.
4. Become goddesses of disobedience . . . Young women tell ... of injustices, from campus rape to classroom sexism. But at the thought of confrontation, they freeze into niceness . . . And at last you'll know . . . that only one thing is more frightening than speaking your truth. And that is not speaking.[7]

We think men and women both need the same advice. It is important to know yourself, to know your partner, your boss; speak the truth and not be put down; be intentional about your future by articulating your dreams; and be aware of how your dreams might subvert someone else's.

Your orientation toward the future always involves a number of interacting questions. How important are the expectations others hold for you: parents, partner, spouse, children? How much risk are you willing to take? Do you need some time out? How solid or open is your own identity?

If Lee, the recent college graduate who was debating medical school, had filled out Exercise 12.1, "Your Future Orientation," it might have looked liked this.

EXERCISE 12.1   *Lee*
                                                      name

YOUR FUTURE ORIENTATION

1. What do you think will happen right after graduation?

   Right after graduation I just want to have fun for a while.

   six months later?

   I hope to have a job but I am not sure what kind. I don't have any
   very clear purposes right now.

   a year from now?

   I'm not at all sure. Maybe a good job, maybe school.

2. In what ways are your expectations about what is next
realistic or unrealistic?

I guess my expectation for having a good job a year from now is not very realistic if I don't know what I want.

3. What are your major concerns? Identify the top three and describe your plans for handling them.

☑ a job?   ☑ a career track?
❏ graduate school?   ❏ where to live?
❏ relationships with friends?   ❏ relationship with a special other?
❏ relationships with parents?   ❏ finances?
❏ a clear sense of yourself—who you are?   ☑ a clear sense of where you are going?
❏ other?

1. Clear sense of where I am going. Until I know where I am going all the other things will be unsettled. The only plans I have are to find a job and see what happens.

2. A career track. But I can't get on a track until I'm clearer about where I'm going.

3. A job. I can get just any kind of job, but it would be nice to begin working with a more long-range plan in mind.

4. In what ways do you expect the next six months to go smoothly? In what ways might there be a downward trend?

I still feel unready to leave college, without a clear direction.
Some of my friends know just where they are going.

5. If you feel as if you are stumbling, where can you garner support?

I might go to the career planning center. Perhaps talking more with friends or my parents would help.

6. What is the transition process as described in this book?

Transitions take time. There will be slippage. My reactions will change. I need to be more clear about my supports and myself. I need to think about particular strategies I can use to deal with the situation I'm in.

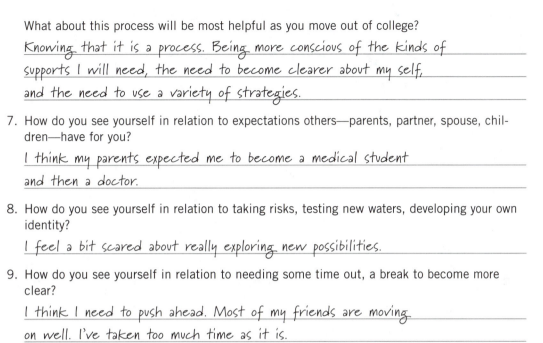

What about this process will be most helpful as you move out of college?

Knowing that it is a process. Being more conscious of the kinds of supports I will need, the need to become clearer about my self, and the need to use a variety of strategies.

7. How do you see yourself in relation to expectations others—parents, partner, spouse, children—have for you?

   I think my parents expected me to become a medical student and then a doctor.

8. How do you see yourself in relation to taking risks, testing new waters, developing your own identity?

   I feel a bit scared about really exploring new possibilities.

9. How do you see yourself in relation to needing some time out, a break to become more clear?

   I think I need to push ahead. Most of my friends are moving on well. I've taken too much time as it is.

10. How solid or open do you feel about your own identity?

    I am pretty unclear. That's why I tell my girlfriend I'm not ready to get married.

11. What are you going to do right after college?

    I'll volunteer in a hospital while I look around.

Lee had quite a struggle. His volunteer job in the hospital did not pay benefits even though it did pay a relatively high hourly wage. After a year of struggling about what to do, envious of some of his classmates who were well employed and getting on with their life, he made some decisions. He decided that social work was more his bent than medicine. That meant he need more training, so he entered a clinical social work program.

Completing Exercise 12.1 helped him gain some perspective. He felt immature, he felt he needed direction, but he also recognized it might take time. It took a year and a half after graduating to decide how to approach the next part of his life. We hope he realizes that there will be many transitions, and that it might take some time to leave one setting and get going in another.

You can use Exercise 12.1 to think through these issues and what they may imply.

EXERCISE 12.1

YOUR FUTURE ORIENTATION   name

Respond to this exercise using a separate sheet of paper.

1. What do you think will happen right after graduation?

   six months later?

   a year from now?

2. In what ways are your expectations about what is next realistic or unrealistic?

3. What are your major concerns? Identify the top three and describe your plans for handling them.

   ❑ a job?

   ❑ a career track?

   ❑ graduate school?

   ❑ where to live?

   ❑ relationships with friends?

   ❑ relationship with a special other?

   ❑ relationships with parents?

   ❑ finances?

   ❑ a clear sense of yourself—who you are?

   ❑ a clear sense of where you are going?

   ❑ other?

4. In what ways do you expect the next six months to go smoothly? In what ways might there be a downward trend?

5. If you feel as if you are stumbling, where can you garner support?

6. What is the transition process as described in this book?

   What about this process will be most helpful as you move out of college?

7. How do you see yourself in relation to expectations others—parents, partner, spouse, children—have for you?

8. How do you see yourself in relation to taking risks, testing new waters, developing your own identity?

9. How do you see yourself in relation to needing some time out, a break to become more clear?

10. How solid or open do you feel about your own identity?

11. What are you going to do right after college?

Wrap-Up

There are clearly many possibilities for the way your life is unfolding. Whose voices are speaking to you as you begin the struggle to move into a new phase of life? Many of our interviewees felt pressure to become "grown up." Many felt their stumbling was unique. This struggle to know who you are, and to be comfortable with yourself, is a lifelong issue.

It seems to us that reading the books of Levinson, Heilbrun, and Bateson could be helpful as you think about this next period in your lives. All of us have many chances to improvise, to reinvent ourselves. Identity issues are never fully resolved. Transitions like leaving college, marrying, obtaining a graduate degree, divorcing, and retiring all evoke questions about who we are and who are we becoming. What we decide today can be changed. We have many chances, many possibilities. We need not fear the next step because we can back up, go forward, rewind, step out.

We would all like certainty in a world of unpredictability. In many ways, the biggest task is learning to live with ambiguity, with emerging possibilities. We might not know what is next, but this book provides a structure for you to assess what you want next, as you look at your resources for dealing with the inevitable ups and downs of life. If nothing else, you know more about transitions now than when you entered college and you can take that knowledge with you.

REFERENCES

1. Seuss, T. (1991). *Oh, The Places You'll Go!* New York: Random House.
2. Bateson, Mary Catherine. (1989). "Composing a Life." *The Atlantic Monthly.*
3. Levinson, D. J. (1978). *The Seasons of a Man's Life.* New York: Alfred A. Knopf, pp. 71 & 78.
4. *Ibid*, p. 79.
5. Josselson, R. (1987). *Finding Herself: Pathways to Identity Development in Women.* San Francisco: Jossey Bass.
6. Heilbrun, Carolyn. (1988). *Writing a Woman's Life.* New York: W. W. Naughton & Co.
7. Wolf, Naomi. (May 31, 1992). "A Woman's Place." *The New York Times,* Op-Ed, p. 19.

Taking It With You

Life and learning will not stop with graduation. You don't get grown up once and for all, at any particular point in time. If you become static, you become, in some ways, dead. Career success and a good life depend on continuous learning and self-development. Coming to college, moving in, and moving through—taking courses, investing in other activities and organizations, getting a job, establishing new relationships, building relationships with faculty friends and dealing with difficult ones, and coping with a frustrating institutional bureaucracy—all these stimulate significant learning. Such experiences, positive and negative, are what keep us alive and growing. Leading a rich full life often depends on your capacity to put yourself in new, challenging situations and then to learn from them.

To stay in charge of your own learning and development and to keep your own development underway, two things are helpful. First, it is useful to have some perspective on what lies ahead, what some have called the "adult life span." Second, it is useful to be clear about the knowledge, competence, and personal characteristics you are taking with you.

We asked senior students what they were taking with them from their college experiences. Their responses covered a wide range of knowledge, abilities, and personal characteristics.

Robin, for example, said, "What I've gained is a better understanding of how the system works, how politics goes, how the world is interdependent. I have learned about new processes of international organizations that I am going to have to know or be able to work with. Much of what I learned has come from outside the classroom. I have learned a lot of business information. I have learned how to write contracts that protect the contractor and contractee. I have probably learned more about computers than I ever care to know because I had to work with them. A lot of the stuff I am taking with me is practical that will help me support myself while I am waiting for a real job."

"What are some things you have learned that are most important for your future?"

"Time management. Time management is a big one. How I can fit all the things that I do into my life. So I am taking away knowing how to manage myself—through time, through business, through personal relationships. I am taking away a great knowledge of how the world runs through governments, because that is what I have studied. I am taking away a greater knowledge of business systems because that is what I have worked in. I am also taking ideas of the way organizations work. I will be able to apply those things no matter where I go."

"What have you learned about transitions?"

"Never be afraid of change. Change can be bad. There is no doubt that change can be bad, but it doesn't mean you have to be afraid of it. A transition is merely a challenge. It is very important to go in with the attitude that I can handle this. It is not going to take me over. It is not going to stop me. I am going to conquer whatever is out there. I think the Army had a lot to do with that. I had to move. I had to meet new people. At one point in time I was a shy person that hid behind my mother's skirts. In Germany, because of transitions, every summer I would have friends come and go. I learned not to be afraid of it and not to worry about it. It was something I could deal with."

"How do you deal with stress?"

"I tell everyone to get out of my face for at least 15 minutes, because if they don't I am going to explode and it is not going to be very pretty. I do a lot of sitting still. Just sit still. I used to dance when I got upset. But I have no knees now. They have been destroyed by too much activity and by genetics. When I am upset I just send the world away, close myself in my room, and close myself within myself. I go inward. I figure out what I have to do to achieve what I am going into. I refuse to let it get the best of me. I stay on top of it. There will be times when a transition is given to me and I have to work through it. I understand that and it doesn't bother me. Somebody else can tell me where to move and when to move, but I am in charge of that transition."

"What have you learned about taking charge of your own learning and future?"

"I didn't take charge of my own learning until I had to fill out the general education requirements. I learned to develop my own agenda, my own program. A lot of it was because the university has expanded its base. I was not only an international studies major, but I was the first to have a minor in history and in European studies. I believe you cannot be a diplomat without knowing the history, and Europe is my area of study. There is a lot I developed on my own just because I needed to."

"What have you learned about your approach to learning?"

"I had to learn how to study. I went through high school with a 4.0 average. I didn't have to study. It was a breeze. I got to the university and there was no structure. No one checked my homework. No one took attendance to make sure I was in class. No one told me I had to do something. There were no quizzes on the readings. I did not work well with this lack of structure. It took my first year-and-a-half to learn to deal with it. But I just had to teach myself to manage my time. I had to teach myself how to study. I had to teach myself how to learn in a different environment."

"What have you learned about relationships?"

"I learned not to compromise myself. I have done that before and [it] ended up hurting me. I learned that no one out there is more important than my own feelings. That may be selfish, but that is the truth to me. But I learned to compromise, also. I learned how to come out of a fight and still turn around and say, 'I'm sorry.' I learned how to have fun with a large group of people. I had groups of friends before but I always felt on the outside, on the fringes. I learned how to manage a relationship that is real personal and a relationship that is professional. I learned to separate the two, which I never had to do before. You can have one person you work with in a professional way and in a personal way, and separate the two without compromising yourself or your ideals, without conflict of interest entering into the relationship. I learned to deal with many aspects of one relationship. I think that is the biggest thing. Because I refuse to put myself in a position where I can be compromised."

"What advice would you give an incoming student about how to get the most out of college?"

"Read Margaret Atwood's *Handmaid's Tale*. Don't let the bastards get you down. Don't let the system kill you. It's a different system, an odd system. It is not a user-friendly system. Find someone who knows, whether it be with the department, with student organizations, or through something else. There is someone out there who knows what to do. Don't go at it by yourself. Don't go at it blind. Find persons with answers and ask them the questions. Then open your eyes and see the world around you. Especially if you come from a small town. There are people who are going to be different from you. That difference is going to aid you in learning more about yourself and about your life. It is not going to hurt you. It is not going to effect you and take you over. Whether that difference is racial, ethnic—even in sexual orientation—there is nothing wrong with being different. You should allow yourself to be exposed to that with open eyes. No matter how different they are, you are going to learn something. Don't shut yourself, don't shut your eyes to change."

It sounds as though Robin has achieved significant learning and personal development during her college years. She now has some practical skills that can help her get immediate employment as she pursues her long-range career plans. She has broad-based knowledge about political systems, historical perspectives, and Europe that is pertinent to those plans. She has developed more sophisticated understandings about how organizations and businesses work; this will serve her well across a wide range of possibilities. She has developed strong self-discipline, the ability to manage her time and herself, and to get where she wants to go. She has a sense of competence that lets her welcome change and tackle transitions, confident that she can handle them in ways consistent with her own purposes and needs. She developed her own program consistent with her particular needs for learning and personal development, and knows how to take charge of her own learning. She has become sophisticated concerning personal and professional relationships. She can handle many aspects of different relationships and maintain her own identity and integrity. She respects individual differences; she appreciates encountering and learning from persons different from herself. If you check the kinds of competence and personal characteristics important for career success and a good life, which we discussed in Chapter 2, she has made significant progress in most of the key areas.

The Adult Life Span

One thing Robin has not learned about in any systematic way is the "adult life span." This is not a new idea. Philosophers, poets, playwrights, and novelists have given us ancient and modern descriptions. Shakespeare sets forth seven acts, from the infant mewling and puking in the nurse's arms, through the whining school boy creeping unwillingly to school, the lover sighing like a furnace, and the capon-lined justice, to the final second childhood/childishness and oblivion. These artistic descriptions singing down through time suggest fundamental chords that underlie the melodies, harmonies, and overtones found by current scholars. Their research findings and theoretical perspectives can help you anticipate some of your future challenges for learning and self-development. With that knowledge you can assess which of those challenges you've already met and dealt with, which may be coming at you soon, and which are still over the horizon. Charts 13.1 and 13.2 share some of the basic concepts and research findings.

More than any other theorist, Bernice Neugarten looks at the role of timing in adult development. Perhaps the most important shift she identified is when you change from thinking about yourself in terms of "time since birth," to thinking about yourself in terms of "time left to live." You change from being oriented toward mastering and controlling the outer world, to self-examination and greater preoccupation with your inner self and sponsoring others. You shift from a focus on achievement to a focus on self-satisfaction. Neugarten found that when events are "on time"—children leaving home, menopause, death of a spouse—they are not experienced as crises. Illness and death of loved ones causes grief and sadness, as does the prospect of one's own death, but when they come at times and in ways consistent with the normal expected life span, most persons manage them without lasting personal consequences.

It is important to recognize that the "timing" Neugarten found was largely determined by male career patterns in a society that was strongly male-dominated. Those historical patterns have been changing slowly during the last 30 years or so as large numbers of women entered the work force and dual career families have become the norm. The comments of all the senior men and women we interviewed were consistent with more broad-based statistics. All the women were oriented toward varied careers, and all the men assumed that their eventual

CHART 13.1   THE LIFE SPAN

Theorist	15	20	25	30	35	40	45	50	55	60	65	70	75

Erickson (1950)

Identity vs Role Diffusion

Intimacy vs Isolation

Generativity vs Stagnation

Integrity vs Despair

Death is no crisis: how and where are important

Neugarten (1971)

Time Since Birth — Future stretches forth: time to do and see everything: achievement orientation: death is an abstractioo

Time Left to Live — Time is finite, time enough only to finish a few important things: sponsoring others: personalization of death

Sense of Self-Determination

Sense of Life Cycle and Inevitability

Neugarten (1963)

Mastery of Outer World

Reexamination

Preoccupation with Inner Self — Withdrawal

Development of social personality, vocation and marital adjustment, home making, child rearing, increased expressivity & expansiveness, reduced anxiety, increaset autonomy, competence, stability

Further stabilization of social personality in family work, recreational patterns. High self-confidence, sense of achievement & mastery. Following outside cues. Energy congruent with opportunities.

Inner drives reexamined, achievement demands questioned. Resistance to coercion.

Outer world seen as complex, dangerous, conflictual. Increasing conformity, passivity.

Introspection, stock-taking, conscious self-utilization, menopause is not a significant crisis, normal events are not crises if timing is appropriate.

Life review, final restructuring, preparatory to death.

Increasingly meek and mild.

WOMEN

Average age women marry

Children
First Last

Last child to school

Last child leaves home, not a significant crisis, increased freedom and home satisfaction

Many women work — Women nurturant, affiliative, conscientious.

Few women work

40% women work

55% women work — Women become more dominant, instrumental, and acceptant of their aggressive impulses, gain increased autonomy, self-confidence.

MEN

Men take the lead in economic, civic, and social activities. They gain competence, autonomy, and self-confidence. They become stabilized for middle age.

Men grow more nurturant and affiliative.

From Chickering, Arthur W. and Associates. *The Modern American College: Responding to the New Realities of Diverse Students and a Changing Society.* Copyright ©1981. Reprinted by permission of Jossey-Bass Inc., a subsidiary of John Wiley & Sons, Inc.

CHART 13.2 LIFE SPAN THEORY

Time Line	15	20	25	30	35	40	45	50	55	60	65	70	75
Levinson (1971)		Leaving the Family		Settling Down			Restabilization						
			Getting into the Adult World		Becoming One's Own Person								
				Transitional Period									
				Mentor Plays Significant Role									
						Midlife Transition							
R.L. Gould (1972)	**Leaving Parents** Breaking out	**Leaving Parents** Staying out		**Becoming Adult** Marriage Work	**Question Life's Meaning** Breaking out	**Continued Questioning** Values, time is finite. Responsible for parents as well as children.		**Occupational Die is Cast** Interest in friends, reliance on spouse.	**Mellowing** Spouse increasingly important, review of contributions.				
		Reliance on Peers											
Sheehy	Pulling Up Roots	Provisional Adulthood		Age 30 Transition	Rooting	Midlife Transition	Restabilization and Flowering						
					Boom								

From Chickering, Arthur W. and Associates. *The Modern American College: Responding to the New Realities of Diverse Students and a Changing Society.* Copyright ©1981. Reprinted by permission of Jossey-Bass Inc., a subsidiary of John Wiley & Sons, Inc.

spouses would be working. Thirty or 40 years ago, college men and women much more frequently assumed that the man would be the "breadwinner" and that the woman would primarily be occupied with children and homemaking, at least until her late 30s or 40s when the kids were on their own. So we need to recognize that Neugarten's findings are anchored in a historical period that is different from yours and different from the one you will live through. But these changes occur slowly. The findings summarized in Chart 13.2 provide a useful way to think about changes you will face, and a good way to recognize differences as they occur.

Levinson and Gould describe a general pattern that begins with the transition from adolescence to adulthood, leaving the parents and getting into the adult world, during the late teens and early 20s. Leaving your family and establishing a new home base can be a time to discover and stretch your newly found independence.

When we asked another senior if it would take long to get settled after graduation he said, "No. I've been fortunate. I prepared myself for that. A lot of people are on campus for four years and after that they're kind of in shell shock. They have to find a place to live. They have to learn to start, you know, buying groceries. I mean just the simplest things. I moved off campus for my senior year. I have a place to live, shop for myself, the whole thing. So for me the biggest change will be the work world, the nine-to-five concept, overtime, and all that sort of stuff." Moving off campus into his own apartment helped this student move one basic step away from family and onto his own.

During the mid-20s—a period of "provisional adulthood"—you first explore commitments to work, marriage, family, and other adult responsibilities. Then you face another transition during the late 20s and early 30s when these initial commitments may be reexamined and their meanings questioned. The long-range implications of continuing with your current work, spouse, community, or lifestyle, have become apparent. At 35, one or more of these may look less challenging or satisfying than it did at 22. You may change one or another of these: your work, your community, your spouse. Or you may simply flirt with other alternatives and recommit yourself to your current combination.

The 30s are typically a time when you settle down, and focus on achievement and becoming your own person. But as you move into your 40s or 50s, that shift from "time since birth" to "time left to live" begins to happen. Time becomes more finite. During these years you may begin taking responsibility for aging parents while responsibilities for children often continue. You become more aware of the likely limits for your career success and achievement. You examine major questions concerning values and priorities for the future. If you don't make a career change now, you will probably continue your current work until you retire. Most persons stick with their general career orientation, but with moderated expectations and drive. Your marriage may be temporarily or permanently upset. Friends, relatives, and your spouse become increasingly important as you "restabilize" during the late 40s and 50s. You begin to give more time to interests and activities that you have set aside while investing heavily in work. During your 50s, you increasingly invest more time and energy in personal relationships.

You need to recognize how women differ from Levinson's findings for men. For women, the first stage, *Leaving the Family*, may be aborted when they leave parental constraints only to enter the family constraints of a husband and children. Similar constraints may work for men, though typically not as powerfully. Leaving parents and college, establishing your own base, can be a time for experimenting with different jobs, a career, developing your own individual talents. But independence, experimentation, and self-development are not usually very congruent with the expected roles of wives and mothers when they exchange being dependent on parents for being dependent on a husband. If you are an older woman going back to college—or to college for the first time after raising a family—you are probably experiencing, a decade or so later, some of the experiences Levinson describes for the men he studied when they were young adults. If you are a young woman, you need to think through the consequences of first choosing the role of wife and mother and pursuing a career later, or making a career a significant part of your life and your identity immediately as you move on from college.

We need to understand that all these research findings and theories reflect our particular historical period. If current social conditions persist—with dual-career families, with women moving into an increasingly wide range of careers and occupations, and with continued legal and public concern for equal rights for women—a study 40 years from now of persons whose lives started during the 1970s will reveal very different patterns. But even though conditions are changing, these findings provide a useful perspective as you think about the mix of family, work, lifestyle, community responsibilities, and avocational interests you want to create during your own adult life. We know that women who find rewarding work and education, as well as the rewards of sharing child rearing and homemaking, enrich their own lives as well as their spouse's. They become stronger, more able to make their own decisions and take charge of their own existence. So, whether you are a man or a woman, how you work through these various issues can have significant consequences.

Life Span Developmental Tasks

One way to apply some of these life-span issues is to use the idea of "developmental tasks." These "tasks" are provoked by internal and external forces. The internal forces are mainly biological and operate primarily during childhood, adolescence, and old age. The external forces come from the pressures and opportunities that are built into the culture and occur because of the particular environments you experience. Other key sources of developmental tasks are your own values and aspirations. These values and aspirations lead you to set goals, to find or create challenging situations that help you achieve what you want to achieve, to become what you want to become. As you become your own self, you gather increasing momentum, you develop your own particular trajectory, your own special characteristics. As you get older, these characteristics become more ingrained, more deeply etched, more important to you. But they can be changed, deflected, or converted. New talents are recognized. New possibilities become apparent. Current conditions may become obsolete, stale, or frustrating. Thus, your developmental tasks emerge from biological changes, social forces, and your own constantly evolving personality. It is important to recognize that many of these developmental tasks are never completed once and for all. Shifting circumstances or powerful new experiences may disrupt a stable situation, challenge your existing values, and require new levels of skill and knowledge.

Vivian McCoy has provided a set of tasks associated with seven different "developmental stages." We use these as the basis for Exercise 13.1. With this exercise you can identify which tasks you have completed, which are in progress, and which you will confront during the next year and the next five years. Here is how Robin might complete this exercise.

EXERCISE 13.1   *Robin*

MY DEVELOPMENTAL TASKS   name

Examine the tasks for all the "developmental stages."

1. Put a **D,** for **Done,** opposite each task you think you have completed.
2. Put an **I,** for **In Progress,** opposite each task currently underway.
3. Put a **1** (one) opposite each task you will undertake during the next year.
4. Put a **5** (five) opposite each task you expect to undertake two to five years from now.

You may have more than one response per task. For example, "Break psychological ties" may be I, for In Progress, 1, because you expect it to continue next year, and 5, because you expect it to continue for two or three years.

DEVELOPMENTAL STAGES   TASKS

Leaving Home   _I_   1. Break psychological ties.
                  _D_   2. Choose career.
                  _I_   3. Enter work.
                  _D_   4. Handle peer relationships.
                  _5_   5. Manage home.
                  _D_   6. Manage time.
                  _1_   7. Adjust to life on own.

Reaching Out   _5_   1. Select mate.
                  _1,5_ 2. Settle in work, begin career ladder.
                  ____ 3. Parent.
                  _1,5_ 4. Become involved in community.
                  _1,5_ 5. Consume wisely.
                  ____ 6. Own home.
                  _1,5_ 7. Socially interact.
                  _I,5_ 8. Achieve autonomy.

DEVELOPMENTAL STAGES   TASKS

Questions/   _l_   1. Search for personal values.
Questions   ___   2. Reappraise relationships.
                    _5_   3. Progress in career.
                    ___   4. Accept growing children.
                    ___   5. Put down roots, achieve "permanent" home.

Midlife Explosion ___   1. Search for meaning.
                   ___   2. Reassess marriage.
                   ___   3. Reexamine work.
                   ___   4. Relate to teenage children.
                   ___   5. Relate to aging parents.
                   ___   6. Reassess personal priorities and values.
                   ___   7. Adjust to single life.

Settling Down   ___   1. Adjust to realities of work.
                   ___   2. Launch children.
                   ___   3. Adjust to empty nest.
                   ___   4. Become more deeply involved in social life.
                   ___   5. Participate actively in community concerns.
                   ___   6. Handle increased demands of older children.
                   ___   7. Manage leisure time.
                   ___   8. Manage budget to support college-age children and ailing parents.
                   ___   9. Adjust to single state.

The Mellowing   ___   1. Adjust to health problems.
                   ___   2. Deepen personal relations.
                   ___   3. Prepare for retirement.
                   ___   4. Expand avocational interests.
                   ___   5. Finance new leisure.
                   ___   6. Adjust to loss of mate.

Retirement   ___   1. Disengage from paid work.
                   ___   2. Reassess finances.
                   ___   3. Be concerned with personal health care.
                   ___   4. Search for new achievement outlets.
                   ___   5. Manage leisure time.
                   ___   6. Adjust to more constant marriage companion.
                   ___   7. Search for meaning.
                   ___   8. Adjust to single state.
                   ___   9. Be reconciled to death.

Exercise adapted from the work of Vivian Rogers McCoy, Director, Adult Life Resources Center, Division of Continuing Education, University of Kansas. Used by permission.

Colin's responses to the "Developmental Tasks" exercise are very different from Robin's. When he left his inner city high school with a mediocre record, he had trouble finding work. He had never been oriented toward college, and neither he nor his parents had the money anyway. He decided to join the Army. He was assigned to a supply depot in Vietnam. When his two years were up he signed on for another three, and was shipped back to manage the motor pool at a small U. S. base. He got married and had a daughter. After five years he had come to like Army life, and so he decided to stay on. With 20 years of service, he became eligible for retirement. He had become a Master Sergeant, as high as he could go as a noncommissioned officer. He had significant responsibilities in his supply depot, but had been doing pretty much the same work for six years. His daughter was graduating from high school. His parents and his wife's mother were getting older; they wanted the flexibility to be more helpful. It seemed like a good time to make a change. He and his wife figured they could manage on his retirement pay until he found a job in some kind of business. He enrolled in some business courses at the nearby community college. At first he was anxious about being able to handle the studies, but soon found that he could do well. He transferred to the state college that was oriented toward a business major. He took math and physics to satisfy his science requirement, and found them fascinating. For the first time, he understood some of the laws and processes underlying the diverse vehicles and machinery he had spent his Army life maintaining. There was a shortage of science teachers, and he decided that profession might offer more of a change and challenge than simply using his Army background to go into business. Now he has completed a five-year program that combines his physics major with teacher preparation. His responses to the "Developmental Tasks" exercise look like this.

EXERCISE 13.1   *Colin*

MY DEVELOPMENTAL TASKS   name

Examine the tasks for all the "developmental stages."

1. Put a **D,** for **Done,** opposite each task you think you have completed.
2. Put an **I,** for **In Progress,** opposite each task currently underway.
3. Put a **1** (one) opposite each task you will undertake during the next year.
4. Put a **5** (five) opposite each task you expect to undertake two to five years from now.

   You may have more than one response per task. For example, "Break psychological ties" may be I, for In Progress, 1, because you expect it to continue next year, and 5, because you expect it to continue for two or three years.

DEVELOPMENTAL STAGES   TASKS

Leaving Home   _D_   1. Break psychological ties.
                    _D_   2. Choose career.
                    _D_   3. Enter work.

DEVELOPMENTAL STAGES		TASKS
Leaving Home	D	4. Handle peer relationships.
(continued)	D	5. Manage home.
	D	6. Manage time.
	D	7. Adjust to life on own.
Reaching Out	D	1. Select mate.
	D	2. Settle in work, begin career ladder.
	D	3. Parent.
		4. Become involved in community.
	D	5. Consume wisely.
	D	6. Own home.
	D	7. Socially interact.
		8. Achieve autonomy.
Questions/	I	1. Search for personal values.
Questions	I,5	2. Reappraise relationships.
		3. Progress in career.
	I	4. Accept growing children.
	5	5. Put down roots, achieve "permanent" home.
Midlife Explosion	I	1. Search for meaning.
		2. Reassess marriage.
	I,5	3. Reexamine work.
	I	4. Relate to teenage children.
		5. Relate to aging parents.
		6. Reassess personal priorities and values.
		7. Adjust to single life.
Settling Down	I,5	1. Adjust to realities of work.
	I	2. Launch children.
		3. Adjust to empty nest.
	5	4. Become more deeply involved in social life.
	5	5. Participate actively in community concerns.
	I	6. Handle increased demands of older children.
	I,5	7. Manage leisure time.
	5	8. Manage budget to support college-age children and ailing parents.
		9. Adjust to single state.
The Mellowing		1. Adjust to health problems.
		2. Deepen personal relations.
		3. Prepare for retirement.
		4. Expand avocational interests.
		5. Finance new leisure.
		6. Adjust to loss of mate.

Retirement		
	____	1. Disengage from paid work.
	____	2. Reassess finances.
	____	3. Be concerned with personal health care.
	____	4. Search for new achievement outlets.
	____	5. Manage leisure time.
	____	6. Adjust to more constant marriage companion.
	____	7. Search for meaning.
	____	8. Adjust to single state.
	____	9. Be reconciled to death.

Exercise adapted from the work of Vivian Rogers McCoy, Director, Adult Life Resources Center, Division of Continuing Education, University of Kansas. Used by permission.

Your "Developmental Tasks" will clearly differ from both Robin's and Colin's. Completing it will give you a sense of where you are now and what you can anticipate in the near future.

EXERCISE 13.1

MY DEVELOPMENTAL TASKS   name

Examine the tasks for all the "developmental stages."

1. Put a **D,** for **Done,** opposite each task you think you have completed.
2. Put an **I,** for **In Progress,** opposite each task currently underway.
3. Put a **1** (one) opposite each task you will undertake during the next year.
4. Put a **5** (five) opposite each task you expect to undertake two to five years from now.

   You may have more than one response per task. For example, "Break psychological ties" may be I, for In Progress, 1, because you expect it to continue next year, and 5, because you expect it to continue for two or three years.

DEVELOPMENTAL STAGES	TASKS	
Leaving Home	____	1. Break psychological ties.
	____	2. Choose career.
	____	3. Enter work.
	____	4. Handle peer relationships.
	____	5. Manage home.
	____	6. Manage time.
	____	7. Adjust to life on own.

DEVELOPMENTAL STAGES	TASKS

Reaching Out
- ____ 1. Select mate.
- ____ 2. Settle in work, begin career ladder.
- ____ 3. Parent.
- ____ 4. Become involved in community.
- ____ 5. Consume wisely.
- ____ 6. Own home.
- ____ 7. Socially interact.
- ____ 8. Achieve autonomy.

Questions/ Questions
- ____ 1. Search for personal values.
- ____ 2. Reappraise relationships.
- ____ 3. Progress in career.
- ____ 4. Accept growing children.
- ____ 5. Put down roots, achieve "permanent" home.

Midlife Explosion
- ____ 1. Search for meaning.
- ____ 2. Reassess marriage.
- ____ 3. Reexamine work.
- ____ 4. Relate to teenage children.
- ____ 5. Relate to aging parents.
- ____ 6. Reassess personal priorities and values.
- ____ 7. Adjust to single life.

Settling Down
- ____ 1. Adjust to realities of work.
- ____ 2. Launch children.
- ____ 3. Adjust to empty nest.
- ____ 4. Become more deeply involved in social life.
- ____ 5. Participate actively in community concerns.
- ____ 6. Handle increased demands of older children.
- ____ 7. Manage leisure time.
- ____ 8. Manage budget to support college-age children and ailing parents.
- ____ 9. Adjust to single state.

The Mellowing
- ____ 1. Adjust to health problems.
- ____ 2. Deepen personal relations.
- ____ 3. Prepare for retirement.
- ____ 4. Expand avocational interests.
- ____ 5. Finance new leisure.
- ____ 6. Adjust to loss of mate.

Retirement
- ____ 1. Disengage from paid work.
- ____ 2. Reassess finances.

DEVELOPMENTAL STAGES	TASKS

Retirement   ____   3. Be concerned with personal health care.

(continued)   ____   4. Search for new achievement outlets.

                           ____   5. Manage leisure time.

                           ____   6. Adjust to more constant marriage companion.

                           ____   7. Search for meaning.

                           ____   8. Adjust to single state.

                           ____   9. Be reconciled to death.

Exercise adapted from the work of Vivian Rogers McCoy, Director, Adult Life Resources Center, Division of Continuing Education, University of Kansas. Used by permission.

Self-Assessment

As part of *Moving In* to college, we helped you "Take Stock" of the knowledge and competence you were bringing with you. That stock-taking provided the base for thinking more clearly about your purposes in going to college and the types of learning and personal development you wanted to emphasize. Now, as you finish college and undertake your next transition, it will be useful if you undertake another thorough self-assessment. This assessment should help you become clearer about the strengths and characteristics you bring to the complex mix of work, family, social contributions, and community responsibilities you create for a good life. It will help you define what you are prepared to cope with successfully and help you identify the kinds of learning and personal development you want to pursue in the near future. Use Exercise 13.2 to identify the key strong points of your personality and to identify other characteristics you would like to develop further.

Robin might have responded like this.

EXERCISE 13.2   *Robin*

MY STRONG POINTS   name

1. Read the following list of personality characteristics and circle those that best describe you. Remember, your purpose here is not to impress others but to undertake an accurate self-assessment. You may find it helpful to discuss your choices with a friend or relative who knows you well. Sometimes it is hard to see ourselves clearly and realistically.

2. Select the five strongest characteristics and rank them from 1 to 5.

3. Identify five characteristics that you would like to improve, and rank them from 1 to 5 in terms of their importance to you. If there are characteristics that do not appear on the list, feel free to add them.

Accurate	Considerate	Fair-minded	(Methodical)	Sensible
(Adaptable)	Cooperative	Friendly	Optimistic	Sensitive
(Adventurous)	Creative	Gentle	(Organized)	Sincere
(Assertive)	Curious	Helpful	Outgoing	Spontaneous
(Broadminded)	Dependable	Honest	Patient	Tactful
Calm	(Determined)	Humorous	(Persevering)	(Thorough)
(Capable)	Eager	(Independent)	Polite	Thoughtful
Careful	Easy-going	(Intelligent)	Practical	Trustworthy
Cheerful	(Efficient)	Kind	(Purposeful)	Understanding
Clever	Energetic	Logical	Reasonable	Versatile
(Confident)	Enterprising	Loyal	Reflective	Warm
Conscientious	Enthusiastic	Mature	(Self-controlled)	

My five strongest points:

1. Adaptable
2. Broadminded
3. Capable
4. Self-Controlled
5. Purposeful

The five characteristics I would like to strengthen:

1. Calm
2. Gentle
3. Warm
4. Easy-going
5. Spontaneous

Your strong points will help you function effectively across many diverse situations. As you pursue future activities and responsibilities, you can try to be more intentional about addressing some of the areas you would like to improve.

EXERCISE 13.2

1. Read the following list of personality characteristics and circle those that best describe you. Remember, your purpose here is not to impress others but to undertake an accurate self-assessment. You may find it helpful to discuss your choices with a friend or relative who knows you well. Sometimes it is hard to see ourselves clearly and realistically.
2. Select the five strongest characteristics and rank them from 1 to 5.
3. Identify five characteristics that you would like to improve, and rank them from 1 to 5 in terms of their importance to you. If there are characteristics that do not appear on the list, feel free to add them.

Accurate	Considerate	Fair-minded	Methodical	Sensible
Adaptable	Cooperative	Friendly	Optimistic	Sensitive
Adventurous	Creative	Gentle	Organized	Sincere
Assertive	Curious	Helpful	Outgoing	Spontaneous
Broadminded	Dependable	Honest	Patient	Tactful
Calm	Determined	Humorous	Persevering	Thorough
Capable	Eager	Independent	Polite	Thoughtful
Careful	Easy-going	Intelligent	Practical	Trustworthy
Cheerful	Efficient	Kind	Purposeful	Understanding
Clever	Energetic	Logical	Reasonable	Versatile
Confident	Enterprising	Loyal	Reflective	Warm
Conscientious	Enthusiastic	Mature	Self-controlled	

My five strongest points:

1. _____
2. _____
3. _____
4. _____
5. _____

The five characteristics I would like to strengthen:

1. _____
2. _____
3. _____
4. _____
5. _____

You also have many areas of competence and knowledge that can serve you across a wide range of future life challenges. Use Exercise 13.3 to clarify your most important transferable skills. On the basis of your personality strengths and your transferable skills, you will be able to think about your personal and professional development from a life-span perspective. Here are some of the accomplishments and transferable skills Robin might identify.

EXERCISE 13.3   *Robin*

MY TRANSFERABLE SKILLS   name

A good way to identify your transferable skills is to list several significant accomplishments and then indicate what skills were involved that helped you succeed. An accomplishment demonstrates that we know how to do something and have the capacity to deliver. It can be paid or unpaid, in college or out, recognized by others or unrecognized. Just choose things that you did well and that gave you strong feelings of satisfaction.

For each accomplishment you identify, list the skills that seem to you to have been required. Some skills will probably be associated with more than one accomplishment. If so, it is probably useful to list them.

Here again, the point is to be as accurate as possible. You are not trying to impress others. You are trying to create an accurate self-assessment. Discussing this with others may help you identify skills that did not occur to you or to delete some which really did not seem to be involved. You will probably want to create your own sheet. Use as much space as you need.

1. Accomplishment

   Completed an International Studies major with minors in History and European Studies.

Associated skills:

   Abstracting and conceptualizing written information; analyzing verbal materials; dealing with time pressures to meet competing deadlines; enduring long hours of work; working at a fast pace; imagining theoretical relationships; obtaining information from diverse written sources; preparing written materials for presentation; reading and assimilating large amounts of information; remembering facts, places, sequences of events and causal relationships; researching information from library sources; organizing time efficiently to meet diverse demands; writing papers and reports.

2. Accomplishment

Administrative Assistant to the V.P. for Product Development,
Business Technologies Inc.

Associated Skills:

Compiling statistical data and facts for executive decisions; dealing with
deadlines; designing draft data processing systems; working overtime to
meet special demands; working fast and efficiently; obtaining information
from business reports and corporate colleagues; operating sophisticated
computer systems; preparing graphs, charts, and diagrams; processing data
concerning business trends and market analyses; creating and debugging
computer programs; organizing work days and work weeks to get priority
tasks completed; handling and following through on numerous details and
short assignments.

3. Accomplishment

Completed a semester-long Policy Research Internship for the
Foreign Policy Association.

Associated Skills:

Analyzing, abstracting, and conceptualizing written reports and statistical
information; answering mail; evaluating the strengths and weaknesses of
various policy recommendations; explaining why some recommendations made
more sense than others; finding information from diverse sources pertinent
to policy issues; interpreting statistical reports, graphs, diagrams, legal
language; digesting large amount of information quickly; writing draft
position papers.

4. Accomplishment

Volunteer for the County Historical Association

Associated Skills:

Meeting the public and interpreting historical exhibits; searching historical
archives for new exhibits being created; doing library research for background information pertinent to local history; designing and managing tours to
fit specific time requirements; writing explanatory notes for different exhibits.

5. Accomplishment

> Three months' summer travel through Scandinavia, Germany, Holland, Belgium, France, and Italy.

Associated Skills:

> Anticipating future needs and potential problems; arranging travel schedules and making appropriate advance reservations; coping with different languages and different cultural conventions; dealing with uncertainties; keeping cool when things go wrong; deciding how to use limited funds wisely; bargaining for market goods and services; observing carefully different customs and ways of behaving; recognizing and accepting misunderstandings and deliberate deceit; sustaining patience in the face of apparently needless delays.

EXERCISE 13.3

MY TRANSFERABLE SKILLS
name

A good way to identify your transferable skills is to list several significant accomplishments and then indicate what skills were involved that helped you succeed. An accomplishment demonstrates that we know how to do something and have the capacity to deliver. It can be paid or unpaid, in college or out, recognized by others or unrecognized. Just choose things that you did well and that gave you strong feelings of satisfaction.

For each accomplishment you identify, list the skills that seem to you to have been required. Some skills will probably be associated with more than one accomplishment. If so, it is probably useful to list them.

Here again, the point is to be as accurate as possible. You are not trying to impress others. You are trying to create an accurate self-assessment. Discussing this with others may help you identify skills that did not occur to you or to delete some which really did not seem to be involved. You will probably want to create your own sheet. Use as much space as you need.

1. Accomplishment
   Associated skills:

_____

_____

2. Accomplishment
   Associated skills:

   _____

   _____

   _____

   _____

   _____

3. Accomplishment
   Associated skills:

   _____

   _____

   _____

   _____

   _____

4. Accomplishment
   Associated skills:

   _____

   _____

   _____

   _____

   _____

5. Accomplishment
   Associated skills:

   _____

   _____

   _____

   _____

   _____

ACCOMPLISHMENT	SKILL
Managed development campaign for local service group that raised over $4,500 for new equipment.	Directing others Organizing Motivating
Sold house sitting as service during summer in order to earn money for college. Earned over $3,100.	Selling Organizing Trouble shooting
Set up bookkeeping system that allowed manager of small business to manage cash flow better.	Analyzing Auditing Classifying Compiling
Organized Cookie Sale for Girl Scouts for entire community.	Organizing Directing others Motivating Advertising

Now you are ready to try to pull all this together. First, review the key concepts and the diverse sets of findings concerning the adult life span presented earlier in this chapter. Then complete Exercise 13.4, "Personal and Professional Development in a Life Span Perspective."

EXERCISE 13.4

PERSONAL AND PROFESSIONAL DEVELOPMENT IN A LIFE SPAN PERSPECTIVE

You will want to use your own paper for this exercise. Take as much space as you need to respond to the different parts and questions.

PART ONE: MY LIFE TO DATE

1. Starting with your graduation from high school, divide your life into coherent time segments, up to and including the present.

2. For each time segment:

   a. Describe briefly the major theme, issue, or events that made it a time segment.

   b. List the major learnings, achievements, developmental tasks.

   c. Describe the most significant relationships.

PART TWO: FUTURE PLANNING

1. Examine your past life span, your current situation, and your future possibilities in relation to key concepts concerning the adult life span that is pertinent to your condition.

   a. Identify what you would predict to be the major time segments in your future, as far into the future as makes sense, given whatever uncertainties obtain.

   b. Give the major theme, issue, or events that will characterize each time segment.

   c. List the major learnings, achievements, or developmental tasks that you expect to be associated with each segment.

2. In the light of your responses to the questions above, and taking account of the developmental tasks you have completed, as well as your personal strong points and skills, identify the key areas in personal and professional development that will be important for you:

   a. During the next year.

   b. During the next major time segment you identified.

Wrap-Up

When you have completed Exercise 13.4, you should be well positioned to build on your college experiences. You should have increased clarity about your own mix of work, family, social contributions, community responsibilities, and avocational activities; a mix that leads to a successful career and a good life. You recognize, of course, that you are involved in a process of continual creation. Your personal and professional development will be challenged throughout life. You can lead a rich and satisfying life to the extent that you say "Yes!" to those challenges. Use them to become a more perceptive, thoughtful, adaptable, effective person and you will be a joy to yourself as well as to others.

We wish you well.

REFERENCE

1. Chickering, A. W., and associates. (1981). *The Modern American College: Responding to the New Realities of Diverse Students and a Changing Society.* San Francisco: Jossey-Bass.

Index